The 20 British Prime Ministers
of the 20th century

In Memory of my Father
Bernard Challis Bates
1912–2002
born during the Asquith administration
and always a Liberal voter

Contents

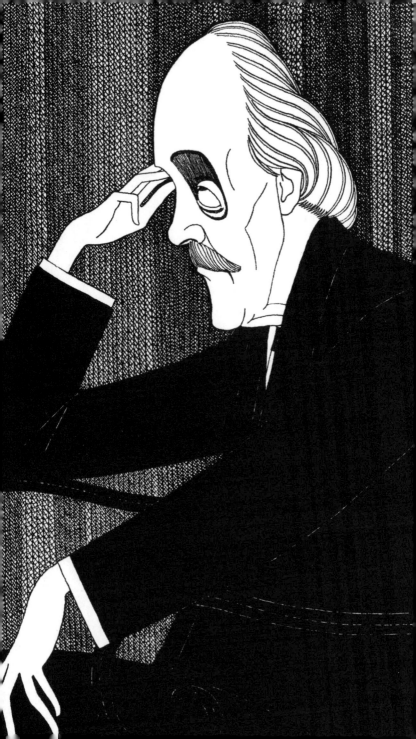

Introduction by Francis Beckett

Arthur Balfour has been treated less than kindly by historians, so I am pleased that the distinguished scholar Ewen Green has done something in this book to restore his reputation. As Green shows, Balfour was a much more substantial politician than he is normally given credit for.

The greatest Prime Ministers are great change-makers – Clement Attlee and Margaret Thatcher spring to mind. But at the next level down are the great change managers, like Stanley Baldwin and Harold Macmillan. And Balfour can put up a respectable argument for joining this second distinguished group, especially if one counts what he did after being Prime Minister into the balance. For in his career, he saw, embodied, and managed, the most profound changes in British society, no less important because they were invisible to many of his contemporaries.

When Balfour was defeated at the 1906 general election, and his successor H H Asquith went to meet the King and kiss hands, the new Prime Minister travelled by himself on the scheduled train to Biarritz where Edward VII was wintering. There was not even a private secretary, let alone a security guard, to accompany him. That's as graphic an illustration as you'll find of the distance we have travelled in those 100 years.

Here's another. Balfour was the last of the Cecils to hold

high office – that great political family whose members had helped to govern the country ever since a Cecil was the key adviser to Elizabeth I. His uncle and immediate Prime Ministerial predecessor, the third Marquis of Salisbury, was the last peer to occupy 10 Downing Street, having been Conservative leader from 1884 to 1902.

The Premiership must have seemed to the Cecils a little like a family business whose proprietors were England's great families. Hilaire Belloc's lachrymose Lord Lundy was told by his ducal grandfather:

'We had intended you to be
The next Prime Minister but three:
The stocks were sold; the Press was squared:
The Middle Class was quite prepared.
But as it is! ... My language fails!
Go out and govern New South Wales!'

Yet less than a decade after Balfour succeeded his uncle as Prime Minister in 1902, the aristocracy was looking on in impotent rage as its powers were drastically trimmed by the *hoi polloi*. Balfour, by then the Conservative Leader of the Opposition, found himself unable to save them from the advance of a democracy which they perceived as something akin to the end of civilisation.

During this crisis Lloyd George called the House of Lords 'Mr Balfour's Poodle' but, as Dr Green shows, the peers were in no mood to take orders from a politician they suspected of being willing to compromise on the sacred rights of the landed gentry. As Stephen Bates writes in the Asquith biography which appears in this series, 'They wanted more vigorous, less scrupulous leadership.'

But as Conservative leader, he was, at least nominally, at

the head of a splenetic aristocracy whose mood was summed up, once again, by Hilaire Belloc. As a Liberal MP, elected in 1906, who lost his seat in 1910 in one of the elections which resulted in the Parliament Act, Belloc knew the people he was writing about :

> During a late election Lord
> Roehampton strained a vocal chord
> From shouting very loud and high
> To lots and lots of people why
> The budget in his own opin-
> -Ion should not be allowed to win.
> He sought a specialist who said :
> 'You have a swelling in the head :
> Your larynx is a thought relaxed
> And you are greatly over-taxed.'
> 'I am indeed! On every side !'
> The Earl (for such he was) replied
> In hoarse excitement. 'Oh ! My Lord,
> You jeopardize your vocal chord'
> Broke in the worthy specialist.
> 'Come ! Here's the treatment ! I insist !
> To Bed ! To Bed ! And do not speak
> A single word till Wednesday week,
> When I will come and set you free
> (If you are cured) and take my fee.'
> On Wednesday week the doctor hires
> A Brand-new Car with Brand-new Tyres
> And Brand-new Chauffeur all complete
> For visiting South Audley Street.
> … A 'Scutcheon hanging lozenge-wise
> And draped in crepe appals his eyes
> Upon the mansion's ample door

To which he wades through heaps of Straw,
And which a Butler, drowned in tears,
On opening but confirms his fears.
'Oh ! Sir ! Prepare to hear the worst !
Last night my kind old master burst.
And what is more, I doubt if he
Has left enough to pay your fee.
The Budget –' With a dreadful oath,
The Specialist, denouncing both
The Budget *and* the House of Lords
Buzzed angrily Bayswaterwards.

No wonder then, as the spokesman and leader of men like that, that Balfour's image today is that of a grumpy aristocrat, rather as though he were one of Bertie Wooster's uncles. And no wonder, since for all their fulminating, the Lords lost, that Balfour as their leader is seen as a rather *louche* public schoolboy. Add to that his dislike of detail and his interest in philosophy, and you have the very model of an English dilettante, as out of place in the driven Downing Street of Lloyd George as he would have been in Harold Wilson's technological white heat.

In his *Defence of Philosophic Doubt*, published in 1879, Dr Green tells us that Balfour 'sought to offer a defence of scepticism against what he saw as the prevailing philosophical trend of scientific naturalism'. And what, the professional politician might ask, does this have to do with the price of fish, or the balance of trade or the growth of the German army? Not a thing, Balfour might have replied, and that is one of the best things about it. Add to this his dreadful, foolish snobbery; the facts that he led his party into three general elections and lost the lot ; and that he is the only sitting Prime Minister in the 20th century to lose his own parliamentary seat (a feat

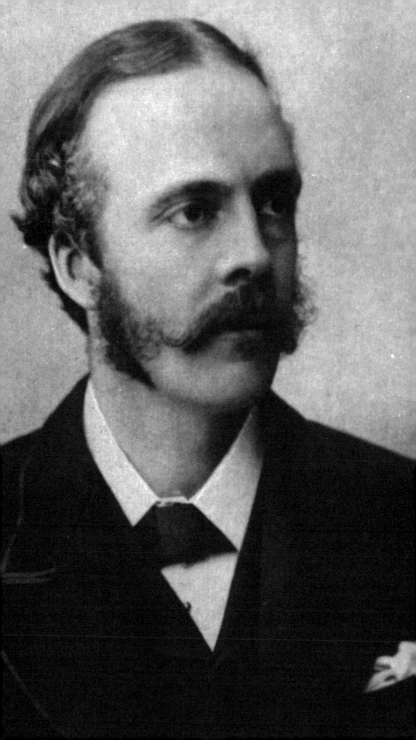

he achieved in the Liberal landslide of 1906). Perhaps it is no wonder that we think of Balfour as a languid amateur.

But we are wrong. He was a substantial politician, an accomplished parliamentarian, an interesting and original economic thinker, and he had real achievements to show for a life in the trade of politics. These achievements began earlier. Eric Midwinter, in the book on Lord Salisbury in this series, notes : 'Balfour won his spurs as Ireland's Chief Secretary, dealing out a mix of coercion and concession with imperturbable flair, despite being branded "Bloody" Balfour by his angry opponents.' He did not settle the Irish question – no one did at the time, and no one has since – but he did, more or less, keep the lid on it during his watch, and he understood better than most Conservatives that Britain could not hold down Ireland forever.

As Prime Minister, Balfour was responsible for the Entente Cordiale with France, bringing to an end the long distrust between the two countries and providing the basis for a formal alliance. The Education Act of 1902 was a real landmark which ensures that historians of the British education system rank the name of Balfour alongside that of R A ('Rab') Butler as creators of landmark legislation. Ewen Green calls this 'the introduction of the first truly national education system in Britain'. And his impact on British society was increased in 1905 when he piloted through Parliament both the Unemployed Workmans Act and the Aliens Act. Quite a record of achievement for one of our shortest-serving Prime Ministers. And it ignores the fact that he held the Conservative Party together when the free trade issue threatened to split it.

During the First World War, though no longer Conservative leader, he took vital decisions as First Lord of the Admiralty on Britain's naval policy and was a key player in the plot to remove Asquith as Prime Minister and replace

him with Lloyd George. And the great Balfour Declaration of 1917 is a real and visionary landmark, and one for which Balfour – by then Foreign Secretary – can claim the credit. Of course – as is the way with great events – one cannot claim it was done entirely from the loftiest of motives, nor that its long term results have been entirely what its author envisaged, but it was done, and it said: 'His Majesty's Government views with favour the establishment in Palestine of a national home for the Jewish people' but 'nothing shall be done which may prejudice the civil and religious rights of existing non-Jewish communities in Palestine.'

Arthur Balfour was the last representative of aristocratic government. It had had its day, and we are much better off without it, but before we get too carried away with how much better things are today, it's worth remembering this. Balfour was born a rich man, and died a much poorer one. In his seventies and eighties he had money troubles for the first time in his life, and was never thereafter free of debt. It is exactly the opposite trajectory from the one we are used to in recent years. I think I might prefer to be ruled by people who were born rich, rather than people who are in the process of making themselves rich.

Part One

THE LIFE

Chapter 1: A Man Born to Rule

Arthur Balfour, as an MP, senior politician, Cabinet Minister and then Prime Minister was a perfect social representative of the late-Victorian Conservative political elite. In terms of his own social status he was a patrician. He was a scion of a wealthy, landed Scottish family and inherited extensive estates at Whittingehame, where he was born on 25 July 1848, and Strathconan. Even the railways acknowledged his and his family's status, for the line from Edinburgh that passed Whittingehame had a stopping point named 'Balfour Halt', which enabled Balfour to be met and more easily transported to his favourite country seat. Furthermore, in 1870 he purchased a large town house in Westminster – an essential prerequisite for membership of 'Society' and political society in particular.

Equally important, Balfour was the nephew of the 3rd Marquis of Salisbury (the Conservative leader *c.* 1884 – 1902) and he was thus part of the close-knit Conservative political hierarchy that found its focus at Salisbury's country seat at Hatfield House in Hertfordshire. This political coterie, which came to be known as the 'Hotel Cecil' (for the simple reason that, either by birth or marriage, most of its members were in the Cecil family), represented the apogee of the Tory hierarchy. Balfour was thus almost born to inherit the Prime Ministerial 'purple'.

His early years were dominated by his mother, Lady Blanche, a daughter of Lord Salisbury. She acted as a quasi-governess in terms of his early education, although he also attended Hoddesdon Grange Prep School in Hertfordshire. As a teenager he attended Eton, although he was not particularly happy there, and from there went up to Trinity College, Cambridge. Balfour secured an indifferent degree result – he obtained a Second instead of the First he had hoped for and expected. This may have been due to the fact that he had developed an aversion to writing by hand, which was to remain with him throughout his life and which was hardly helpful when it came to examinations. Nevertheless, he gained the respect of one of his tutors, the philosopher Henry Sidgwick, and was also influenced in terms of both religious and economic thought, by the College's Clerical Dean and Tutor in Moral Sciences, the High Churchman and historical economist William Cunningham. Balfour's voracious reading and his close relations with celebrated tutors in philosophy earned him a reputation for studied 'high-mindedness', and this in turn helped earn him to gain the College nick-name 'Pretty Fanny', which satirised his bookish and scholarly predilections.

It was Balfour's family connections that provided him with his entry into parliamentary politics, for he was returned, unopposed, as Conservative MP for Hertford in February 1874 – Hertford being a constituency where the chief local political potentate was Balfour's uncle, Lord Salisbury. During his first six years in the Commons Balfour made little impact. He was, in part because of his social rank and connections, respected, and he was generally liked and viewed as 'clubbable'. But apart from some contributions to debates on obscure religious questions, and even more obscure economic issues, he made few speeches in Parliament. Indeed, the rela-

tively abstruse nature of his interventions appeared to confirm the 'high minded' reputation he had gained as a student at Cambridge, as did the fact that most of his energies seemed to have been devoted to writing his *Defence of Philosophic Doubt*, which was published in 1879.

In this work, Balfour sought to offer a defence of scepticism against what he saw as the prevailing philosophical trend of scientific naturalism. For Balfour, who was deeply religious, only sceptical questioning could provide a basis for true faith, which was beyond scientific reason and which, in 1895, he was to outline as the *Foundations of Belief*. Politically his philosophy was interesting as an insight into his mode of thought, but it served him little in his career in Parliament. His colleagues, especially his uncle, respected his intellect, but for most backbenchers he was perhaps the first of a line of senior Tories who were 'too clever by half', as in 1961 Lord Salisbury's grandson famously damned the Colonial Secretary Iain Macleod. In the late 1870s a hard-headed parliamentarian rather than a 'philosopher-king' would have seemed more useful to a party that faced difficult political situations on both the domestic and imperial fronts, for taxes had risen to unpopular levels in order to finance costly imperial adventures, notably in Southern Africa.

It was in the early 1880s that Balfour's political reputation began to take off. Following the Liberal victory at the 1880 General Election, and Disraeli's death in April 1881, the Conservative Party and its leadership in particular were in some disarray. Not all Conservatives would have accepted Disraeli's epigrammatic conclusion that their Party could only 'die like gentlemen', but many Conservatives saw the political situation as grim. It was in these circumstances that Lord Randolph Churchill emerged as a Conservative political hero, with a series of rhetorically invigorating Parliamentary

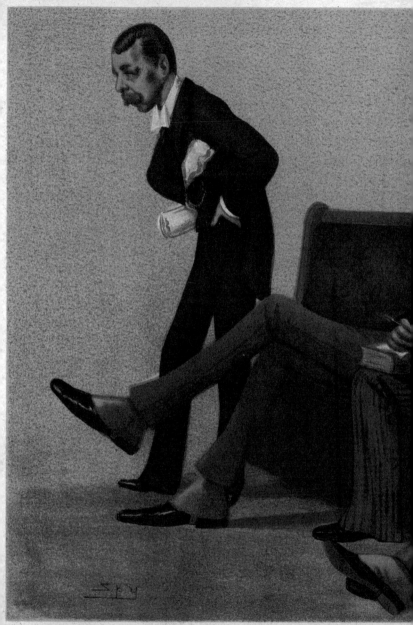

" Th

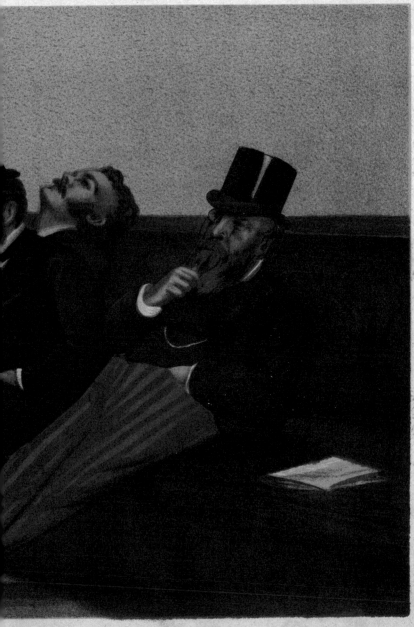

attacks on Gladstone and his administration and also through his mobilising of local Conservative constituency activism with his vague, but politically exciting notion of 'Tory Democracy'. Balfour played very little role in shaping or promoting Tory Democracy', but in the Commons he joined with Churchill, Henry Drummond-Wolff and John Gorst as a key member of the so-called 'Fourth Party', which carried out a form of Parliamentary 'guerrilla warfare' against the Liberals in Commons debates and energised an otherwise demoralised Conservative Party. For Churchill the 'Fourth Party' and 'Tory Democracy' were key elements in his attempt to promote his own political career and establish his credentials as a possible future Conservative leader. Balfour's priorities were, however, very different. His membership of the 'Fourth Party' undoubtedly served to enhance his parliamentary reputation, but his underlying political objectives were to quieten party discontents rather than, as in Churchill's case, exploit them for personal ends.

> **Lord Randolph Churchill** (1849–95), the father of Winston Churchill entered Parliament as a Conservative MP in 1874, and advocated a progressive conservatism called Tory Democracy which favoured popular social and constitutional reform. An effective orator, he opposed Home Rule for Ireland and famously coined the phrase 'Ulster will fight and Ulster will be right'. He became Secretary of State for India (1885–6) in Lord Salisbury's first government and Chancellor of the Exchequer and Leader of the House of Commons (1886–7) in his second. When the Cabinet rejected his budget proposing cuts in the armed services, he resigned, and never again held office. He died of syphilis at the age of 45.

Churchill's political strength in the early 1880s was a result of the fact that there was a core of discontent within the

Conservative Party among the new, urban and suburban Tory elites who, since the founding of the party's National Union of Conservative Associations (NUCA) in 1867, had provided the key voting and organisational basis of local Conservative activity in borough seats. These 'new' Tories, who came to be known as 'Villa Tories', were resentful about the way they had been condescendingly treated and even ignored by the party's aristocratic hierarchy in the 1870s. The fact that John Gorst, the Chief Agent of the National Union, had resigned his party post and joined the 'Fourth Party' was a most eloquent expression of the depth of this 'Villa Tory' resentment. Intriguingly, Salisbury and Balfour seemed to appreciate the socio-political power-base of Churchill's position better than he did. Certainly, Salisbury and Balfour worked assiduously to ensure that these 'Villa' discontents were assuaged. It was Salisbury as Prime Minister who was primarily responsible for appeasing 'Villa' or Conservative middle-class sentiment. His primary tool was the Honours system, which he used systematically to grant knighthoods and other lesser 'baubles' to urban Tory notables. Perhaps the clearest evidence of the politically placatory role of the Honours system is the fact that almost half of Salisbury's correspondence with the Party's Chief Agent, R N Middleton, involved discussion of Honours and their most appropriate and politically useful recipients.

Naturally it was not possible to fulfil every request and/or hope for an honour. To have done so would have undermined the rationale of Honours, which were, after all, supposed to confer or confirm distinction. Furthermore, Honours may have been political recommendations but they were the gift of the monarch, and Queen Victoria did not always co-operate fully – in December 1898, for example, the Queen unilaterally cut the number of knighthoods and Orders of the Bath in the New Year's Honours List by one-third, with the result,

as Salisbury's secretary noted, 'that there will be many sore backs'. Furthermore, elevating an MP to a peerage could, depending on the timing, cause an awkward by-election, and, in terms of the prevailing protocols of status, the recipient of a baronetcy was expected to enjoy a particular income and social standing. But when faced with obstacles such as these the Conservatives found other lower-order rewards to offer their supporters and activists.

The Primrose League, which had been created in the early 1880s as part of the 'Tory Democratic' apparatus of the period, has been viewed as part of an institutional attempt to foster popular, working-class participation in Conservative politics. This may have been part of the League's rationale, but arguably it was just as important as a means of integrating urban Tory elites into the 'social politics' of Conservatism. The 'officers' of the local Primrose League 'habitations' tended to be a blend of local gentry and middle class, and many League meetings were not mass affairs but social and business engagements for local notables. It was doubtless for this reason that the League's local officers were known as 'Knights' and 'Dames' – allowing them to enjoy such titles even though they did not qualify for the real thing.

Here the League's involvement of upper and middle-class women took on a particular significance, for it provided a (suitably domestic) political role for Tory women, but also a political 'Society' which mirrored and reinforced male association in the upper echelons of Westminster politics and local Conservative associations and clubs. It seems that a key function of the Primrose League was to forge links not only between the Conservative Party and 'the democracy' but also to bond old and new Conservative elites who were seeking to control 'the democracy'.

Another 'participatory' reward in the gift of the Conserva-

tive hierarchy was membership of the Carlton Club or, failing that, the Junior Carlton. A good example, one of many, of how this worked was provided by Salisbury's son Lord Cranborne, then MP for Darwen, who told the Conservative Chief Whip in July 1886 that:

'A Mr William Huntington, one of my constituents, is very anxious to get into the Junior Carlton … He is a county magistrate for Lancashire and rather an important man in Darwen – being a partner of Potter who stood against me in '85 and brother of Charles Huntington who really came out against me this time … William Huntington is, however, a Tory and supported me, but it would be very useful to confirm him in his faith. He is not, I take it, a very convinced Tory. I may add that the firm of Potter and Huntington is the most important firm in Darwen and influences a large number of votes.'[1]

All of the ingredients of the management of urban Toryism were discussed in this letter: a local notable from an essentially Liberal background, needing to be confirmed in the Conservative faith in order that his local influence would be committed to the Conservative cause – all this to be achieved by holding out a simple but vital symbol of political recognition and social acceptance.

The attempts made by the Conservatives to blend their traditional, landed and gentry support with their new, bourgeois 'Villa' supporters were assiduous and continuous. However, they did not always flow smoothly, for the simple reason that social tensions were often as prominent as harmonies. Thus in 1888 Balfour told the Conservative Chief Whip about *a great idiot in my country, who … Is burning to become a member of the Carlton Club*.[2] Likewise, when Balfour suggested that the prominent Leeds businessman, W L Jackson, be made Postmaster-General he felt it necessary to tell Salisbury that Jackson *has great tact and judgement – middle class tact and*

judgement I admit, but good of their kind. He justly inspires great confidence in businessmen and he is that rara avis *a successful manufacturer who is fit for something besides manufacturing*. Balfour concluded his 'glowing' appraisal with the comment that: *A Cabinet of Jacksons would be rather a serious order no doubt, but one or even two would be a considerable addition to any Cabinet.*[3] As it happened Jackson entered the Cabinet, and in 1898 he was created Baron Allerton as a further reward for his, albeit middle class, tact and judgement. Equally important, Jackson's town, Leeds, where he was President of the Chamber of Commerce, was granted a City Charter and Lord Mayoralty by Salisbury's second government, thereby confirming that it was the locale and not only a prominent individual that was being recognised and honoured.

He [the manufacturer W L Jackson] *justly inspires great confidence in businessmen and he is that rara avis a successful manufacturer who is fit for something besides manufacturing.*

BALFOUR

This glimpse at what one can best term the 'social history of Conservative politics' places Balfour's parliamentary career in context. In late 1885, for example, he gave up his safe seat in the Salisburyian fiefdom of Hertford to became MP for East Manchester, which was a largely suburban constituency but which also contained, in its outlying districts, a substantial mining vote. Nor was Balfour the only Conservative grandee to locate himself in this manner, His brother Gerald took on a constituency in Central Leeds, whilst Salisbury's sons Lord Cranborne, and Lords Hugh and Robert Cecil took on, respectively, Darwen and two metropolitan London constituencies. There was by no means overwhelming respect shown to middle class representatives by Tory grandees, but remarks such as those made by Balfour, cited above, were contained in private correspondence. In public the patrician hierarchy kept

their snobberies and prejudices more than well contained. Salisbury, unlike his supposedly more populist-minded, or even demotic, predecessor Disraeli, always attended and addressed the annual NUCA conference. Furthermore, he set aside time to attend, for example, the South-Eastern Oyster Catchers' Feast and the Sheffield Master Cutlers' convention. Salisbury's correspondence with his secretary indicates that he found such events extremely tedious, but he regarded his attendance as a socio-political necessity, and his nephew was wholly in accord with Salisbury on this point.

Balfour was first given office in Salisbury's relatively short-lived first administration of 1885–6. He was not appointed to a Cabinet post, but was made President of the Board of Local Government. This was hardly a giant stride, but the period in which he held the post was important insofar as Balfour had to lay the foundations for the reform of local government in the counties. There was no immediate legislation – the issue was too complex and what parliamentary time there was too taken up with other matters. But Balfour's proposals were to form the basis for the introduction of elected County Councils by Salisbury's second

Robert Cecil, Lord Salisbury (1830–1902) was Prime Minister a total of three times (1885–6, 1886–92 and 1895–1902). In his view 'The use of Conservatism is to delay changes till they become harmless'. He was against the tide of democratisation and social reform, opposing Factory Acts, temperance laws and leasehold reform. His expertise was in foreign affairs and for most of his time as Prime Minister he was also Foreign Secretary. A believer in 'Splendid Isolation', he nevertheless presided over a vast expansion of the British Empire in Africa, largely to forestall rival countries and to defend existing possessions, notably India and Egypt. (See *Salisbury* by Eric Midwinter, in this series.)

6. The Story of the Pushful One.

ONE day said Uncle: "Arthur dear
I must recruit and leave you here.
But O my nephew, concentrate
Your thoughts upon affairs of State,
The Pushful One's a dreadful schemer
He hates a sportsman and a dreamer,
And if you waste your thoughts on golf
He'll cut your pretty hands clean off;
And then, how shall my Arthur try
To keep his finger in the pie?"

Now Uncle scarce had turned his back—
He snatched a gingham from the rack
And gave a paper-weight a whack!

(15)

administration in 1888. Conservative concerns, and Liberal hopes, that this would end the dominance of the 'old order' in the counties did not materialise – partly because Balfour had structured the distribution of votes with care, and partly because the Liberals were in some disarray. The 'old order' did very well until after 1900, when the combination of their own socio-economic troubles and a Liberal political revival changed the situation quite dramatically and the unchallenged dominance of the 'knights of the shires' was ended.

Chapter 2: Ruling Scotland and Ireland

By the time Balfour's local government blueprint was implemented he had been holding high office for two years. In August 1886 he had been appointed Secretary of State for Scotland, principally to deal with the Land League in Scotland, which had formed a focus for social protest against the aristocracy's engagement in the Highland Clearances. Having dealt with the Scots to Salisbury's satisfaction, Balfour was promoted, at the age of 38, to the Cabinet in November 1887 as Chief Secretary for Ireland, to deal with a still more pressing land agitation, and one with profound political implications. The campaign of the Irish Land League had been ongoing since the late 1870s and had involved significant levels of political violence – ranging from attacks on landlords, to cattle maiming, crop destruction and refusal of payment of rents – the famous 'Boycotts'. The land agitation had formed the focus of the Home Rule movement and also for some more extreme Irish Nationalist organisations, such as the Irish Republican Brotherhood.

When Balfour took office the war of attrition between Irish tenants and their landlords had taken the new form in the shape of the 'Plan of Campaign', which was a demand for the withholding of rent co-ordinated by members of the constitutional campaign for Home Rule, and with, for the first time, local priests acting as 'trust-fund' agents to gather withheld rents,

which gave the campaign both some legal footing and moral *gravitas*. Furthermore, 1887 had seen the Irish Home-Rulers in jubilant mood. One of their foremost opponents, Randolph Churchill, had resigned as Chancellor of the Exchequer and the Irish detected hints of government weakness or at any rate hesitation. They mounted 17 nights of obstruction against the proposals of Sir Michael Hicks Beach, the then Irish Chief Secretary ('Black Michael' as the Irish Nationalist MPs called him) for strengthening the law against the Plan of Campaign. When Hicks Beach, afflicted with eye trouble, resigned from the Irish Office, there was some sense of crisis. Salisbury reiterated his belief that the future of the British Empire was at stake in the Irish struggle, and yet to ride the political storm, he chose a man for long seen by parliamentarians as (according to Henry Lucy) as 'a sort of fragile ornamentation', namely Balfour. On 5 March 1887 Balfour was examined by the physician Sir William Jenner and pronounced 'a sound man'

The term 'boycott' derives from the name of Captain Charles Cunningham Boycott (1832–97), the land agent of the Earl of Erne, an absentee landlord in County Mayo. In 1880, the Irish Land League led proposed that those landlords who refused to reduce rents should be socially ostracised. Boycott became the test case for this new policy. He refused to reduce the rents and ejected the protesting tenants from their land. Boycott was shunned. He had no servants and farm hands, local shops refused to serve him and his mail was not delivered. His crops had to be harvested by volunteers from the North guarded by 900 troops. Boycott returned to England.

and destined to enjoy 'a first-class life' (although no Chief Secretary could overlook that one recent holder of the office, Lord Frederick Cavendish, had been assassinated in 1882!). Balfour became Secretary of State on 8 March, and his Secre-

taryship was to prove both controversial and the making of his political reputation.

Balfour's main, immediate goal was to quell the Irish members at Westminster and restore 'law and order' in Ireland. In this respect his views were archetypically Unionist. Discussion of constitutional questions, demanded by Parnell and his followers, had to be preceded by their renouncing of all forms of illegality. Balfour thus introduced a new sense that Unionism could consist of more than mere opposition to Home Rule. He offered a policy of energetic coercion, in the form of the Criminal Law Amendment Act of 1887, which gave the State and the police draconian powers against Irish activists in Ireland and on the mainland. Indeed, there is a case for seeing this legislation as an early forerunner of the similarly illiberal Prevention of Terrorism legislation of the 1970s.

But Balfour combined his coercion with a variety of forms of constructive social relief – ironically, a return to Gladstone's policy in his pre-Home-Rule years, though Balfour, it must be said, made much more of the moral and political importance of coercion. As Charles Townshend has pointed out, Conservative Governments felt less compelled than Liberals to explain or excuse their illiberality. He took on, and faced down, Irish opposition in the Commons: the Parnellites 'cannot make much of Balfour who foils them by his skill and coolness and indeed leaves no just opening for their rancour', Cranbrook told Salisbury on 1 September 1887. Balfour was deliberately antagonistic to what he saw as the constitutional pretensions of the Parnellites, for he regarded them as, in effect, worse

'{The Parnellites} cannot make much of Balfour who foils them by his skill and coolness and indeed leaves no just opening for their rancour.'

THE EARL OF CRANBROOK

than open Fenians. He turned their tactics against them and had considerable success in breaking up the National League. He treated with cool contempt the outcry which followed the violence which occurred at Mitchelstown on 9 September 1887, when police fired on and beat demonstrators. Indeed, it was as a result of this incident that he became known as 'Bloody Balfour'.

Balfour's actions in 1887 heartened his party, but in 1888 Balfour took a decision that was to backfire on both him and the government, the decision to prosecute Parnell and other Irish Nationalists before a special commission of English judges on the basis that they had actively encouraged criminality – as 'revealed' by letters purporting to be written by Parnell and 'discovered' by and published in *The Times*. This attempt to discredit Home Rule boomeranged when it became clear that the case was based on forgeries and when their true author, the forger Richard Pigott, killed himself. Balfour had become cautious about the commission, but too late. *The Times* was discredited and the government could only appear to be a party to the newspaper's folly. Balfour needed all his debating skills in the censure debate in February 1890, the 12th vote of censure during his Secretaryship.

Balfour had little hesitation in deploying tough, coercive measures in Ireland. But there was another important dimension to his policies – a series of constructive, conciliatory measures. He passed two Land Purchase Acts, in 1887 and 1891, which were designed to enable tenants to become small proprietors – the idea being that landlord-tenant tensions would dissolve if, in effect, the rural population were all landlords! A Light Railway Act, passed in 1889, was designed to lower the cost and improve the transport and export of Irish produce. Then in 1891 Balfour presided over the establishment of the Congested Districts Board, which

sought to bring about internal migration in Ireland and move elements of the population from over-crowded and agriculturally exhausted areas – notably the western districts – to less populated and potentially more productive areas.

Some of these ideas had been put forward in 1888 by Joseph Chamberlain and his 'small-holding'-obsessed lieutenant Jesse Collings, but both Salisbury and Balfour accepted that a Conservative government should, given the critical circumstances in Ireland, gamble on these radical constructive policies despite their cost to the taxpayer. This strategy was to be labelled 'killing Home Rule with kindness', but this slogan was rarely used in Ireland. It was rather designed to explain the rationale and cost of the policies to an English audience. Balfour was at one with Salisbury in believing that Home Rule could not solve the Irish problem. It would, they thought, merely stoke the fires of a distinctive Catholic nationalism in Ireland. In persisting for years to come with his policies of reconciliation within the Union, Balfour was, however, sustained by a touch of optimism, which stood in contrast to his uncle's deep underlying pessimism.

Balfour's years in Ireland were regarded as a great success by his Party, and in 1891, when Salisbury's great ally W H Smith died, there was little doubt that Balfour would replace him as Leader of the House of Commons, and this was exactly what happened. When Balfour became Leader of the House Randolph Churchill is said to have responded that 'Tory Democracy is dead'. Churchill was, of course, both unwell and bitter, but, even allowing for this, his remarks were simplistic. When the Conservatives went into opposition in 1892 a number of Conservatives and Unionists advocated innovative programmes of social reform as a route to recovering popular appeal. The best-known of these was promulgated by Joseph Chamberlain, who constructed a comprehensive

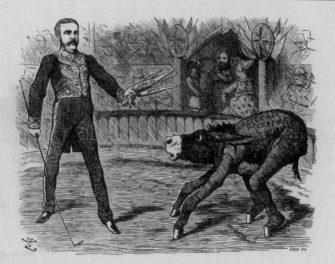

BALFOUR'S "IRREPRESSIBLE" DONKEY.

labour programme and also embraced Charles Booth's call for the introduction of old age pensions. Nor was Chamberlain a lone voice, and the Scottish NUCA in particular brought forward a series of ambitious schemes for social reform. But neither Salisbury nor Balfour would endorse these proposals. They had nothing in principle against state-sponsored social reform, and indeed Balfour stated publicly that Socialism and social reform were as distinctive as bain and antidote. The problem was that increased state action required higher taxation, and Balfour agreed with Salisbury that this was as likely to alienate existing support as much as attract new friends, and hence caution was the best option.

Balfour was to be Leader of the Commons, in both Government and also for the Opposition from 1891 until he became Prime Minister in 1902. He was in many ways a slightly idle Leader of the Commons, and bored by the routine of patient attendance the post required. Indeed, after the Liberal victory at the general election of July 1892, he was noticed at Westminster 'beaming like a boy about to have a long-deferred holiday'.[1] Balfour wanted a rest after his spell in Ireland, which had been very arduous. Moreover, as he had often confessed to his close friend, Lady Elcho, he had a tendency to enjoy being an *idler*[2] and found Parliamentary business particularly tiresome. Certainly, Balfour had numerous distractions which he indulged. At College he had become keen on both 'Real' and 'Lawn' tennis, and he was to play the latter until the year before his death. After College he also became a golf enthusiast. He achieved a handicap of eight, which made him an average player, but he was frequently to be seen on the great golf courses on the East Coast of Scotland – St Andrews, Carnoustie and Gleneagles – and a follower of what came to be known as 'the Golf Stream'. For the most part golf was personal relaxation, but he also frequently

partnered newspaper editors and fellow politicians, and in this last respect Balfour was one of the originators of golf as *the* political game.

Tennis and golf were essential to Balfour, and the former had more than sporting significance, for, along with croquet and clever conversation, it was one of the main pastimes of 'The Souls'. The Souls were a youthful aristocratic coterie with some bohemian sexual and personal pretensions and a penchant for modernist architecture, but above all who saw themselves as aesthetes. They circulated around each other's country houses, and some of the younger male members were to enjoy significant political futures, for example George Wyndham and George Curzon, as well as Balfour himself. It was through the Souls that Balfour established a close platonic relationship with Wyndham's sister, Mary (from 1883 the wife of Hugh Elcho, a member of the Wemyss family, another aristocratic Scottish Tory clan) maintained from 1886 by regular correspondence (see *The Letters of Arthur Balfour and Lady Elcho*, edited by J Ridley and C Percy). The Souls reached their zenith in the period from the mid-1880s to the mid-1890s, and Balfour, with his graceful charm, was its chief adornment.

In spite of his sporting and social distractions Balfour blossomed as opposition Leader of the House after 1892. He presented an attractive contrast to his future parliamentary rival on the Liberal front bench, H H Asquith, then the Home Secretary. Asquith was nearly four years younger than Balfour, but he seemed prosaic in comparison, whilst Henry Lucy found Balfour's 'sunny nature' and 'light-hearted humour' of 'inestimable value' to a Party Leader in the Commons. Balfour may have found his post tiresome, but he was by no means unconscientious. In 1893, for example, he fought Gladstone's second Home Rule Bill clause by clause. There were

RIGHT HON. ARTHUR GOLFOUR, M.P.

As Irish Secretary known to fame,
Golfour, links-eyed, pursues his favourite game.

no Liberal Unionists to bring over in 1893, and the rejection of the Bill was to be carried out by the House of Lords in September 1893. Indeed, most of the serious rejection/defeat of Liberal measures that could be deemed 'sectional' was done in the Lords under Salisbury's aegis – Balfour's role was necessarily secondary.

It was perhaps because his workload was not overly burdensome and/or tedious, that Balfour found time in Opposition to write his second philosophical work, *The Foundations of Belief*, which was published in 1895. Only a politician working effectively part-time could have produced a piece of work on this scale. But things changed after June 1895, when Salisbury and the Conservative/Liberal Unionist 'coalition', as it had effectively become, returned to office. Balfour again became Leader of the House of Commons, with Chamberlain and the Liberal Unionists, 71 in number, sitting on the government benches alongside 340 Conservatives. Chamberlain became Colonial Secretary and, by dint of his charisma and powerful platform oratory, was often seen as a serious rival to Balfour for the succession to Salisbury. Balfour tended to present set speeches poorly through lack of preparation, but after Gladstone's retirement there were few in the Commons to match his finesse in debate. Moreover, Conservatives continued to value the aristocratic and Anglican Balfour precisely because they saw him as an obstacle to the Unitarian Birmingham manufacturer's hopes of becoming Unionist leader. Indeed, there had been some Conservative opposition to Chamberlain's elder son Austen being given a formerly Conservative seat, purely on the grounds that he was a Nonconformist – something which confirmed that confessional as much as any residual political differences were a source of tension within the Unionist coalition. Here, Balfour was an ideal Leader of the Commons, insofar as he was known to

be a devout Anglican – which was reassuring to Conservatives – but he was also a member of the Church of Scotland and appeared ecumenical enough in his doctrinal outlook to appease, or at any rate not alienate, devout Nonconformists in the Liberal Unionist ranks.

As Leader of the House Balfour also found parliamentary means of appeasing Liberal Unionist sentiment. In 1897 the Workmen's Compensation Act was passed which provided automatic financial assistance to labourers injured at work, and which precluded the necessity of their pursuing compensation through the courts under the 1881 Employers' Liability Act. This act of social reform, much welcomed by trade unionists in particular, was presented in Parliament by Joseph Chamberlain and in this way Balfour, who shaped the Parliamentary timetable, provided Chamberlain with a perfect set-piece opportunity to demonstrate that his days as a radical social reformer were not over.

Balfour's work before he succeeded to the Premiership was focused on three particular areas – Ireland, education and Britain's imperial position. Balfour agreed with his uncle

Joseph Chamberlain (1836–1914) was a successful Birmingham businessman who turned to politics. As Mayor of Birmingham Chamberlain introduced 'municipal socialism' by taking over the local gas and water utilities, clearing slums and founding Birmingham University. He became a Liberal MP in 1876 but split from Gladstone over Irish Home Rule. As leader of the Liberal Unionists he allied himself with Lord Salisbury, becoming Secretary of State for the Colonies in 1895. An ardent imperialist, he led Britain into the Boer War and supported protectionism and Imperial preference in trade to combat the economic rise of the United States and Germany. He resigned in 1903 over tariff reform and split the Unionist alliance.

on the need for persistent constructive work in Ireland to save the Union. From 1895 to 1900 he worked in close co-operation with his brother Gerald (an MP since 1885) who had been appointed as the new Chief Secretary for Ireland. In 1896, with Parliamentary help from his elder brother, Gerald Balfour introduced and secured the passage of a Land Law which further eased the purchase of land by Irish tenants; and in 1898 he followed this with an important Irish Local Government Act. The latter provided a local legislative context within which moderate, constructive Irish reformers, as best represented by Horace Plunkett and his followers, could pursue ground-level reforms, including the spread of new agricultural techniques, to improve the lot of small, tenant farmers. In this respect Arthur Balfour worked with his brother in an attempt to continue and extend the constructive side of his own work between 1887 and 1891.

Balfour's interest in foreign affairs and, increasingly, in defence policy can be traced back to 1878, the year he acted as Salisbury's private secretary at the Congress of Berlin. In the Commons he had also contributed to debates on relations with Turkey and Afghanistan, and he had also spoken, in public and in private about his concern about the Russian advance towards India. British naval supremacy, which Balfour saw as fundamental to Britain's imperial position, was increasingly a matter of concern in the 1890s. On the one hand it was challenged by the emergence of various industrialising states as naval powers. By the early 1890s a potential military combination of France and Russia seemed the principal threat to the British Empire – a point given popular expression in William le Queux's novel *The Great War in England of 1897*. The conventional strategic assumption was that Britain needed to maintain the so-called 'two-power standard', where the British fleet would match the size of the next two

largest fleets. The cost of maintaining this commitment was becoming increasingly difficult to meet, and it had really not been wholly surprising that the trigger for Gladstone's resignation in 1894 had been a Cabinet dispute over the size of the Naval Estimates – rising military costs were threatening Gladstonian budgetary orthodoxy and balance.

At the same time a number of disastrous British naval exercises had raised question marks about the efficiency of British seamanship. The navy – Britain's great pride – had, it seemed, become a source of embarrassment. Nor did the army offer any compensation for the navy's failings. Britain's small volunteer army was, in numerical terms, almost insignificant compared with the conscript armies maintained by the leading continental states. Furthermore, its performance in the Zulu wars of the late 1870s, in South Africa in 1881 and in the Sudan in 1885, had not inspired confidence in the troops or, more particularly, the officer corps. On all fronts, the British Empire seemed a weak as well as a weary titan.

Soon after the Unionists took office in June 1895, Balfour made serious efforts to innovate a much-needed scheme for the co-ordination of defence policy. But Salisbury was largely uninterested and offered little support. Consequently Balfour oversaw the initial steps towards the creation of the Committee of Imperial Defence, which was, in theory, to co-ordinate military policy across the board, but which had few powers over the military and functioned more as a high-level 'talking shop' rather than as an effective Cabinet committee – certainly, contrary to his own recommendations, it did not provide for the attendance of the professional service chiefs. Its failings were to become all too apparent during the Boer War of 1899–1902, when the mightiest Empire the world had seen, took three years, lost tens of thousands of troops and spent £150,000,000 in beating a bunch of farmers.

The education question was at one level bound in with the issue of Britain's international position. In 1894 E E Williams, in his widely-read book *Made in Germany*, argued that one reason German industrialists and manufacturers had stolen a lead over their British counterparts was because of the higher levels of education and in particular technical education available in Germany. As a consequence the development of education in Britain was often discussed as a means of countering British 'decline'. But the education issue also carried a crucial domestic political dimension. The provision of education had, throughout the 19th century, been overlaid with confessional differences and in particular by a conflict between the Established Church and Nonconformity. Following the 1870 Education Act, and the creation of the Board Schools, confessional conflict over the provision of education had continued but had at least been relatively contained. By the 1890s, however, the situation was changing. In part this was as a result of the falling funding levels available to all voluntary, and most notably Church, schools. At the same time the Cockerton Judgement of 1896 had raised the thorny question of whether schools could or should be permitted to provide education beyond the elementary level. By the mid 1890s issues concerning the funding of education were thus bubbling beneath the surface of British politics, and important question marks were being raised about both the adequacy and structural rationality of Britain's education system. Salisbury's third administration signally failed in its attempts to address education and it was not until the early 20th century that the nettle of comprehensive reform was to be grasped.

Part Two

THE LEADERSHIP

Chapter 3: Prime Minister

Balfour succeeded his uncle as Prime Minister in August 1902. He was seen as the natural successor: in part because of his familial link, but also because his record in office was highly regarded. Also, there were no serious challengers. The only politician who enjoyed a more outstanding public reputation was Joseph Chamberlain, and, as a Liberal Unionist and former Radical, he was unacceptable to the Tory old guard backbenchers. Furthermore, Chamberlain had suffered a serious cab accident, injuring his head, shortly before Salisbury retired, and thus Balfour's only rival (albeit an unlikely one) was *hors de combat* at a crucial time.

The situation Balfour faced when he became Prime Minister was by no means an easy one. The Boer War had been brought to an ostensibly successful conclusion, but the military inadequacies the war had exposed demanded that Britain's military establishment be thoroughly examined and reformed. Indeed, one of the first processes that Balfour set underway was army reform – to be carried out following an investigation by the new Minister of War, H O Arnold-Forster.

The Boer War had revealed Britain's diplomatic isolation in that its only support during the war had come from the major Colonies. In the late 19th century Salisbury had famously referred to Britain's 'splendid isolation', insofar as it had no need for foreign entanglements and alliances. However, by the

Europe

'As early as 1916, Lord Balfour, then British Foreign Secretary, fore-saw at least a part of the danger that lay ahead for Europe when he warned that an independent Poland might leave France defenceless in another war: if "Poland was made an independent kingdom, be-coming a buffer state between Russia and Germany, France would be at the mercy of Germany in the next war, for this reason, that Russia could not come to her aid without violating the neutrality of Poland" – exactly the dilemma in 1939. To contain Germany, France needed an ally in the East that could force Germany to fight a two-front war. Russia was the only country strong enough to fulfil that role. But with Poland separating Germany and Russia, Russia could only pressure Germany by violating Poland. And Poland was too weak to play Russia's role. What the Treaty of Versailles did was to give an incentive to Germany and Russia to partition Poland, precisely what they did twenty years later.

Lacking a Great Power in the East with which to ally itself, France sought to strengthen the new states to create the illusion of a two-front challenge to Germany. It backed the new East European states in their effort to extract more territory from Germany or from what was left of Hungary. ... Yet these infant states could not possibly assume the role that up to this time, Austria and Russia had played. They were too weak and racked by internal conflicts and mutual rivalries ...

Thus the stability of the Continent came to rest on France. It had taken the combined forces of America, Great Britain, France, and Russia to subdue Germany. Of these countries, America was again isolationist, and Russia was severed from Europe by a revolutionary drama and by the so-called *cordon sanitaire* of small Eastern Europe-an states standing in the way of direct Russian assistance to France. To preserve the peace, France would have to play policeman all over Europe. Not only had it lost the stomach and the strength for so interventionist a policy but, had it attempted one, it would have found itself alone, abandoned by both America and Great Britain.'

[Henry Kissinger, *Diplomacy* (Simon & Schuster, New York: 1994) p 243]

early 20th century this isolation no longer seemed quite so splendid and it was during Balfour's Premiership that it came to an end. In 1902 Britain formed an alliance with Japan, and although the negotiations had begun under Salisbury it was Balfour's premiership which saw the agreement formally ratified. More important still it was Balfour's premiership which saw in 1904 the forging of the Entente Cordiale. Although the Entente was not a formal alliance it brought to an end significant Anglo-French tensions which had in the 1890s come close to armed conflict in Northern Africa. Furthermore, the Entente did serve as the basis for the formal Anglo-French alliance that was to be signed and then extended in 1907–8, and which was to be the basis of the alliance of the two nations during the Great War.

But if Balfour's premiership was very active in the sphere of foreign relations it was similarly full on the domestic front. Here the first major piece of legislation was the 1902 Education Act. This saw the abolition of the School Boards and the transferral of responsibility for the provision of elementary education to local government, with schools being funded out of local taxation. After 1902 all children were to attend school until the age of 14, and voluntary schools were also to be able to apply for rate aid if they fulfilled certain criteria in provision for their pupils – essentially the 'three Rs'.

It was once thought that this legislation was a quasi-Fabian measure insofar as the chief civil servant at the Board of Education, Robert Morant, was relatively close to, and admired by, Sidney and Beatrice Webb. Given that the 1902 Act removed the School Board structure, which the Webbs undoubtedly saw as a prime example of the 'administrative nihilism' of Victorian administration, it is perhaps understandable that the 1902 Act could be seen in these terms.

But Morant was not simply a Fabian *manqué*, for his background was much more complex. In fact Morant had once been intending to become an Anglican priest and of course one of the major results of the 1902 Act was that voluntary schools, most notably Anglican schools, could apply for local government funding. In this respect the 1902 Act, both by removing the School Boards, which had been havens of Nonconformist influence, and by providing under certain conditions subsidies to Anglican schools, could be seen as an effective prop for the beleaguered Anglican voluntary system. Certainly this was how militant Nonconformists regarded the Act, with the result that the following general election witnessed what one could term the last great kick of the 'Nonconformist Conscience'.

Nevertheless two things in particular are worth noting here about the 1902 legislation. The first is that Joseph Chamberlain, whose Liberal Unionist followers were the members of the government most concerned over the fate of the School Boards, supported the passage of the Act and indeed went so far as to say he

Social reformers and pioneers of social science, **Sidney** (1859–1947) and **Beatrice Webb** (1858–1943) helped to bring the Fabian Society to prominence, to create the *New Statesman* political magazine, and to found the London School of Economics. Although Sidney Webb had a short parliamentary career and served in the first two Labour governments, the couple were most influential through their writings. Balfour was a frequent visitor to their home from 1902. He appointed Sidney as a member of the Royal Commission of Trade Union Law (1903) and Beatrice to the Royal Commission on the Poor Laws in 1905. They were instrumental in the relaunch of the Labour party in 1918 and they provided the intellectual basis for the moderate reformism of Labour governments.

would resign rather than see the legislation lost. The second is that whatever one makes of the confessional political complexities of the legislation, the 1902 Act did see the introduction of the first truly national education system in Britain.

Balfour's last year as Prime Minister also saw the introduction of two novel pieces of legislation which were to have relatively significant long-term implications. The first of these was the 1905 Unemployed Workmen's Act, which permitted local authorities to engage in public works to provide employment for workers rendered 'idle' by seasonal or other forms of trade dislocation. This legislation was, as already noted, permissive and thus there is no way in which it could be presented as 'pre-Keynesian' but it did represent an important acknowledgement by central government that unemployment was a systematic rather than an individual-based problem.

The second significant piece of legislation was the Aliens Act of 1905, which was the first attempt by a British government to control and even prevent certain groups from gaining entry into the country. The principle objective of this legislation was to prevent Jewish immigration and to halt the inflow of Eastern and Central European Jews who were fleeing from the pogroms that had burgeoned in those regions in the 1890s and early 20th century. Concern over the mass immigration of 'pauper aliens' had been expressed at NUCA Conferences since the 1890s and two Conservative MPs, Captain William Shaw and Major Evans-Gordon, had flirted with the activities of the British Brothers League in the East End of London. Balfour's legislation, although it was counter to the long-standing British tradition of open immigration, was in some ways an attempt to moderate potentially more extreme expressions of 'anti-alien' sentiment.

The most large-scale domestic legislation that was passed

under Balfour concerned his old stamping ground, Ireland. As noted earlier, Balfour himself and his brother, Gerald, had sought to encourage and extend land purchase by Irish tenants to transform them into small-holders. This strategy reached new heights in 1904 with the passage of what came to be known as the Wyndham Act – named after the then Chief Secretary for Ireland, George Wyndham. Wyndham, who was a close friend of Balfour, took what was in effect the simple view that the Irish landlords should be made an offer they could not refuse. In effect the state offered to buy landlords' property, at a good price given that land prices generally and in Ireland in particular were falling, and then sell the land on to the tenantry on the basis of low, long-term mortgages.

This was an extraordinarily ambitious policy. To begin with, it demanded large-scale capital expenditure by the Treasury with the fundamental aim being to remove the Irish landlord class. Never in European and certainly not in British history had state intervention on this scale been devoted to such an overt act of social engineering. The rationale of the policy was that if landlord-tenant tension lay at the root of 'the Irish Question' then the Wyndham Act would sever that root. At first glance it seemed as if the policy might succeed in that take-up of the scheme by both landlords and tenants was widespread, and by 1910 two-thirds of land in Ireland had changed hands. But, much to the disappointment of Wyndham and especially Balfour, support for Home Rule did not decline and indeed manifestations of extreme Irish nationalism, such as the founding of Sinn Fein in 1906, seemed to indicate that the problem was growing more intractable. Moreover, problems emerged in that in certain areas of Ireland, notably in the west, graziers purchased large tracts of land and made them unavailable for small-scale mixed

farming. This led to conflicts between the so-called 'bullock men' and disaffected former small tenants who felt excluded from the land – what became known as the 'Ranch War'. The complexities of Ireland's rural structure and relations seemed to have thwarted Balfour's best-laid and most ambitious plans.

The Irish Question had of course been a long-running issue for British governments of all political persuasions since the 1840s, but a new issue Balfour had to confront, which was ultimately to splinter his government, concerned British trade and economic policy. It was thought that British trade policy had been settled in the 1840s with the repeal of the Corn Laws in 1846. Indeed, Benjamin Disraeli, who himself had been a protectionist in the 1840s, stated in 1852 that protectionism 'was not only dead but damned'. Yet in the late 19th century, particularly after the German re-introduction of protection in 1878 and the breakdown of the Anglo-French 'Cobden-Chevalier Treaty' in 1881, protectionist sentiment resurfaced in the United Kingdom. Some of this sentiment took the old-fashioned form of agricultural protectionism – almost a recrudescence of the pro-Corn Law lobby of the 1840s. But there were also new and more varied forms, best expressed in the National Fair Trade League, which argued that Britain's unilateral adherence to Free Trade in an increasingly protectionist world was systematically disadvantaging British industry and manufacturing. Given that in the mid-1880s Salisbury's first government had felt it necessary to establish a Royal Commission on the Depression of Trade and Industry, the notion that British economic policy, and more particularly trade policy, was synonymous with prosperity came increasingly under question. Economic policy nostrums that were once regarded as at best erroneous and at worst straightforwardly heretical began to gain a public airing, and

more surprising still a school of economists began to emerge who were willing to question the received wisdoms of liberal political economy.

In the 1880s Arthur Balfour emerged as one of the few mainstream politicians willing to question the received orthodoxies of economic policy and economic thought, although this seems utterly to have escaped the notice of those who penned Balfour's entry in the *New Dictionary of National Biography*. He had studied political economy at Cambridge under the tutelage of Henry Sidgwick, and never lost his interest in the subject. From the outset of his political career this interest was evident. He had made his maiden speech in the Commons on the subject of Indian currency, and in the 1880s and 1890s Balfour showed a pronounced sympathy for the bimetallic cause.[1] Bimetallism proposed that the Gold Standard be replaced by a joint Gold and Silver Standard, with the two metals fixed at a value ratio. The basic rationale was that this would raise the world's money stock, and thereby reverse the price fall that had hit the global economy since the early 1870s. Moreover, it was to remove the competitive advantage enjoyed by manufacturers in countries on a silver standard. This was particularly troubling to Lancashire cotton producers, who found themselves confronting competition from Japanese and domestic Indian producers in their crucial Far Eastern and Indian markets. Bimetallism was, in effect, to remove the advantage of devalued currencies that manufacturers on a silver standard enjoyed.

Balfour was one of the voices sympathetic to bimetallism on the Royal Commission on Currency in the late 1880s. This could be attributed to the fact that he sat for a constituency in Lancashire, where bimetallism had a powerful appeal to the cotton industry.[2] But it is difficult to see local interests as more than a partial explanation for Balfour's involvement

with the currency question. He was one of the most inquisitive members of the 1887–8 Royal Commission on Currency, and during Salisbury's third administration Conservative bimetallists looked to Balfour as the senior figure who would press their case in Cabinet.

Balfour's interest in and support for bimetallism is significant for two reasons. First, here was an economic issue renowned for its abstruse, even arcane, arguments which Balfour mastered and pursued with intelligence, tenacity and some relish. Second, prior to the tariff controversy bimetallism was the most important debate with implications for Britain's commitment to 'orthodox' liberal political economy. In 1898 Robert Chalmers, one of the Permanent Secretaries at the Treasury, told T H Farrer: 'The more I have to do with these heterodox people [bimetallists], the more I realise the unity of the principles which lead you to maintain the two things – Free Trade and sound currency. One is the obverse of the other, the reverse of the same coin'.[3] Although there was by no means a simple correlation between advocates of bimetallism and critics of Free Trade there was an implicit willingness on the part of currency 'heretics' to question received economic wisdom. In this respect Balfour's support for bimetallism was indicative of his acceptance that all was not right with Britain's economy, especially the agricultural and manufacturing sectors, and showed his readiness to consider alternatives to prevailing policy orthodoxies.

The reasoning that allowed Balfour to countenance economic 'heresy' was made clear in his 'formal' writings on political economy. His first significant intervention in this field was published in the *National Review* in 1885. In this essay Balfour noted that political economy, as a discipline, had lost much of its cachet over the previous decade. This, he argued, was due to misguided efforts to establish the notion

of economic orthodoxy. The net result had been that political economy *cease*[d] *to be a living science, and petrifie*[d] *into an unchanging creed.*[4]

Balfour felt that political economy was a vital science, in that *the study of economic facts is a necessary preliminary to any judicious treatment of some of the most important problems of the day*, but he was also clear that it was necessary to limit the claims of political economy *qua* science to be an absolute guide to policy. Political economy, he contended, only dealt with one aspect of life, the pursuit of wealth, whereas politicians had to consider society's needs in the round. Hence any conclusions produced by political economy had to be *subject to revision*, and notions like Free Trade and *laissez-faire* had to be seen as *maxims*, not *truths*.[5] This line of thinking led Balfour to declare that *there is no question concerning either the method or the results of political economy which I for one am not prepared to question.*

There is no question concerning either the method or the results of political economy which I for one am not prepared to question.

BALFOUR

With regard to the unfolding of Balfour's premiership, the key issue was how far he was prepared to question Free Trade. Indeed, this was to be the dominant issue of his time in office. On 15 May 1903 Joseph Chamberlain, speaking at Birmingham Town Hall, declared that Free Trade should no longer be seen as sacrosanct and that in particular Britain should examine the possibility of establishing special trading relations with its major colonies on the basis of preferential tariff agreements. This marked the opening of the tariff reform campaign, which was to broaden and deepen as, in a series of speeches in the autumn of 1903, Chamberlain 'carried the fiery cross' to the constituencies and announced a programme of tariff proposals which included preferential

tariffs on colonial agricultural produce and protective tariffs on imported manufactured goods. By the early autumn of 1903 Chamberlain's proposals had already split Balfour's Cabinet, with the result that five Cabinet ministers – Chamberlain and four of his Free Trade opponents – had resigned. However, it remained open as to what position Balfour took on this crucial question, and Balfour famously remarked that he had *no settled convictions* on tariff reform.

After 1885 Balfour did not publish any formal thoughts on the nature of political economy. His *Economic Notes on Insular Free Trade* of 1903 did contain some important theoretical implications, which will be touched upon later, but it was largely a 'tract for the times'. But between 1907 and 1911 Balfour worked on the manuscript of a projected major treatise on political economy, and although it was never published (and probably did not deserve to be) it contains some interesting insights into his thinking. In his manuscript Balfour argued that the *fundamental* problem was, *we live in a changing world, and in a world where economic changes are at least as striking as any other ... by what causes are economic changes affected? and can these causes, or any of them, be reduced to law?* His answer was pessimistic. He noted that: *Merely to state them {the above questions} is to show how small a fraction of the economic problem can ever come within the scope of economic theory, or for the matter of that, of any theory. New methods of manufacturing material, new methods of transporting it, the exhaustion of old supplies, the discovery of new ones, war, conquest, colonisation, the diffusion through Eastern nations of Western knowledge, revolutions in taste, in science, in organisation – who shall deny that these are among the great causes of economic change? who shall assert that they can be reduced to law? Evidently the task is hopeless.*

But Balfour felt that some had mistakenly sought to establish such laws. The culprits were the Classical economists,

and he declared that, *where I venture to think Classical Economics has been to blame ... is in the arbitrary emphasis it places on certain causes of change, in its defective account of them, and in the one-sided theory of economic development which has been the inevitable result.*[6]

Balfour underscored this argument by further arguing that *some economists have been haunted by the notion that the infinite variety of economic effect exhibited in different stages of culture, display the workings of a single set of eternal and unchanging principles, which it was their business to disengage from their temporary setting ... For my own part ... I doubt whether much is gained in any branch of sociology by searching after laws of universal validity. The field of economic theory, at least, is no regime of unalterable outline, retaining its identity through every stage of social development. It depends for its content upon such variable elements as custom, law, knowledge, social organisation; nay on human nature itself which ... is not necessarily the same from generation to generation ... Every phase of civilization requires its own political economy.*[7]

Balfour's manuscript on political economy represented a deepening and strengthening of the views he had articulated in 1885, and as such it indicates the consistency of his outlook over time. The scepticism which informed his views was perhaps to be expected, but of even greater importance is the historical relativism of his approach, for this brought him very close to the historical school of British economists.

The historical school, whose leading lights were William Cunningham, W J Ashley, H S Foxwell, L L Price, and W A S Hewins, first came to prominence in Britain in the 1880s, and from that point on developed a sustained critique of Classical economics and what they saw as its vulgarized derivatives, Manchesterism (a commitment to Free Trade and *laissez-faire*) and Socialism.[8] Their basic objections to the Classical school were, first, the deductive method used by the Classical economists which had led them to 'isolate certain motives and

measure them, and formulate laws according to which these motives act'.[9] This, the historical economists argued, was a fallacious procedure because 'no economic principles have this mathematical character of being true for all times and places alike ... [but were] approximately true as statements of the facts of actual life under certain social conditions'.[10] Their second, related, objection was to the Classical economists' abstraction of economic phenomena from the surrounding context. This 'immense simplification' of 'isolating wealth as a subject for study' was regarded by the historical economists as in some respects a good thing, but only as long as it was 'not forgotten that it was a tool of convenience'.[11] Where the Classical school was seen to have gone wrong was in thinking that the 'science of wealth' represented the be-all and end-all of political economy, and ignoring the wider social, cultural and historical influences on economic development.

For the historical economists the Classical school's deductive, abstract reasoning had ensured that they had 'lost touch with the actual phenomena of the present day'.[12] This was seen to be most evident in the individualist assumptions underpinning Classical economics. Looking at the late-19th and early-20th century world the historical economists saw trusts, trade unions, and empire states as the characteristic features of economic life. In short they saw *collective* agencies as the key actors on the economic stage. More particularly they saw nationalism exercising a pervasive influence on the economic policies of Britain's rivals. The resurgence of protectionism was regarded by the historical economists as evidence of the desire of Britain's competitors 'to organise [their] economic life ... in independence of [their] neighbours',[13] and therefore a comprehensive rejection of the 'cosmopolitan' assumptions of Classical economics which saw 'the interests of particular individuals'.[14] Looking at Britain's

response to this environment, however, the historical school saw economists and governments still wedded to individualistic shibboleths of *laissez-faire* and Free Trade, based on notions of the comparative advantage of individual 'economic men' in an international division of labour. In terms of both theory and practice, Classical economic orthodoxies were seen to be out of step with contemporary conditions.

The net result of Britain's misconceived and misaligned thinking and policies was, the historical economists contended, a deterioration in the nation's relative economic performance. In particular they drew attention to the problems faced by Britain's 'productive' sector, by which they meant agriculture and manufacturing.[15] Here Free Trade was seen to have allowed unrestricted import penetration to weaken Britain's farming and industrial interests.

Equally damaging, foreign manufacturers, aided by the state assistance of tariffs, had formed themselves into capital-rich trusts and cartels which had enabled them to adopt trading practices, such as 'dumping', which were driving British producers from foreign, 'neutral' and even home markets.[16] At no point did the historical economists contend that Britain was becoming poorer in an absolute sense. But they did argue that the nation's wealth was becoming imbalanced through an increasing reliance upon service sector and investment income.[17] This, they felt, brought home in practical terms the distinction between individual and collective/national prosperity. The historical economists frowned upon investment income on the grounds that it produced fortunes in the City of London but created only 'values in exchange'[18] for the nation, and did not lead to the diffusion of economic activity and employment that attended upon production.[19] They prioritised *productive* wealth as the basis of a nation's economic prosperity *vis-à-vis* other nations in a competitive world.

Just as wealth in itself was an inadequate subject of study, so wealth in itself was no measure of a nation's economic health – what mattered most was *how* that wealth was created and what contribution it made to national well-being.

In terms of policy this emphasis on the need to foster Britain's productive capacities led the historical economists in the late 19th century to support, like Balfour, the bimetallic cause. The price fall of the late 19th century, which the historical economists attributed to the gold standard, was seen to have benefited banking and investment interests at the expense of producer profits. Likewise the historical economists felt that Free Trade had boosted *international* commerce and provided increased service income for 'the City', but left Britain's *national* productive base vulnerable.[20] Both the Gold Standard and Free Trade were seen as having committed Britain to a 'cosmopolitan' political economy which was out of keeping with the prevailing climate of cut-throat national rivalries, of benefit only to the 'unproductive' *rentier* element in society and damaging to the interests of employers and employees in the productive sectors. As an alternative the historical economists advocated a neo-mercantilist approach, which culminated in their support for the tariff campaign. Tariffs were to provide British producers with a defence against their competitors and, through Imperial Preference, establish a large, sheltered market which would enable them to expand their activities. Britain's productive forces were to be actively encouraged by abandoning an economic strategy which had left them exposed to the whims of a market that was biased against them.

A close examination of Arthur Balfour's position indicates that he not only shared the historical economists' relativism but also many of their broader assumptions. This reflected his own independent thought, but it is also noticeable that his

papers include extensive correspondence with W J Ashley's brother, Percy (a senior official at the Board of Trade), and an even fuller exchange with W A S Hewins. Indeed, between 1906 and 1910, Hewins, who was Secretary of Chamberlain's Tariff Commission, was Balfour's closest economic adviser. He viewed the separation of economic phenomena from their wider context as an 'artificial simplification',[21] agreed that 'the industry of the world is evidently a corporate process',[22] and accepted that 'the State is something more than the individuals composing it'.[23]

Equally important, he shared many of the historical economists' ideas about the nature of economic organisation and the practical effects of contemporary economic developments. Like the historical economists, Balfour had no truck with the Smithean idea that 'the merchant has no country'. In his *Economic Notes on Insular Free Trade* he remarked that nations *have not felt themselves bound to consider arguments drawn from cosmopolitan economics*, and argued that this indicated that they were *both unable and unwilling to turn the natural resources of the world to the best economic account*. Balfour thus rejected the notion that there was a functioning international division of labour, and accepted that national interests were the basis of economic policy-making in the modern world. When he addressed more particular issues, Balfour was also close to the historical economists. For example, on the effects of falling prices he argued that *the fall of prices acts differently on the different members of the {social} group ... On whom will fall the loss? Evidently on contributors who cannot withdraw their contribution and not on those who can.*[24]

Money makes nothing: therefore saving money does not accumulate the means of making anything ... From all this it follows that an investing nation does not thereby become a producing nation.

BALFOUR

Balfour underlined his position by noting that ... *A man who merely serves does nothing for production. A man who merely invests, i.e. buys someone else's shares or stocks, does nothing ... for production ... Money makes nothing: therefore saving money does not accumulate the means of making anything ... From all this it follows that an investing nation does not thereby become a producing nation.*[25]

This was in keeping with Balfour's and the historical economists' bimetallist thinking, and it shows that Balfour accepted the historical economists' distinction between productive and unproductive groups. Furthermore, in his *Economic Notes on Insular Free Trade,* Balfour was clear that, *As regards the national income from foreign investments, it has to be observed that while it must always be better for the inhabitants of any country to own capital than not to own it, it is better that the capital they own should be earning a profit at home,* and he concluded that capital export could represent a loss to domestic capital and labour.[26] Balfour thus took the view that domestic production was of greater value in a national economic context than, 'invisible', service income.

With regard to Free Trade Balfour also adopted a historicist position. In April 1902 he declared that *the doctrine of Free Trade is not a mere speculative hypothesis ... it is not a metaphysical theory, and it is not even a theological dogma, but ... a practical thing.*[27] The implication of this argument was that *circumstances* rather than principle determined the efficacy of Free Trade, which paralleled the historical economists' view that if a policy had worked in the past *there must be a strong presumption that it would be unsuitable in the present condition of society.*[28] In virtually all of his early statements on the tariff question Balfour insisted that the debate was not a repeat of the controversies of the 1840s, for the simple reason that circumstances were entirely different, and he demonstrated

great impatience with those who spoke of *heresy* or who *find some formula in a book of authority, and throw it at their opponents' head*.[29] In his *Economic Notes* he explicitly referred back to the 1840s, and declared that Cobden and his supporters had *failed to foresee that the world would reject Free Trade and ... failed to take account of the commercial possibilities of the British Empire*.[30] His message was constant and consistent – time and circumstance had changed and policy makers needed to take note of that rather than rely upon a-historical formulations.

If in general terms Balfour acknowledged that changed circumstances required a re-think of policy, it was also the case that he felt that some changes in economic conditions were of particular importance. The development of trusts and their trading practices was one which he singled out for attention. In June 1903 Balfour stressed *the provision of adequate capital for carrying on great modern industries*[31] as a *sine qua non* in an industrial world dominated by large-scale corporations. Here, again, he was in step with the historical economists who felt that 'capital has become the dominating influence on production'.[32] In Balfour's view Britain's ability to attract the level of capital necessary for its industries had been *imperilled by the fact that foreign nations, under their protective system, are able and willing to import into this country objects which are largely manufactured in this country at below cost price either in the country of origin or in the country of importation*.[33]

The advantage that protection gave Britain's competitors was, according to Balfour, that it enabled them to *run their works evenly* [and] *... design their works on the scale which shall serve the greatest economy of production*.[34] In short, tariffs gave foreign industrialists the economies of scale and home-market security that enabled them to pursue 'dumping' tactics abroad. Balfour's analysis and description of the causes and effects of dumping was rarely matched, either by the

historical economists or indeed by committed tariff reform propagandists, and they provide an interesting example of his acceptance of the reasoning which underpinned a central element of the case for tariffs.

Balfour's basic precepts of political economy, and his arguments about the nature of economic developments in the late 19th and early 20th century, were very close to those propounded by the 'house intellectuals' of the tariff campaign. Moreover, there was very little in his analysis of what was wrong with the British economy that the most ardent tariff reformer would have found alien. This makes it difficult to see his position as anything but sympathetic to the tariff cause. But if this is the case, he seems to have behaved in a rather surprising manner, as we will see in the next chapter.

Chapter 4: Balfour the Enigma

If Balfour was sympathetic to the tariff cause, why did he not translate this intellectual sympathy into a more clear-cut support for the Chamberlainite campaign? The question becomes all the more puzzling if one examines Balfour's position in the prologue to, and initial phases of, the tariff campaign. In his speech to the House of Commons of April 1902 Balfour had signalled his view that Free Trade was not an immutable policy, and his behaviour during the rest of that year confirmed his position. Here it should be remembered that before he left for South Africa in November 1902, Joseph Chamberlain had, to his satisfaction, secured majority Cabinet support for using the 1-shilling duty on imported corn imposed in spring of that year for the purposes of Imperial Preference.[1] Had Balfour as Prime Minster and chairman of Cabinet not been in agreement it is difficult to see either how the issue could have reached such an advanced stage of Cabinet discussion. Likewise it is difficult to understand why Chamberlain should have reacted so angrily when, on his return, he found that the Chancellor of the Exchequer, C T Ritchie, had effectively blackmailed the Cabinet into accepting the duty's repeal. Unless Chamberlain was engaged in an extraordinary act of self-delusion there is no alternative but to accept that the Cabinet, with Balfour at its head, had indicated its

acceptance of the principle of Chamberlain's argument in the autumn of 1902.

The discussions and machinations that followed on from the repeal of the corn duty in the early summer of 1903 appear to confirm that Balfour was closer to Chamberlain than to the Free Trade element in the Cabinet. Following a key Cabinet discussion in early May, Balfour informed the King that he was due to meet a deputation objecting to the corn duty's repeal later that month, and that he would speak *in such terms as would indicate the possibility of a revival of the tax, if it were associated with some great change in our fiscal system* (my emphasis).[2] Given that Prime Ministerial correspondence with the sovereign is normally anodyne, this was an important statement, for it implied that Balfour had not discarded the idea of either Imperial Preference or a more comprehensive alteration in Britain's Free Trade stance.

On 15 May Balfour met the deputation against repeal, and told them that he was not *one of those who can flatter themselves that our existing fiscal system is necessarily permanent.* He added that he was not a protectionist and that any policy change would require the consent of *the great body and mass of the people,* but he very much left the door open for critics of Free Trade.[3] On the same day Chamberlain made his famous 'demand for an enquiry' in Birmingham – the speech that has gone down as the public starting point of the tariff debate.

That both Balfour and Chamberlain spoke on the same day on essentially the same subject was a coincidence, and it would be wrong to assume some sort of conspiracy concerning either the content or reception of their respective statements. However, given that Balfour and Chamberlain *knew* that they were both due to speak, it stretches the bounds of credulity to think that they had not reached *some* form of agreement before announcing their respective positions. That Balfour

and Chamberlain did have an agreement seems eminently plausible. In his diary for 15 May 1903 Edward Hamilton of the Treasury noted that Balfour's speech 'hinted obscurely at possible changes ahead fiscally', that 'such changes ... could not be made without the express concurrence of the people' and that 'this was presumably or intended to be what he and Chamberlain have agreed upon'.[4]

Likewise Balfour, in writing to the Duke of Devonshire in late August 1903, referred to the Cabinet meeting of early May and noted that *Chamberlain, if you remember, took the occasion to observe that he proposed to say at Birmingham much the same as what I proposed to say to the deputation, only in a less definite manner* (original emphasis)[5] – a description of the two speeches of 15 May that was entirely accurate. However, Balfour added that Chamberlain's comments in the House of Commons in late May, referring to the use of tariff revenues to fund social reform, was *a direct violation of an arrangement with me*, a strange remark to make unless there had been some form of 'pact'.

Piecing together evidence from the documents and events of 1902–3, and assessing it in the light of both Balfour's personal disposition and his statements on political economy, an intriguingly plausible story emerges. On the one hand there is Chamberlain: a dynamic personality well-versed in the arts of popular politics and committed to a radical restructuring of Britain's commercial policy. On the other there is Balfour: a cautious man who fought shy of 'demagogic' appeals but who was also deeply sceptical about Britain's unilateral free-trade stance. In many ways the political division of labour between the two was perfect. Both felt that the time had come for a change in British trade policy, and both accepted that popular support had to be gained if such a change were to be politically viable. Balfour was not in a position, nor was he able,

to engage in a popular crusade to persuade the electorate, but Chamberlain had greater freedom and the requisite political talents to pursue such a course of action. With Balfour as chief, Chamberlain could provide the Indians.

At first glance the idea of such a political partnership may seem unlikely, but it would explain a great deal. To begin with it would explain Balfour's tetchy remarks about Chamberlain's *violation of an arrangement* which would otherwise make little sense. It would also explain Balfour's seemingly duplicitous behaviour in the late summer and autumn of 1903 over the Cabinet resignations, when he kept Chamberlain's resignation secret until he had secured those of the Free Trade Ministers. Balfour's public position on the tariff question in late 1903 was the *Economic Notes on Insular Free Trade*, which foregrounded a 'retaliationist' argument. However, two of the Free Trade ministers who resigned in September, Lord George Hamilton and C T Ritchie, cited Balfour's so-called 'Blue Paper' to the Cabinet of 13 August as a major cause of their disquiet. In this paper Balfour, according to Lord George Hamilton, not only advocated retaliatory tariffs but also accepted 'food taxes' as a basis for Imperial Preference.[6] This, along with the Prime Minister's action in concealing Chamberlain's resignation until he had received the resignation of the Free Trade members of his Cabinet, was taken to indicate that Balfour was closer to Chamberlain than he had been willing to admit. Given that there was a great deal of bitterness surrounding the Cabinet resignations of September 1903 it could simply be that sour grapes were being pressed particularly hard. But the fact that Balfour replaced Ritchie at the Exchequer with Chamberlain's son, Austen, hardly indicated even-handedness. More important, Balfour's public statements on the tariff question in late 1903 and over the next year tended to confirm the Free Traders' concerns.

Balfour's public exchange of letters with Chamberlain on the latter's resignation was hardly reassuring to Free Trade opinion, with the Prime Minister saying that *the time has come when a change should be made in the fiscal canons by which we have bound ourselves in our commercial dealings with other governments.*[7] This message was to be a consistent theme of Balfour's utterances from the autumn of 1903 onwards. At the Sheffield meeting of the National Union in October Balfour stressed that whilst the move towards Free Trade in 1846 had been *necessary and appropriate to the times*, it had to be acknowledged that *those times are not our times.* Balfour went on to point out that Cobden had made an important error. *Few who have studied ... [Cobden's] life and writings*, Balfour argued, *will pretend that the sentiment of nationality had any large place in his philosophy of politics.* This, he declared, was a particularly relevant oversight insofar as *the sentiment of nationality has received an accretion of strength of which no man then living* [1846] *could have dreamed; and that contemporaneously with this growing sentiment of nationality we have found protection in foreign countries.* For Britain and the Colonies not to take cognisance of this nationalist trend was, in Balfour's view, to live in an ideal world fit only for *dreamers.* Having neatly summarised the basic historical case against Free Trade, Balfour went on to point out the more particular dangers inherent in the contemporary situation, stating that *in the alliance of tariffs and trusts there is a danger to the enterprise of this country which threatens not merely the capitalist ... but ... the artisan and labouring classes.* In the light of these developments Balfour posed himself a question. He asked: *Do you desire to alter fundamentally the fiscal tradition which has prevailed*

The time has come when a change should be made in the fiscal canons by which we have bound ourselves in our commercial dealings with other governments.

BALFOUR

during the last two generations? To that, he replied: *'Yes, I do.* Mindful of the issue that had brought about the resignation of his Free Trade Ministers, and concerned about the electoral implications of the 'food tax' aspect of the argument for Imperial Preference, Balfour entered some important caveats in his Sheffield speech. Whilst accepting that the idea of closer economic relations with the Colonies was an essential part of the case for tariffs, he contended that it was not a practical proposal at that time because *the country will not tolerate a tax on food.* For this reason he felt that tariff reform could not be *tried in its integrity*, and emphasised that he proposed to amend Britain's Free Trade stance only in order to deploy 'retaliatory' tariffs for the purposes of commercial negotiation.[8]

Speaking at Manchester in January 1904 Balfour reiterated his view that times had changed since 1846 and that this demanded a re-thinking of Free Trade. He also went out of his way to launch an attack on H H Asquith, who had pursued Chamberlain around the country in the autumn of 1903 in an attempt to repudiate the case for tariff reform. Balfour in turn repudiated Asquith's arguments.

Herbert Henry Asquith (1852–1928) was Prime Minister from 1908 to 1916. First elected to parliament in 1886 as a Liberal, he took over as Prime Minister on Campbell-Bannerman's death. His government introduced old age pensions, unemployment insurance and an expansion of the navy. Conflict over the 1909 budget with the House of Lords led to the passing of the Parliament Act 1911 which removed the House of Lords veto on legislation. In 1915 he headed a coalition government, but was seen as an ineffective wartime leader, and he was forced out by Lloyd George in 1916. Asquith remained leader of the Liberal Party until 1926 and became a peer in 1925. (See *Asquith* by Stephen Bates, in this series.)

He denounced Asquith's optimistic description of Britain's economic situation under Free Trade, and described the Liberal spokesman as a pseudo-Free Trader, on the grounds that retaliatory tariffs were the only means in the current climate of bringing about 'real' Free Trade through negotiation.[9]

With regard to Imperial Preference Balfour described this as *the greater half of fiscal reform* which was motivated by *more unselfish and nobler instincts than mere negotiation about tariffs*, but he also stressed the obstacles in its path. At the same time he denounced the Free Trade argument that imperial tariffs would lead to arguments with the Colonies and asked *did anybody ever put his ideal of domestic felicity in a perpetual judicial separation?*. Balfour was particularly keen in this speech to emphasise the need for Conservative Party unity, but his argument in this context was an interesting one insofar as he stated that *fiscal reform itself will suffer more than any other cause if undue impatience or any other motive ... forces a change so great either upon the Party or the country in a manner which threatens even for a moment that there shall be a reaction*. The very next day he underlined this message, declaring that *Conservatism ought not to resemble Radicalism* and whilst stating that the Conservatives were *a Party and a Government of fiscal reform* urged caution.[10] Timing as much as principle was Balfour's concern.

Through all of his major set-piece speeches on the tariff question in 1904 and 1905 Balfour sang from the same hymn sheet. He consistently stated that Britain had to revise its tariff policy in order to bring protectionist nations to the negotiating table, counteract the effects of 'dumping' and, if possible, bring about closer commercial links with the Colonies. His main emphasis throughout was on the retaliatory aspect of tariff reform, with Imperial Preference in close, if always qualified, attendance. It is important to note, however, that Balfour also consistently and explicitly rejected

protectionism which he flatly described at Edinburgh as *not the best policy*.[11]

Balfour's caution on the tariff question is most easily explained in terms of his desperate desire to ensure party unity, but there is an alternative explanation. Balfour's views on the general nature of political economy, and at his stance on tariff reform, were remarkably consistent, and indicated that Balfour had clear and strong views on these subjects.

To begin with Balfour evidently had no faith in Free Trade as an established wisdom. For him there was simply no such thing. He accepted the historical economic viewpoint that economic policy had to be shaped to its particular social, cultural and national context. By 1903 Balfour had come to the view that 'old fashioned' Free Trade had had its day and that a new commercial policy better fitted to the prevailing climate had to be designed. Thus in July 1903 he was able to tell his cousin, Lord Hugh Cecil, that *the serious mistake into which you have fallen is that of supposing that the Unionist Party were put into office for the purpose of preserving, in every particular, a version of Free Trade doctrine which … I at all events, have never accepted*.[12] In this respect he was completely in agreement with Joseph Chamberlain that Free Trade in its established form had to go.

The question remained, however, as to what was to replace it, and it was on this question that Balfour and Chamberlain's 'partnership' unravelled. Balfour accepted Chamberlain's and the historical economists' critique of Free Trade and their analysis of the damage it had done to the British economy, but he did not endorse their neo-mercantilist remedy.

With regard to Imperial Preference Balfour was in principle supportive. Had he not been then, as noted above, it is unlikely that the Cabinet would have approved the principle of preference at the Cabinet of 2 November 1902. Like Chamberlain,

Balfour was struck by the voluntary support the Colonies had given to Britain during the Boer War and also by the unilateral 'Colonial Offer' of trade reciprocity at the Colonial Conference of 1902, and he clearly hoped to exploit this outburst of 'imperial spirit'. In his Birmingham speech of May 1903, Chamberlain told his audience that the Colonies' outlook gave them 'an opportunity' which they had to seize or perhaps lose for good.[13]

In a memorandum to Cabinet only six weeks later Balfour issued a similar warning. He criticized any dogmatic rejection of preferential duties on the grounds that *if a tax is otherwise sufficiently desirable, the mere fact that it carries with it some flavour of Protection is by no means a conclusive argument against it*, and he told his colleagues that if they rejected Canada's offer then this would lead the Canadians *to an ultimate fiscal alliance with the United States* and do untold harm to the Empire, a contingency he described as *not only probable ... [but] almost inevitable*.[14] Balfour had told his own audience of 15 May that he saw economic ties, rather than constitutional and political bonds, as the best means of securing imperial unity and stated that *if it were possible I should look forward to such a consummation with unfeigned pleasure*. For Balfour the key phrase was 'if it were possible', and in this context his particular concern was popular antagonism to 'food taxes'. In Parliament at the end of May Balfour had agreed that *you will never have a tax on food ... accepted by the people of this country except as an integral part of a large policy on which their hearts are set.*

You will never have a tax on food ... accepted by the people of this country except as an integral part of a large policy on which their hearts are set.

BALFOUR

This, however, does not indicate that Balfour was *against* Imperial Preference. Rather it reinforces the argument,

developed earlier in this book, that Balfour looked to Chamberlain's campaigning abilities to deliver *the heart, and conscience and the intellect of the great body and mass of the people.* All the indications are that Balfour thought that Imperial Preference was *right,* but that he felt an 'educative' campaign was necessary before the Party could embrace it as official policy. The problem that arose for Balfour was that, partly as a result of Chamberlain's personal disposition and partly as a result of the complex political economy of the tariff argument, the 'educative' campaign got out of hand. Once the lid had been taken off the tariff issue Chamberlain found that balancing the various demands and interests affected by the campaign required additions to the initial 'big idea' of preference. The question of whether social reforms were necessary to sweeten the 'food tax' pill for the working class electorate; whether domestic producers would accept the export emphasis of the argument for preference; whether rural and urban interests in tariffs could be reconciled. All of these issues came out of the woodwork once the tariff issue had been raised, and Chamberlain's impulsiveness, and the fact that at 67 he was 'an old man in a hurry', only added to the problems. The considered, constructive debate that Balfour desired was thus lost in the heated controversy that surrounded the issue. Balfour's almost angst-ridden pleas for 'moderate' debate that marked his statements in early 1904 may well have been motivated by concerns about his own Party's unity, but they also expressed his frustration that the sane, disinterested reappraisal of Britain's commercial policy which he desired had become submerged in a sea of factional dispute.

What was particularly worrying for Balfour, and ultimately to be instrumental in his downfall, was Chamberlain's endorsement of protective tariffs for British industry and indeed agriculture in the autumn of 1903 and the

prominence of these issues in the tariff campaign thereafter. Politically Chamberlain had very little option, and personally very little inclination, to avoid these issues, but Balfour regarded them as unnecessary and unwanted distractions from what he saw as the core issues at stake. For Balfour Imperial Preference was a *noble*, *unselfish* and eminently desirable goal, but protectionism, which raised the spectre of American-style interest politics, was fraught with *squalid* possibilities, and in December 1904 Balfour complained that Chamberlain had, through protectionism, hitched *all sorts of particular and selfish interests to his Imperial car*.[15]

But this was not Balfour's only objection. As noted above Balfour saw protection as a *wrong* policy, for the very good reason that he was a *committed* retaliationist, that is to say he believed in imposing tariffs on other protectionist nations in order to force them to the negotiating table. This position had an obvious, and oft-referred to, political *raison d'etre*. But to see it simply as a politically convenient 'half-way house' between the 'whole hog tariff reform' and 'free food' positions is a one-dimensional view. Balfour himself dismissed this description of retaliation and argued that it was a cogent policy in its own right.[16]

Balfour's defence of his policy was understandable, for he had adhered to it for many years. In June 1880, in the context of Anglo-French trade relations, the young Balfour had argued that circumstances had changed since Cobden had negotiated his famous commercial pact with Chevalier. It was not true, he declared, that foreign countries had moved towards Free Trade spontaneously in the past, but rather that they had done so in exchange for mutual tariff reductions. But in 1880 he saw Britain at a disadvantage in any negotiations because, having no tariffs of its own, it could only use *threats instead of bribes*. A possible way out of this problem,

he suggested, was for Britain to introduce retaliatory tariffs as a bargaining instrument, a suggestion he repeated a year later when Parliament debated the new Anglo-French commercial treaty. Likewise during the election campaign of 1892 he stated that: *I am not a Fair Trader nor a Protectionist, but I am of the opinion that, if foreign nations deliberately attempt to screw up their duties against English manufactured goods, there will be occasions on which it would suit us to bring them to a better state of mind by, in our turn, placing duties upon their manufactures.*[17]

I am not a Fair Trader nor a Protectionist, but I am of the opinion that, if foreign nations deliberately attempt to screw up their duties against English manufactured goods, there will be occasions on which it would suit us to bring them to a better state of mind by, in our turn, placing duties upon their manufactures.

BALFOUR

These arguments from the 1880s and 1890s were precisely the ones Balfour used in the early years of the tariff campaign. In his speech of 15 May 1903 he stated that: *New conditions have arisen since the old Free Trade policy was fought out; and I can imagine contingencies under which, not so much by way of protection as by way of retaliation, it might conceivably be necessary for this country to say that it will no longer remain a passive target for the assaults of other countries living under very different fiscal systems.*[18]

Similarly in his Sheffield declaration he was clear that he looked to tariffs to provide *liberty to negotiate.* Balfour took what was in many ways an 'international relations' view of the tariff question, arguing that *international commerce is largely regulated by treaty, in which trade flows along channels engineered not by Nature but by diplomacy.* For Balfour, very much his uncle's protégé, national diplomacy, rather than bellicose economic nationalism, was the way forward. This required

that Britain had something to negotiate with and hence the necessity of retaliatory tariffs, but protectionism *tout court* was a complete anathema to this approach and had no place in Balfour's schema.

When in August 1904 Balfour told the House of Commons *I am a Free Trader*, there was in terms of his own definition of tariff political economy an internal logic to his position. He accepted that many self-professed Free Traders did not acknowledged him as an adherent of their creed, but this he attributed to his being a *new fashioned Free Trader* rather than a devotee of the old school. In Balfour's view his 'Free Trade' critics, unlike him, had failed to adjust to the times and could not appreciate or understand his idea of *freer* trade. Balfour saw no problem in reconciling his pursuit of freer trade with his support for Imperial Preference. Apart from contending that imperial reciprocity would produce freer trade within the Empire as the Colonies lowered their tariffs, Balfour also argued that retaliation would inhibit other countries from inflicting tariff 'punishment' on the Colonies for their actions. In Balfour's view a combination of retaliation and preference would act to weaken protectionist barriers all round.

Unfortunately for Balfour the subtlety of his position was lost on devout Free Traders, and also failed to please the more autarky-minded imperialist and protectionist sections in the tariff campaign. In this respect Lord Robert Cecil was right in arguing that although Balfour wished to be 'all things to all men', he ended up by being not much to hardly anyone. Balfour's formula was a subtle and sophisticated contribution to the debate on Britain's commercial policy. It undoubtedly did represent a critique of crude Free Trade, but it also avoided the cruder aspects of the tariff campaign. The consequence of Balfour's subtlety, however, was that his arguments failed to garner *immediate* support, but a strong case can be made for

seeing his retaliationist position as gathering strength over time. In the long run Britain's business community proved more receptive to Balfourian than Chamberlainite logic, and the creeping success of retaliationist sentiment was to be an important indicator of weakening business faith in Free Trade.[19] But time, although it was what he wanted, was precisely what Balfour did not have.

Between 1903 and the general election of 1906 the tariff campaign shifted rapidly. For as soon as one aspect of tariff reform had been raised it was impossible to avoid opening the whole can of tariff worms. Balfour had looked to engage in a comprehensive and hopefully subtle debate on the merits and demerits of both tariffs and Free Trade and in this context his emphasis on retaliatory tariffs as a route to freer trade seemed to him to offer a plausible *via media*.

Given the intensity of the tariff debate and the strength of feelings expressed on both sides of the controversy Balfour was desperate to find a way of soothing and smoothing Party divisions. In many ways it could be said that Balfour fudged, fudged and fudged again to save the party he loved.

Part Three

THE LEGACY

Chapter 5: Leader of the Opposition

The 1906 general election, at which the Conservatives were decisively defeated, and electoral developments between 1906 and 1910, strengthened the hands of those within the Conservative Party who favoured a positive, tariff-based approach to the electorate.

That the Conservatives lost so heavily in 1906 was largely because, for the first time since 1892, they faced a united, fully active Liberal Party that was fighting in alliance with the newly-formed Labour Party. Moreover, the Conservatives themselves were divided over tariffs, and in some seats presented two candidates. Before 1906 the wholehearted tariff reform had had two rivals for the affections of the Conservative Party. The most important was the strategy promulgated by Balfour and Conservative central office.

As noted above, the 'Balfourite' option was not opposed to tariff reform on principle but emphasised the pragmatic issue of Party unity. Balfour emphasised Party unity as an important issue in its own right while simultaneously trying to construct a workable compromise on the tariff question. Here he stressed the retaliatory aspect of the tariff argument which acknowledged the need for a 'reconsideration' of Britain's Free Trade stance but showed the Free Trade contingent in the Party that he wished to secure a more genuine system of international Free Trade. The 'Balfourite' position had stood

as 'official' Conservative policy before 1906, although there were enormous difficulties in sustaining the complex logic of this position. As Robert Cecil was to note in his memoirs, the result of Balfour's stance was that 'sometimes both sides … claimed him as an adherent. At others both rejected him … if anyone could reconcile the irreconcilable it would be he. But it [could] not be done.'

The difficulty of defending the 'Balfourite' position was, however, not solely confined to reconciling the irreconcilable. Again, as Robert Cecil pointed out, there were problems in presenting the 'Balfourite' position to a wider audience: 'the body of electors regard[ed] his attitude as either intentionally ambiguous or else motivated by a culpable levity'. Others describe the basic problem in less coded terms. Writing to Lord Lonsdale in January 1904, E H Currie, the Secretary of the Northern Region NUCA, stated that 'in the North, as far as I am able to judge, … there is no use in … halting at the half-way house of retaliation as among working men the issues are too complex for them to grasp … with them it is just one or the other, Protection or Free Trade.'

That Balfour lost his own seat at the 1906 election – thereby establishing the unenviable record of being the only prime minister to lose his seat at a general election – did not exactly strengthen his electoral plausibility and other 'Balfourites' expressed clear disillusion. In short, Balfour's famed subtlety was deemed beyond the understanding of the mass electorate. Balfour remained leader of the party and a safe seat was procured for him by the early resignation of a Balfourite loyalist: otherwise he would have had to go to the Lords, and this was thought an inappropriate option.

Balfour's unwillingness to embrace the 'full tariff programme', as developed by Chamberlain and his followers between 1903 and 1910, did not stem solely from his desire to

preserve Party unity, or from his intrinsic inability to commit himself to a cause. To see Balfour's actions solely in these terms is to do a disservice to Balfour's ideas and to the history of the tariff debate. Balfour was committed to a particular conception of tariff reform, and his real problem was that he was asked to commit himself to another conception which he did not believe was *right*. In 1903 Balfour had hoped to bring about a change in public opinion on Free Trade which would open the door to retaliation, a 'rational' readjustment of Britain's trading relations, and, if possible, closer commercial ties with the Colonies. Instead the tariff campaign developed into a semi-autarkic programme of preference and protection linked to further schemes of domestic reform. Balfour may have been at fault for not realising that this would happen, but in this respect he was by no means alone among his contemporaries. The net result was that Balfour became the leader of a party that had embraced a conception of tariff reform that was unrecognisable from his own and which he did not believe in. It may be a general assumption that politicians are good at saying and doing what they do not really believe, but the field of history is littered with the political corpses of those who have tried and failed to achieve this feat – and Arthur Balfour's is one of them.

After the electoral debacle of 1906 Balfour shifted his position, perhaps because he realised that his subtleties were indeed lost on both the electorate and the mass of the Conservative grass roots. But it was also perhaps because the overwhelming majority of Conservative MPs who had retained their seats in 1906 were fully committed tariff

'Tariff reform means work for all.'

JOSEPH CHAMBERLAIN

reformers. At any rate Balfour announced at successive NUCA conferences in 1906, 1907 and 1908 that tariff reform was *the*

first constructive work that a future Conservative government would undertake. Furthermore, he was clear in all of these speeches that it was the full tariff programme and not merely retaliation that the party would pursue.

Balfour may not have been an enthusiastic convert to the tariff cause but political circumstances between 1906 and 1910 left him very little room for manoeuvre. Apart from the fact that the balance of power within the Conservative Party had shifted decisively towards the tariff reformers, developments on the Left of politics militated in favour of the tariff option. The tariff slogan, coined by Chamberlain in 1903, that 'tariff reform means work for all' seemed to have an extended appeal when unemployment was seen to be rising in 1907–8. Certainly this was deemed to lie at the heart of a number of Conservative by-election successes in 1908. Equally important, however, the argument that tariffs both directly and indirectly would provide a boost to government revenues without recourse to increased direct taxation began to take on added political significance in the wake of the Liberal government's willingness to utilise high direct taxation.

Asquith's budget of 1908, which differentiated between earned and unearned increments in people's incomes and which taxed the latter heavily, indicated that a radical Liberal regime was prepared to adopt a redistributive fiscal strategy. This was underlined by the Liberal government's radical social reform initiatives, such as free school meals for children introduced in 1906, the creation of old age pensions in 1908 and the introduction of medical and dental inspection for school children in 1908–9. All of these reforms demanded high levels of government revenue and the Liberal choice was to levy high direct taxation.

Balfour and his party were genuinely appalled at the

radical fiscal regime that was developing under the Liberals and against the backdrop of an increasingly high direct tax regime the appeal of indirect taxes – that is, tariffs – became even greater. Balfour himself described Asquith's 1908 budget as *socialistic* but the Conservatives' splenetic hostility to Liberal fiscal policy reached its peak in 1909 as the party raged against the 'People's Budget' introduced by Lloyd George. The fact that Ramsey MacDonald, Philip Snowden and other Labour leaders welcomed the budget only confirmed the Conservatives' belief that the Liberal Party had gone over 'bag and baggage' to socialism. Likewise the Conservatives were confirmed in their belief that the only viable alternative to the Liberal direct tax regime was the introduction of tariffs – a point summed up in a pamphlet produced by the Conservative editor of the *Observer* J L Garvin which was simply entitled *Tariff or Budget*.

Prime Minister from 1916 to 1922, war leader and orator David Lloyd George (1863–1945) entered Parliament as a Liberal MP in 1890, and was Chancellor of the Exchequer from 1908 to 1915. It was his 'People's Budget' of 1909 with higher taxes for the rich that brought the conflict with the House of Lords leading to the 1911 Parliament Act. During the First World War, by successfully manoeuvring to remove Asquith as Prime Minister of the coalition government, he split the Liberals. He won the 1918 general election at the head of the coalition, but in 1922 he was forced to resign when the Conservatives withdrew support. For the next 20 years, he campaigned in Parliament largely without a political party to support him. (See *Lloyd George* by Hugh Purcell, in this series.)

So visceral was the Conservative loathing of the People's Budget that the House of Lords, which of course contained an overwhelming Conservative majority, voted to reject the

budget. This led the Liberal government to resign and to call a General Election on the basis that the country faced a clash of 'the Peers versus the People'. Although the Conservatives recovered some of the electoral ground they had lost in the Liberal landslide of 1906, they did not secure a majority, and the Liberal government had secured a mandate for the re-introduction of the radical budget.

The rejection of the 'People's Budget' was arguably Balfour's greatest blunder as Conservative leader. In 1906 he had made the extraordinary political statement that no matter which Party held a majority in the Commons the Conservative Party would still govern the British Empire – a remark noteworthy as much for its arrogance as its crude view of political relations between the Commons and the Lords. At the same time, however, his predecessor, Lord Salisbury, had used the Conservatives' inbuilt majority in the Lords systematically to mutilate Liberal legislation between 1892 and 1895. But Salisbury had been very careful to select legislation that could be deemed sectional. For example, the Lords had thrown out Gladstone's second Home Rule Bill but had left untouched Harcourt's introduction of death duties in 1894 and the introduction of Parish Councils in 1894. In short Salisbury had deliberately avoided attacking Liberal legislation which could have opened the door to a 'Peers versus the People' campaign.

At first glance it seemed as if Balfour after 1906 would pursue a similarly subtle mode of assault. Balfour's Lords had effectively mutilated Liberal education and Irish legislation but had left untouched social reforms, such as, notably, old age pensions and the Trade Boards Act. The trouble was that the People's Budget went too far for Balfour's erstwhile followers amongst the aristocracy. Lloyd George's 'People's Budget' was carefully targeted, with the rise in income tax

to 1s 2d (7p) in the pound, hitting only about one million voters. But there were other causes of grievance. The full rate of tax was targeted at earned incomes over £3,000 per annum and unearned incomes over £700. Those with an earned income not in excess of £3,000 were to pay only 9d (4p) in the pound on the first £2,000 and 1s (5p) between £2 and £3,000. In addition, Lloyd George introduced a 'Supertax' of 6d (2.5p) in the pound on incomes over £5,000, higher death duties, and duties on the value and sale of undeveloped non-agricultural and some country estates land. The budget was unapologetically class-discriminatory, with Lloyd George declaring that he was 'robbing hen-roosts' to help the poor.

In particular the taxes on land and land development hit the Liberals' oldest adversaries, the aristocracy. The British aristocracy, especially those dependent upon relatively small-scale agricultural and rental income, regarded themselves as a social class pressurised by economic hardship and socio-political prejudice. Like Oscar Wilde's Lady Bracknell they felt that their land 'gave them position and prevented them from keeping it up' and indeed that land had 'ceased to be either a pleasure or a profit'. In these circumstances it was virtually impossible for a Conservative leader to control the violent antagonism which the self-styled beleaguered aristocracy felt towards Lloyd George and his budget.

One result of the rejection of the 'People's Budget' was that the Liberal government decided to prevent the House of Lords from ever again being in a position to reject legislation that had been passed by an 'overwhelming' Commons majority. Thus 1911 saw the introduction of the Parliament Act whereby the veto powers of the House of Lords were effectively to be abolished. This in itself of course raised an obvious problem, namely what to do if the House of Lords vetoed the Parliament Act. Here the Liberal government

refused to be cowed and Asquith obtained a promise from the new King, George V, that if necessary he would create enough new Liberal peers to guarantee a majority in favour of the Parliament Act in the Lords. This in turn presented the Conservatives with a dilemma. Many Conservative peers felt that their only options were either to vote in favour of the Parliament Act or to abstain, with either of these courses ensuring the passage of the Act. However, there were those who felt that opposition *à outrance* was necessary and indeed obligatory. These Conservative peers became known as 'the Ditchers' on the basis that they would die in the last ditch to preserve the Lords' powers.

Balfour, much to the irritation of the 'Ditchers' in the Lords and his more volatile supporters in the Commons, advocated abstention, which simply served to confirm the view of many Conservatives that their leader lacked backbone. Balfour himself felt that opposition to the Parliament Act was pointless. He told one 'Ditcher': *You object to your tailor being made a peer, [but] you mean to vote in such a way that your hatter and barber shall be ennobled also.*[1]

> *You object to your tailor being made a peer, [but] you mean to vote in such a way that your hatter and barber shall be ennobled also.*
>
> BALFOUR

Perhaps Balfour and the Conservative peers who abstained, or who indeed voted for the Parliament Act, could be deemed to have been guilty of a politically supine snobbery, in that they preferred to retain the social exclusivity of the Lords as a 'club' rather than its constitutional privileges. But whatever the motivations were which led the Conservatives ultimately to acquiesce in the passage of the Parliament Act, the episode served further to undermine Balfour's standing, and the fact that he was out of the country on the day on which the vote

took place diluted the little respect he still enjoyed within his own party. Had Balfour perhaps been more imaginative he could have attempted to counter the Parliament Bill with an alternative scheme of House of Lords reform. Several such schemes were drawn up by Conservatives, with the most imaginative formulated by Lord Selborne (full details of the scheme can be found in Selborne's papers in the Bodleian Library) but Balfour seemed hardly to consider the possibility of offering a positive alternative.

Given that the Parliament Act was from the outset essentially a lost cause, its passage need not in itself have fatally undermined Balfour's leadership. His real problem was that his decision-making and positions during the general elections of January and November 1910 had seemed to many Conservatives to be poor and ultimately damaging to the party's prospects. To begin with Balfour had announced in the run-up to the January election that a Conservative government, albeit committed to tariff reform, would allow Colonial corn to enter the British market duty free. At one and the same time this sold the pass on the idea that the 'food taxes' intrinsic to the tariff programme, as the Liberals had always claimed and the Conservatives denied, threatened to increase the working-class cost of living. Then in the summer of 1910, between the two elections, Balfour had challenged Asquith to put Home Rule to a referendum if the Conservatives promised to do the same thing with the 'food taxes'. Many Conservatives saw this as, in effect, a cowardly presentation of their Party's policy and indicative of Balfour's generally indecisive approach to politics and his lack of real commitment to the Party's central policy.

At best Balfour could be deemed to have committed some major policy *faux pas* in 1910 and these, taken together with his hesitancy over the Parliament Act, led to a growing

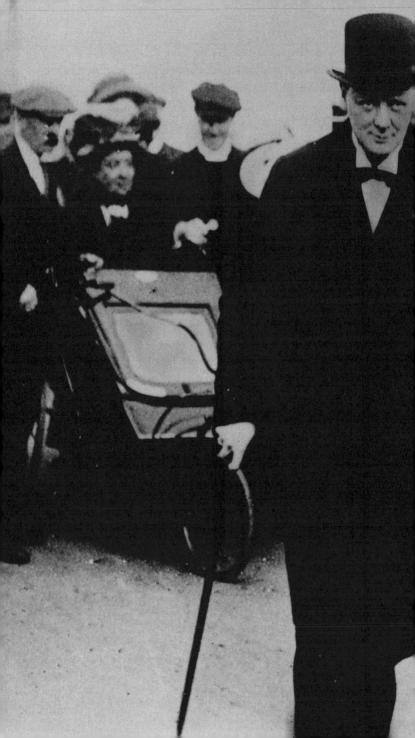

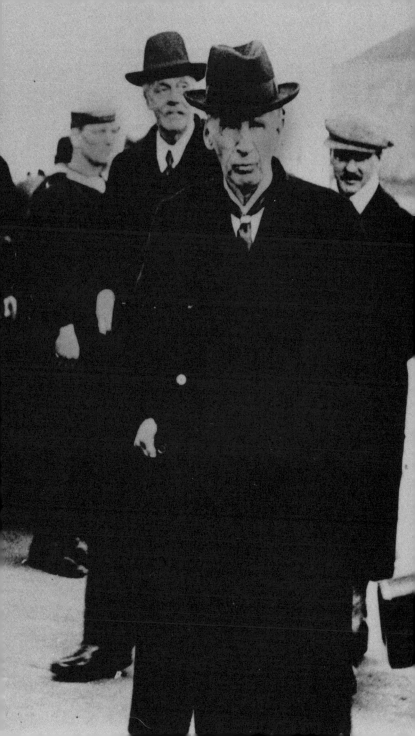

disillusionment with his leadership. At one level it was not surprising that a long-time critic of Balfour's, the editor of the *National Review*, Leo Maxse, should have begun a 'B[alfour] M[ust] G[o]' campaign but by mid-1911 such thoughts were not confined simply to extremists like Maxse. In 1908 the Conservative MP for Ludlow, Rowland Hunt, complained that Balfour could not 'bring himself down from the Olympian heights of philosophy and golf' to address the electorate effectively, and even Balfour's cousin by marriage, Lord Selborne, felt that Balfour's Parliamentary talents were not matched by his ability to appeal to the general public, and in a political environment in which 'the democracy' was the decisive element this weakness was crucial.

Although much of Balfour's time in 1911 was taken up with the Parliament Bill and intra-party tensions over the issue, he did find time look at other questions. In particular he examined and pursued the question of the reform of the party's organisation. Party machinery was a traditional scapegoat for electoral failure, and, in spite of the party's relatively high vote in 1910, the two defeats of that year were no exception. Balfour set in train a series of changes, but, unlike earlier organisational reforms, they focussed on the Party's central administration rather than the localities.

To begin with Balfour's reforms saw the creation of a new, high-level position – that of Party Chairman. The occupant of this post was to be in overall charge of party finance, election strategy and to oversee policy debate within the party in order that 'loose cannons' could be kept under control and embarrassing proposals minimised. At the same time a central Publicity Department was created to ensure that party materials placed before the public all, as it were, 'sang from the same hymn-sheet'. Furthermore, this new Department was to liaise with organisations that were sympathetic

to the Conservative cause, but which were not affiliated to the Party, such as the anti-Socialist Union, in order that their material harmonised with the Tory stance. In the mid-1920s this Department was to play a crucial role in providing the party with an advantage in electoral campaigns. So, Balfour's administrative reforms were, arguably, to be his longest-lasting legacy for the party – at any rate they were in place before he resigned in November 1911.

Balfour's 'failure' as a party leader seemed to be particularly pronounced in terms of the Conservative Party's electoral malaise, which of course did not compare favourably with the success enjoyed under his predecessor. Balfour fought three general elections as party leader and lost all three, whereas Salisbury had fought six and won four with the last two victories in 1895 and 1900 having produced very large Conservative majorities. However, Balfour's 'failure' can be overstated for the simple reason that so too can Salisbury's success. Salisbury's great triumphs of 1895 and 1900 had largely been due to the fact that the Conservatives had faced a demoralised and ill-organised Liberal Party. Bereft of both funds and morale the Liberals had left 117 seats uncontested in 1895 and 149 in 1900.

Thus when one sees that the Conservatives in 1900 obtained 50.3 per cent of the popular vote one needs to ask: 50.3 per cent of what? In 1900 the total poll had been 3,523,482 with 35.1 per cent of the electorate residing in seats that returned unopposed MPs. When the Liberals achieved their landslide victory in 1906 the total number of voters had risen by over two million since 1900 and only 12.6 per cent of the electorate was represented by an unopposed MP. In spite of the fact that their Parliamentary contingent was so drastically reduced in 1906 the actual number of Conservative voters had actually risen. Likewise in January 1910 the Conservatives obtained

their highest share of the popular vote that they obtained under the electoral system that had been introduced by the Third Reform Act of 1884.

In the light of these figures Balfour's 'failure' and Salisbury's 'success' as popular politicians have both been overstated. In many ways Balfour had sought to deploy political and electoral strategies that were very similar to those employed by his uncle, but the political circumstances had completely changed. Balfour, unlike Salisbury, faced a revitalised and united Liberal Party which enjoyed constructive relations with the newly formed Labour Party, which precluded any repetition of the low working-class turnouts that had characterised the elections of 1895 and 1900. Furthermore, the Edwardian Liberals were as close as their predecessors to the Irish Nationalists in Parliament. Rather than focussing on Balfour and the Conservatives' failings it is perhaps more accurate to speak of British politics in the Edwardian period as indicative of the *success* of their opponents.

Nor was it simply in the context of electoral turnouts and the number of contested seats that Salisbury passed a poisoned chalice to Balfour. When Joseph Chamberlain wrote to Balfour in January 1906 to commiserate with him on the loss of his own seat he remarked 'you have gone down in the Labour wave'. Leaving aside the fact that Chamberlain, like many others on the Conservative side, emphasised 'the Labour wave' rather than the 'Liberal landslide' he was in many respects accurate, for Balfour's defeat in East Manchester had in no small part been due to the full mobilisation of the mining vote against him.

Nor was Balfour the only defeated Conservative who felt that the labouring vote had been a decisive factor. For example Lord Stanley, explaining his own defeat, attributed it to the fact that he had had 'the black mark of the trade

unions against me'. That the unions were so committedly anti-Conservative in 1906 was not simply due to the fact that many Conservative MPs, especially in urban areas, were businessmen. Rather it was a consequence of the fact that the Salisburyian regime had presided over a series of legal decisions that had damaged the trade union movement. The most famous of these decisions had occurred in 1901 when the Law Lords, chaired by the ultra-Conservative Lord Chancellor, Lord Halsbury, had decided that actions for breach of tort could be brought against trade unions that had engaged in strike action, and that their employers could bring suit for damages resulting from industrial action. This was the Taff Vale Judgement, and it did more than any other single event to politicise the trade unions and build the Labour vote. Salisbury and his colleagues could claim that this was a legal and not a political decision but not surprisingly the trade union movement found it difficult to see any real difference. In 1906 Balfour and his party picked up the electoral tab that had been run up by the Salisburyian regime.

Chapter 6: War in Europe and Westminster

Balfour was 63 years old when he resigned as Conservative leader. He remained a member of the Shadow Cabinet, but he played very little active part in Party debates, even though between 1911 and 1914 the political focus was on Ireland and was leading towards the passage of Home Rule.

At first it seemed that Balfour was inclined to return to his first intellectual love, philosophy. During his years as opposition leader he had served on the council of the Royal Society, both in 1907–8 and again in 1912–14, and an invitation to give the Gifford lectures at Glasgow University allowed him to develop his intellectual justification of a theistic philosophy. Paradoxically Balfour saw the foundations of doubt and of belief as closely related, insofar as both depended upon reasoned scepticism. Balfour delivered these lectures in the winter of 1914 and they were to be published in 1915 in *Theism and Humanism*.

Apart from philosophy Balfour also turned his attention to his extended family, in which he took great pleasure and which included three nephews and eight nieces – the children of his brothers Gerald and Eustace – most of whom had grown up. Much as in the past, Balfour aired his lines of philosophical thought and discussed them with these young people who often stayed at Whittingehame. Fortunately he seemed to

avoid the tense arguments which had tended to characterise his debates with his cousins, Hugh and Robert Cecil. In her biography (published in 1936) Blanche Dugdale describes this as a particularly happy time in Balfour's life.

Between 1912 and 1914, particularly in the light of Austrian aggression in the Balkans, the threat of war was looming large. From 1912 Balfour was heavily involved with the Committee of Imperial Defence, which of course he had set up when Prime Minister. By 1912 Maurice Hankey had begun his long career as the Committee's secretary, and Balfour tried to use his contacts with Hankey to influence strategic thinking. In 1904 Balfour had called into being a Parliamentary Committee to examine the security of the nation's food supply, which had come to the conclusion that Britain was in effect a raft moored in the North Sea with six weeks food supply on board. The issue of blockade was paramount in British strategic thinking in the decade leading up to the outbreak of war, with the key question being whether Britain was more vulnerable to such a strategy or Germany.

Balfour's concern, relatively advanced for its time, concerned the possibility of the threat of submarine warfare. Balfour tried without success to get Winston Churchill, the First Lord of the Admiralty, to appreciate that submarines were essentially the weapon of the weaker naval power; and, in correspondence with Admiral Lord Fisher, he pointed out that, if war should come, U-boats would probably sink British and other merchant shipping without restraint – *for a submarine could not capture*, he wrote on 20 May 1913.

Balfour, as always sensitive to correct protocol, did not attempt to act as an adviser to his successor as Conservative leader, Andrew Bonar Law. He did become somewhat involved as the Home Rule issue moved into its final and most dangerous pre-war phase. For Southern Ireland, Balfour

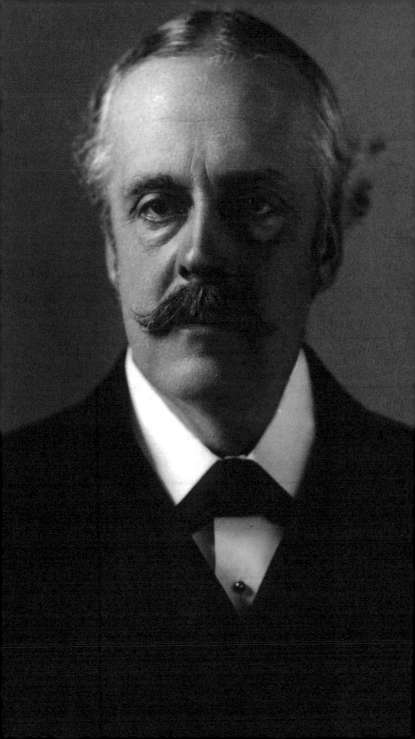

was willing to accept, as a last resort, a grant of independence rather than Home Rule for the whole country, and supported the exclusion of Ulster from governance from Dublin. In this respect he came close to Bonar Law in supporting an 'Ulsterisation' of the Irish Question, but as he well knew this was a strategy that was not warmly approved of by Southern Unionists.

In 1913 Asquith invited Bonar Law to secret talks at Cherkley on the question of Ulster exclusion. Balfour seemed alarmed that Asquith might find a solution and thereby spoil the chances of a Unionist victory at a general election. If this was a real concern it was an extraordinarily naïve reading of the situation. The likelihood of the Conservatives winning a general election was extremely low and their winning one over the issue of Ireland was even lower. In fact between 1912 and 1914 the Conservatives were split more profoundly over the Irish issue than were the Liberals, and Balfour's attempt to wave the Orange flag in a speech at Aberdeen on 3 November 1913 was the action of a man who seemed not to have grasped that the situation had changed since 1885 when Randolph Churchill had famously declared that 'Ulster will fight and Ulster will be right'.

The moderate Unionist reformer, Horace Plunkett, once noted of Balfour that 'sometimes he plays the game when he ought not', but in fact Balfour and the Conservative Party were playing wholly the wrong game. When Bonar Law declared that there was no level of resistance Ulster could undertake which he would not support, he was in effect countenancing resistance and perhaps armed resistance to government legislation. On this issue Bonar Law and Balfour were in accord but, leaving aside the constitutional improprieties of their position, it is extremely doubtful that it was proving politically and electorally successful. Certainly the Chairman of the

Conservative Party, whom Balfour had appointed and who was respected by Bonar Law, saw the Irish issue as a whole and the Ulster Question in particular as extremely dangerous questions with which to tangle, in that the electorate was likely to turn against those who could be deemed responsible for civil disturbance, and in 1912–14 the party advocating such behaviour was the Conservative Party. Equally damaging, there were strong divisions within the Conservative Party itself over the position that would be occupied by Ulster if Home Rule was to pass. Many Conservatives advocated the exclusion of Ulster from Home Rule but many did not wish to see this become permanent separation of the North from the South. On Ireland, as on most other issues before 1914, the Liberals held the strongest hand, and Balfour's old Orange trumps could no longer win the trick.

After the outbreak of war with Germany in August 1914, the Government of Ireland Act was set aside for the duration. Balfour supported the British decision to defend Belgium. Asquith appointed him a full member of the Committee of Imperial Defence and in November he became a member of Asquith's War Council – the only member of the Shadow Cabinet thus

In spring 1914, with civil war threatening in Ireland as both Nationalist and Unionist militias were readying for battle over Home Rule and the government likewise preparing to use force, 57 British Army officers based at the Curragh outside Dublin stated that they would sooner resign their commissions than coerce the Ulster Protestants into accepting Home Rule. The so-called 'mutiny' was badly handled by the government, which sent out mixed messages, implying that Ulster-born officers might be able to avoid service against their kinfolk. The scandal forced the resignation of Field Marshal Sir John French as Chief of the Imperial General Staff.

appointed. Perhaps somewhat unexpectedly he showed in this position qualities of imagination and foresight. This seems to indicate that Balfour was at his best when policy making was under the control of others. As had been the case under Salisbury, Balfour proved to be a better second-in-command than a leader. On home defence he wrote an important paper in January 1915 on the effect of high army recruitment on the economy (*'Limits of Enlistment'*) and he proposed a set of what came to be known as 'reserved occupations' from which troops were not to be enlisted. Balfour was an early high-level critic of the loss of life on the Western Front and largely as a result he was a keen supporter in the War Council of Churchill's proposal to attack the Dardanelles. Balfour did not share Churchill's hubristic hopes for the Dardanelles campaign but he did feel that the strategic possibilities made the venture well worth the likely cost.

In May Churchill, at the time leaving the Admiralty, suggested that Balfour should replace Lord Kitchener at the War Office. Bonar Law, for his part, asked Lloyd George, who was still at the Exchequer, to demand a new Prime Minister, either Balfour, Grey or Lloyd George himself. A coalition was duly formed, with Asquith still as Prime Minister. But Balfour, on 25 May 1915, became First Lord of the Admiralty, the most important of the six cabinet posts offered to Conservatives. Indeed, his status in the new Cabinet was second only to that of Asquith himself. For the first time since 1905 the Conservatives were back in the corridors of power, albeit having entered through the back door, and Balfour had played a key role in unlocking the door.

With regard to naval matters Admiral Fisher declined to serve under Balfour, blaming him even more than Churchill for the Dardanelles disaster. Fisher was replaced by the undynamic Admiral Sir Henry Jackson, who as a fellow of

the Royal Society, like Balfour himself, was a more congenial First Sea Lord, with whom Balfour could work. In the North Sea the sound, unadventurous policy followed by Admiral Jellicoe in the early days of the war was maintained, but Balfour remained unduly optimistic about the Dardanelles campaign, despite the ongoing and severe military setbacks experienced in that theatre.

With regard to wartime politics Balfour established a good working relationship with Lloyd George, whom he had long admired as a political opponent. In the summer of 1910 there had been brief consideration of a possible coalition to be headed by Lloyd George, and Balfour had not been wholly unresponsive to this suggestion. Balfour's willingness to work with Lloyd George was strengthened by the war as he was much impressed by the Welshman's work, from May 1915, at the Ministry of Munitions. Balfour, however, differed from Lloyd George by opposing conscription, which was perhaps surprising as it was Liberals rather than Conservatives that blenched at the idea of forcing people to fight. Furthermore, in December and January he argued against further great offensives being mounted on the western front before the British forces had reached their peak. But he could not prevail against the

Admiral Sir John Jellicoe (1859–1935), commander of the Grand Fleet at Jutland, had had several narrow escapes before reaching high rank. In 1893 he had survived the sinking of HMS *Victoria*, accidentally rammed by HMS *Camperdown* off Beirut, and in 1900 he had been badly wounded during the first failed attempt to relieve the besieged Peking legations during the Boxer Rising. After Jutland, he became First Sea Lord, but was sacked by Lloyd George in 1917 for failing to get to grips with the U-boat problem. After the war he was Governor-General of New Zealand.

military policies which culminated in July 1916 at the Battle of the Somme.

But Balfour's chief concern had necessarily to be Britain's naval position and earlier in the summer of 1916 Balfour had had to face an embarrassing situation with regard to reports concerning the major naval engagement at Jutland. Balfour himself drafted a public communiqué based on Admiral Jellicoe's report of ships lost on either side of the battle. It was difficult to see the respective tally of losses as anything but disappointing to the Royal Navy even though the battle could not be described as a defeat. In fact the German High Seas Fleet was to remain in port for the rest of the war and Britain's naval command of the North Sea was to remain unshaken in spite of the fact that Jutland had been a disappointing engagement. Nevertheless the fact that Balfour published the disappointing tally of British and German losses without any further reassuring comment was, in terms of his own position, somewhat injudicious. This was, his niece wrote, 'a supreme example of Balfour's faulty understanding of the psychology of the common man',[1] a failing which had, as noted above, attracted comment on numerous occasions before the war.

> At the Battle of Jutland on 31 May 1916 the Royal Navy lost three battlecruisers, three armoured cruisers and eight destroyers, to the Germans' one battlecruiser, one pre-dreadnought battleship, four light cruisers and five destroyers. As the three British battlecruisers and two of the armoured cruisers had exploded and sunk with almost all hands, the losses in men were far more one-sided, 5,914 British to 2,195 German. Many German ships had been damaged, but it is thought that their less volatile ammunition saved them from the explosions that had sunk the British capital ships lost in the battle.

Towards the end of 1916, the U-boat problem was assuming serious proportions. Convoys had been introduced for the protection of troop ships and cross-channel traffic, but Jackson and his advisers believed that a general system of convoys was obviated by a number of considerations. Of these one carried special weight, the lack of a sufficient number of escorts. On this, as on all naval matters, Balfour remained open to suggestion and plied his professional advisers with searching questions. The problem of escorts was not to be fully solved until the United States entered the war but other inventive efforts to protect British shipping were introduced. Perhaps one of the most intriguing of these was the use of 'dazzle camouflage' invented by Norman Wilkinson, which was first used with no little success under the aegis of Balfour's Sea Lordship.

In the summer of 1916 Balfour supported the solution proposed by Lloyd George, on Asquith's prompting, of immediate Home Rule for the South of Ireland, with Ulster deferred for the duration. But although this suggestion may have seemed superficially straightforward the situation in Ireland had changed somewhat after the Easter Rising of 1916. It may have been the case that the rising was carried out by 'a minority of a minority' but the British response, most particularly the summary execution of a number of those who had participated in the occupation of Dublin's Post Office, had lent strength to the Irish Nationalist and indeed Republican cause. Furthermore, the introduction of conscription in Ireland had hardly been a politic move. It was thus unsurprising that Balfour was unable to persuade his Unionist colleagues that Asquith and Lloyd George's proposed settlement was acceptable and it collapsed.

In these circumstances the way was clear for the growth of Sinn Féin, which had been a minor force in Ireland before the war but which now began to replace the Irish Nationalists as

the main political force in Ireland. Balfour himself was ready to accept the idea of an Irish Free State, for he always favoured independence for Ireland rather than Home Rule as long as Ulster was exempt. In many respects this was precisely the form of Irish Free State that was to come into being in 1921 and its essential foundations had been laid out by the logic of events during the war and the British attitude towards the governance of Ireland.

Balfour opposed proposals for a negotiated peace in Europe, notably when Lord Lansdowne, his erstwhile colleague, presented his 'peace memorandum' to Asquith in November 1916, an initiative that was partly responsible for triggering the political crisis of the coalition. By December 1916 Balfour agreed with those who thought that a more decisive prime minister was required, and he began to draw close to those who were in effect planning a *coup d'état* to replace Asquith with Lloyd George, in spite of the fact that Asquith was determined to keep Balfour as First Lord. In fact Balfour emerged as somewhat of a key piece in the game of chess that was being played out by Asquith and Lloyd George and their respective supporters. Realising that Lloyd George, as part of his move to take over the running of the war, wanted a change at the Admiralty, Balfour pressed his own resignation, from his sickbed, on Asquith on 5 December. Asquith asked him to reconsider. There were some hints of a possible Conservative-led coup, which became evident when Asquith declined to serve in a cabinet led by Bonar Law. Balfour, in turn, asked Asquith to reconsider, but on 6 December Balfour attended a meeting at Buckingham Palace and was unsuccessful in requesting Asquith to serve under Bonar Law. The upshot was the Lloyd George coalition. Many high-ranking sailors were sorry to see Balfour leave the Admiralty, Admirals Jellicoe and Beatty included.

Outstanding among Balfour's wartime services was his part – rated by Bonar Law as the most significant – in the resolution of the Cabinet crisis ending with the formation of Lloyd George's coalition in December 1916. After Lloyd George became Premier Balfour remained in the ministerial first rank, but he accepted Lloyd George's wish that he leave the Admiralty. That he supported the installation of his pre-war political adversary as Prime Minister was not wholly surprising. As noted above, Balfour had not been wholly unreceptive to the idea of forming a political coalition with Lloyd George in 1910 and some historians, notably Robert Scully, have seen the origins of the Lloyd George coalition as predating the Cabinet crisis of 1916. Such an argument can be overstated but it is nevertheless crucial to realise that Balfour and Lloyd George, and other members of the 1916 Coalition, shared more common attitudes than would at first glance seem to be the case. Had this not been so, it would be difficult to explain why the Coalition lasted until the autumn of 1922 and also why many leading Conservatives objected so strongly and negatively to its break-up in the latter year.

But to return to Balfour, it is fair to say that in December 1916 his selfless conduct – not matched by Asquith – was entirely in the interest of a more energetic and decisive running of the war. Lloyd George, for his part, wanted a greater show of energy at the head of the Admiralty, but he deemed Balfour ideally suited to the Foreign Office, and had suggested him as a temporary substitute for Grey as early as March 1915.[2] Balfour accepted the Foreign Office, and in his memoirs Lloyd George was later to pay tribute to the quality of Balfour's whole wartime contribution: 'his unfailing courage' which 'steadied faltering spirits in hours of doubt and dread'.[3] But in spite of this later praise, Balfour's role had been somewhat diminished under Lloyd George. While,

America

'Balfour, who had taken over from Sir Edward Grey as foreign secretary, substantially less interested in humouring the president, believed with others in the Cabinet, including the prime minister, that peace could be achieved only by the defeat of the Central Powers. What Lloyd George had said in an interview in late September remained the government's fixed policy. No offer of help by the recently re-elected president changed the prime minister's view that "the fight must be to the finish to a knock-out".

Wilson refused to be dismayed by these evidences of recalcitrance and continued to preach for "a league of peace", adding a memorable phrase when he spoke of "peace without victory" on January 22, 1917. The British, angered by the president ignoring the bill of particulars they had prepared to support their charges about Germany's aggressive behaviour, found such words almost offensive. Spring Rice, in one of this last dispatches as ambassador – he was dying of Graves' disease – sought to explain why the president spoke and acted as he did, and wrote: "The President is a transitory being. His glory is effulgent but brief. The temptation to play a great part before the authority is over is overwhelming. The Democratic Party for many years has not had consecutive terms of office. It is a one man party. It is the permanent glory of the party in the person of its head. A man who was quite recently rejected by a local university and who becomes the arbiter of the destinies of the world, a partner with Pope and Kaiser, is naturally the object of admiration ... The President's great talents and inspiring character fit him to play a great part. He feels it and he knows it. He is already a mysterious, rather Olympian personage and shrouded by darkness from which issue occasional thunderbolts. He sees nobody who could be remotely suspected of being his equal should any such exist in point of intellect or character."'

[Stephen Graubard, *The Presidents* (Allen Lane, London: 2004) pp 181–2]

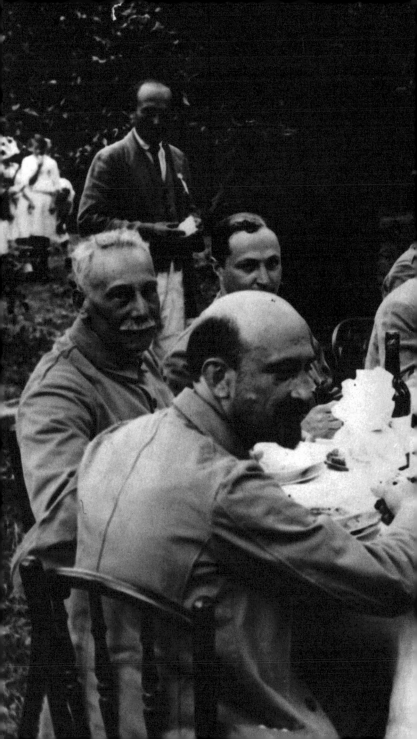

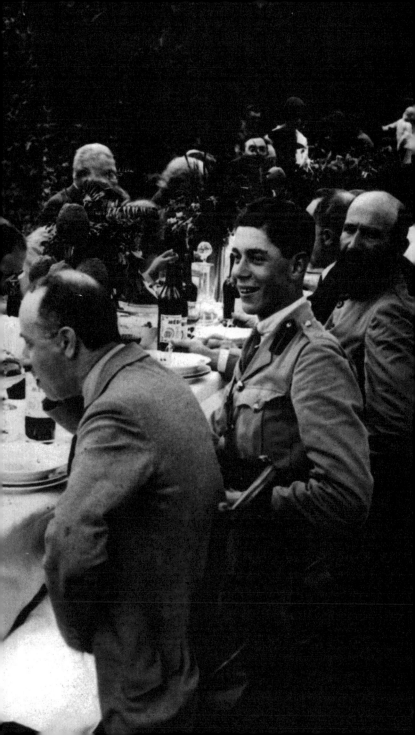

uniquely, he had unrestricted access to Lloyd George's small War Cabinet, he was not a member of it, and his political base within his own party had been seriously eroded. At one level Balfour's continuance in one of the great offices of state testifies to Lloyd George's confidence in him but it was also indicative of Lloyd George's desire to keep the Foreign Office from the Asquithian Liberals and from Bonar Law's more hard-line Conservatives.

George Nathaniel Curzon (1859–1925) became an MP in 1886 and was Viceroy of India between 1898 and 1905. An Asian specialist, he introduced major administrative changes to British rule, reforming the police, the railways and the education system. He resigned in 1905 over a dispute with Lord Kitchener over control of the Indian army. He became a peer in 1908. During the 1914–18 war Curzon was leader of the Lords and President of the Air Board. After the war he became Foreign Secretary in Lloyd George's government. Curzon was favoured to succeed Bonar Law as Prime Minister, but lost out to Stanley Baldwin. He established the Remembrance Day service at the Cenotaph held annually on 11 November.

The first memorable episode of Balfour's term at the Foreign Office occurred in April 1917 when, at the age of 68, he went at the head of a mission to Washington. Balfour had long been an advocate of close Anglo-American relations – perhaps remembering how close Britain and the United States had come to conflict during the Venezuelan Crisis of the 1890s. By early 1917 it was clear that an American declaration of war on Germany was imminent and the War Cabinet decided that 'someone of the highest status' in Britain 'who would have the entrée to all circles, should proceed to Washington'.[4] Balfour 'very sportingly' (thought Hankey) agreed to go: he sought to establish a good rapport with President Wilson and to smooth the way for American co-operation,

Foreign Office,
November 2nd, 1917.

Dear Lord Rothschild,

I have much pleasure in conveying to you, on behalf of His Majesty's Government, the following declaration of sympathy with Jewish Zionist aspirations which has been submitted to, and approved by, the Cabinet.

"His Majesty's Government view with favour the establishment in Palestine of a national home for the Jewish people, and will use their best endeavours to facilitate the achievement of this object, it being clearly understood that nothing shall be done which may prejudice the civil and religious rights of existing non-Jewish communities in Palestine, or the rights and political status enjoyed by Jews in any other country".

I should be grateful if you would bring this declaration to the knowledge of the Zionist Federation.

Y. ...

Arthur James Balfour

MB

to

Tring Park.
Tring.

4 Nov. 1917

Dear Mr Balfour,

I write to thank
you most sincerely
for your letter — &
also for the great
interest you have
shown in the wishes
of the large mass of
the Jewish people
& also for the efforts
& trouble your have

taken o
I can a
that the
of ten
people
for the
Govern
opinio
messag
of safe
to lar
of peo
much
it. I h
have be

behalf.
you
tude
ons of
be your
lish i
—has
g their
spect
omfort
mes
ho are
of
you
ould

that already in
many parts of Russia
renewed persecution
has broken out.
With renewed
thanks to you
& His Majesty's
government.
I remain
yours sincerely
Rothschild

especially in resisting the unrestricted onslaught of U-boats against shipping. Balfour did all that was asked of him. He was well received in the House of Representatives when he addressed it, even by its Irish Catholic members who had expressed strong concern about the British response to the Easter Rising in Ireland. From the USA Balfour went on to Canada, where he was received enthusiastically in Ottawa, Toronto, and Quebec.

The question of Britain's role in the Middle East as the Ottoman Empire disintegrated exercised the government from the start of the war. Balfour was much less enthusiastic about an extension of British responsibilities in the Middle East than some of his colleagues. This was perhaps somewhat ironic as Britain had secured a monopoly of the production of crude oil in Iran in the Edwardian period and the government had established a 51 per cent share-holding in the Anglo-Persian Oil Company precisely in order to ensure a secure source of fuel oil for the navy which was rapidly converting its ships to the use of oil rather than coal. As First Lord of the Admiralty Balfour could have been only too aware of how important Middle Eastern oil was to Britain's strategic interests. In 1918 his one-time fellow Soul, George Curzon, declared 'we are floated to victory on a wave of oil' and that 'wave' had its origins for Britain in the Middle East. By the time that he became Foreign Secretary the de Bunsen committee had reported, recommending a British sphere of influence in Palestine to the exclusion of France, and Mark Sykes had made his notorious agreement with Picot (in May 1916) for partitioning the area after the war, with Britain getting Palestine.

Initially British policy was shaped by traditional strategic concerns, but as the war progressed the support of Jews in the USA and Russia became important. Balfour, like Lloyd

George, was sympathetic to Zionism. When Prime Minister, he had supported Joseph Chamberlain's plans for Jewish resettlement in east Africa (although in part this was motivated by a desire to stem the flow of Jewish immigration to Britain), and in the aftermath of those plans he had met Chaim Weizmann on 9 January 1906, in Manchester during the election campaign. In his house in Carlton Gardens, he

'{Balfour} said that, in his opinion, the {Jewish} question would not be solved until either the Jews became completely assimilated here or a normal Jewish society came into existence in Palestine.'

CHAIM WEIZMANN

again met Weizmann in December 1914. Weizmann reported: 'Our talk lasted an hour and a half. Balfour remembered everything we had discussed eight years ago... . He said that, in his opinion, the {Jewish} question would not be solved until either the Jews became completely assimilated here or a normal Jewish society came into existence in Palestine'.[5]

Further conversations between Balfour and Weizmann followed in 1916 and 1917, and while in the USA Balfour also met influential Zionists, impressing Justice L D Brandeis with his 'quietly emphatic remark: *I am a Zionist*'.[6] In the summer of 1917 strategic and Zionist concerns coincided to encourage the Foreign Office, Balfour, Lloyd George, and, from 3 September 1917, the War Cabinet to contemplate a public statement. A delay occurred through the strong opposition from Edwin Montagu, who represented an important section of British Jewry, and who argued that a Jewish national home would be disadvantageous to the position of Jews in their present national locations, and from Curzon, who drew attention to the problems that a 'national home' would cause with and for the existing Islamic population in and around Palestine. Although not represented at the highest level, this was also the view of T E Lawrence (Lawrence of Arabia) who felt that

the Arab peoples and as a consequence British interests in the Middle East were being ill-served by British policy.

Nevertheless, on 5 October Balfour consulted the American government on a cautious draft proposal. He gained the Americans' agreement (on condition that they were not publicly associated with the declaration), and on 2 November 1917 what was at once known as the Balfour Declaration was published in the form of a letter from Balfour to Lord Rothschild; it stated that the British government favoured 'the establishment in Palestine of a national home for the Jewish people' on the clear understanding that there should be no disadvantage to 'the civil and religious rights of existing non-Jewish communities in Palestine, or the rights and political status enjoyed by Jews in any other country'.

Of the many initiatives of the British government in the First World War, and indeed of the many initiatives taken by Balfour personally during his career, this is the one that perhaps has cast the longest shadow. Balfour told the Cabinet that it implied a *British, American, or other protectorate* and not the early establishment of an independent Jewish state. Nevertheless, Balfour pressed for the acceptance and publication of the Declaration with unwonted energy.

Chapter 7: Elder Statesman

As the war ended, Balfour and the Foreign Office prepared a British approach to the peace. Balfour had always hoped the German and Austrian empires could survive defeat, and initially stated *I don't want to trample her* [Germany] *in the mud*,[1] though he later modified this view, and he backed the Carthaginian peace of the Versailles settlement. He supported the maintenance of the Coalition led by Lloyd George to oversee the peace and the aftermath of war, announcing his views in an exchange with Bonar Law in November 1918.

In the 'coupon' election in December 1918, Balfour was again returned for the City of London. At the Paris peace conference of 1919 Balfour inevitably played second fiddle to Lloyd George (they both had apartments at 23 rue Nitot). Early in the conference, during the temporary absence of the national leaders, Balfour expedited preparations for their return. Hankey, by then Secretary of the Cabinet, commented on 'Balfour's extraordinary aptitude', despite recent ill health and his 70 years, 'for rising to the occasion'; and Robert Vansittart, a member of Balfour's diplomatic team in Paris, conveyed in his memoirs the respect and affection which Balfour inspired

'It was hopeless to avoid devotion to AJB, and I never tried.'

ROBERT VANSITTART

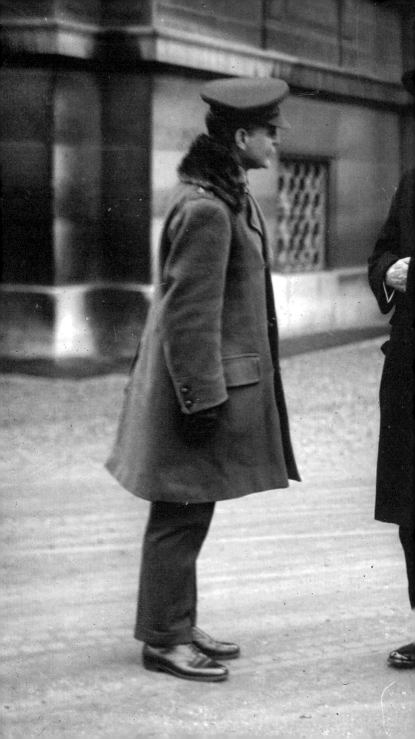

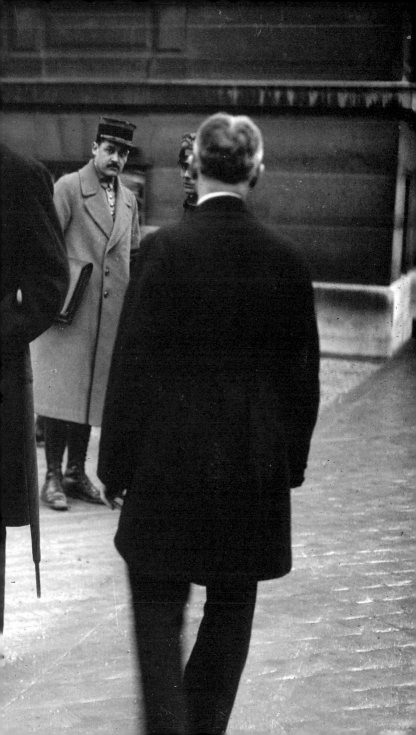

in his subordinates. He noted that 'It was hopeless to avoid devotion to AJB, and I never tried.'

Yet Balfour's reputation during the negotiations was that of a man withdrawn who allowed others to set the pace. But his absence of significant intervention may have been conditioned by his recognition that the conference had to make rapid progress if it was to secure legitimacy, and that the prevarication by the Europeans might weaken the attachment of the USA to the settlement.

Balfour remained less hostile to the Germans than some of the British delegation, and he certainly never accepted that they should 'Hang the Kaiser'. He accepted the need for reparations but recommended the easing of the blockade. The German treaty was signed in June, but Balfour remained as leader of the British delegation until the Austrian treaty was concluded in September. Minority treaties were negotiated with the many successor states. Ironically, Balfour negotiated for Eastern Europe a settlement based on just the recognition of nationalities which his political career at home had been dedicated – in the case of the Irish – to preventing. Overall, in an extremely difficult and frequently tense situation Balfour had proved to be a patient but above all able Foreign Secretary – a satisfactory conclusion to his career in high office.

On 23 October 1919 Balfour exchanged offices with Lord Curzon and became Lord President of the Council, but this did not bring an end to his prominent role in foreign affairs (nor did he, as many expected, take a peerage). While Lord President he represented Britain on the council of the League

'AJB dominates the Assembly, easily and without effort.... It is partly mere charm and unassuming dignity, partly his great prestige, partly a real diplomatic power of making almost anyone do what he wants.... He makes no effort and is irresistible.'

GILBERT MURRAY

of Nations. He realised that the League was weakened from the outset by the absence from its ranks of the United States, but he still felt that it had its uses. Thus, despite ill health and a disinclination to travel to Geneva, he led the British delegation there each autumn in 1920–2. Indeed, according to Gilbert Murray, who was a delegate to the League from 1921 to 1923, 'AJB dominates the Assembly, easily and without effort... . It is partly mere charm and unassuming dignity, partly his great prestige, partly a real diplomatic power of making almost anyone do what he wants... . He makes no effort and is irresistible'.[2]

Balfour's commitment to the League was marked. Its underlying idealist rationale may have seemed distant from Balfour's characteristic scepticism, but he had been Honorary President of the League of Nations Union from 1918. Here he had close contact with his cousin, Lord Robert Cecil, who was deeply involved with the Union, and as Foreign Secretary he left many of the details of the negotiations about the League's formulation to his cousin. Balfour's presence and support were

The celebrated Cambridge economist and member of the Bloomsbury group of artists and authors, **John Maynard Keynes's** 1936 book *The General Theory of Employment, Interest and Money* changed how the world viewed economics. He advocated that in depressions, governments should stimulate demand by fiscal measures and deficit budgeting. He was a member of the British delegation to the Versailles Peace Conference in 1918. In his book *The Economic Consequences of the Peace*, he opposed the reparations imposed on Germany. In 1944 he led the British delegation to the Bretton Woods International Conference that set up the World Bank and the International Monetary Fund. Keynes died in 1946 shortly after negotiating an American loan to the United Kingdom.

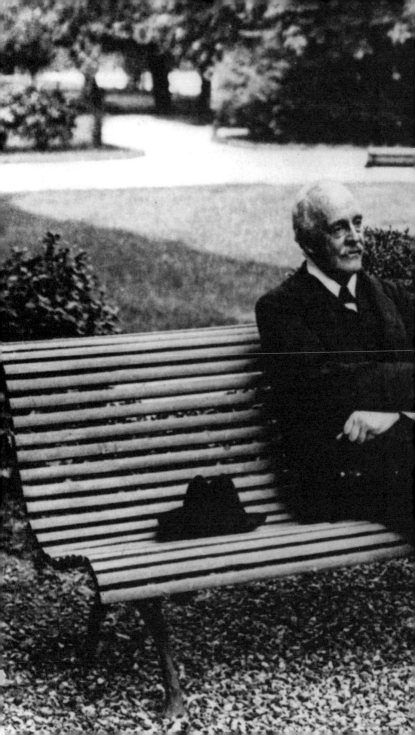

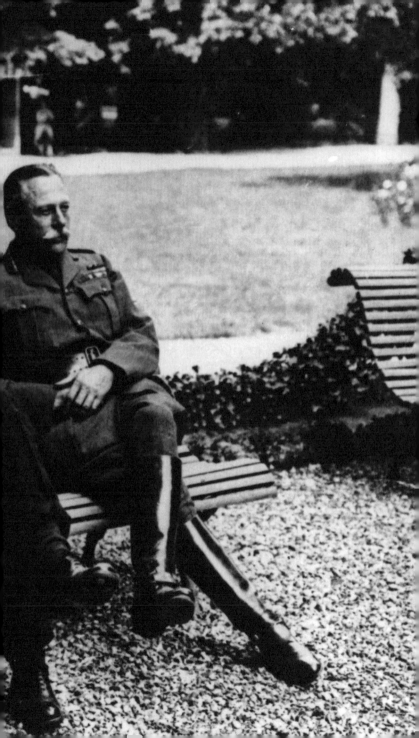

of importance in establishing the status of the League as a body with wider support than merely its enthusiasts. He was sceptical about many of the tenets of the League, but he none the less thought it worth a try.

In 1920 the Committee of Imperial Defence was revived with Hankey again as its secretary, although he also remained Secretary of the Cabinet, and Balfour, too, again took on a prominent role. In 1921, with Lloyd George preoccupied with negotiating the settlement in Ireland, Balfour was the key British representative at the Washington Naval Conference, which was to be the most successful arms limitation agreement reached in the early 20th century. Although the treaty marked the formal end of British naval superiority, American willingness to accept parity with Britain was quite a national success, in the light of the superior shipbuilding capacity enjoyed by the United States.

On his return to Britain in March 1922, Balfour was feted, and the King made him a Knight of the Garter and he was created Earl Balfour. Balfour regretted leaving the Commons but his elevation did not bring an end to his governmental career. Curzon was ill for much of the summer of 1922 and Balfour acted as Foreign Secretary in his absence. As such he issued the 'Balfour Note' of 1 August 1922 which advocated the cancellation of all war debts but, failing that, argued that Britain needed to exercise her own claims simply to the extent whereby it could pay its own debts to the United States. There were some slight echoes here of Keynes's *The Economic Consequences of the Peace* and its critical views of the punitive nature of the Versailles Settlement. But Balfour's note was as poorly received as had been Keynes's treatise.

Balfour's hopes for domestic reconstruction were to be as disappointed as were his hopes for international settlement. He had offered consistent support to the Lloyd George

Coalition from the time of its inception, and he believed, along with Austen Chamberlain, Lord Birkenhead (F E Smith) and some other Conservatives, that it offered the best available counterweight to socialism in Britain. But from the spring of 1921 through 1922 grass-roots Conservative hostility to the Coalition grew uncontrollably – finding expression in the creation of local organisations such as the Anti-Waste League in the constituencies, and an anti-Coalition memorandum circulated amongst Conservative MPs at Westminster.

Things came to a head in October 1922 when at a famous meeting at the Carlton Club on 19 October the Conservative Parliamentary Party rejected the continuance of the Coalition by 188 to 88 votes. Balfour himself spoke in favour of the Coalition at the meeting, and he was furious with Bonar Law and Stanley Baldwin for their disloyalty to the Coalition and to the then Conservative leader, Austen Chamberlain, who was also pro-Coalition. But, with the Conservative Party at Westminster and in the constituencies hostile to the Coalition and more particularly to Lloyd George, the government came to an end, and the 'Welsh Wizard' and his ministers left office.

Balfour did not go over to the new Prime Minister, Bonar Law, and indeed he did not support his new Conservative government in the general election of November 1922. In terms of domestic politics he remained loyal to his 'official' leader, Austen Chamberlain, and the Coalition Conservatives. He was pessimistic about the Conservative Party's chances as an independent force, although their comfortable victory in November 1922 proved him wrong. Nevertheless, although he was unwilling to join Bonar Law's government, he again became British representative at the League in Geneva, and only resigned in February 1923, largely as a consequence of ill health. In spite of his health problems, he agreed in March 1923 to play a part in an extensive inquiry into

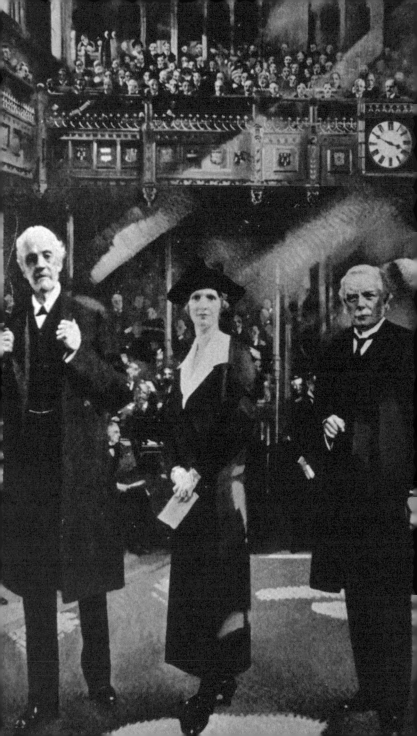

defence policy. This was a critical moment for such discussions insofar as Bonar Law had announced months before the fall of the Coalition that 'Britain could no longer act alone as policeman of the world'. Having entered the Great War as the world's largest creditor nation, Britain after 1918 was a net debtor, and as a consequence was having to cut its imperial and military coat according to the smaller amount of cloth it had available.

In May 1923 Bonar Law's health was failing – he had an untreatable throat cancer – and he announced his intention to give up the Premiership. The King asked Balfour for his advice as to whether Lord Curzon should succeed Bonar Law. Balfour advised against, and felt himself qualified to answer the enquiry as to whether 'dear George' would be chosen with the reply: *No, dear George will not*.[3] This was in fact a somewhat self-important piece of Balfourism for it was not his advice but that of Bonar Law which was decisive in the King asking Stanley Baldwin to form the next government.

The Royal Air Force (RAF) was created as an independent service on 1 April 1918, from the merging of the Army's Royal Flying Corps (RFC) and the Royal Naval Air Service (RNAS). Between the two World Wars, the RAF was involved in using aircraft for Imperial policing, particularly in what is now Iraq, and in the development of long-range strategic bombing, somewhat neglecting the development of naval aviation. Although the Fleet Air Arm was returned to Royal Navy control in 1937, it suffered from a shortage of modern aircraft and the service that had pioneered naval aviation in the First World War had fallen to third place behind the US and Japanese naval air arms.

Baldwin, although Balfour gave him public support, did not offer his first-ever leader a Cabinet post. However, when Curzon died in April 1925 it was Balfour who filled his place

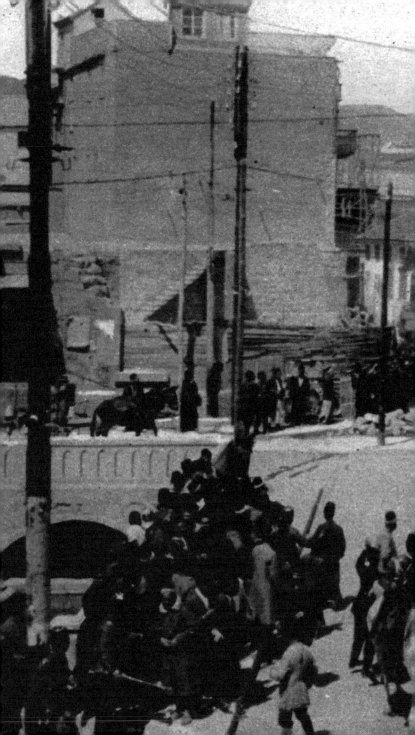

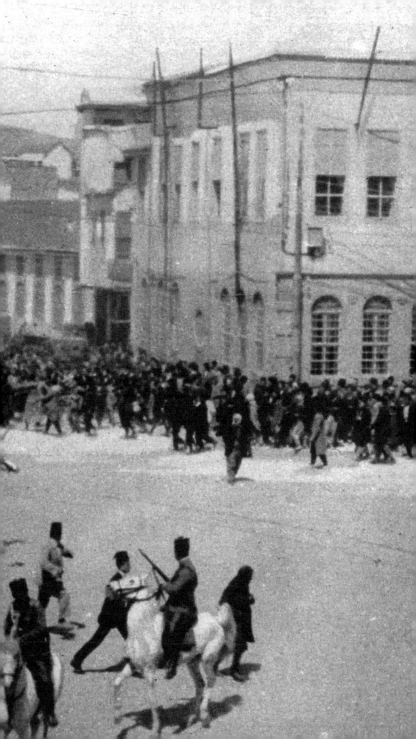

as Lord President of the Council. By then Baldwin, having won a substantial victory at the 1924 general election, was more politically secure, and Balfour, as a peer and an increasingly deaf 76-year-old, could not be seen as a possible Prime Minister and challenger to Baldwin. But Balfour continued to illuminate the proceedings of the Committee of Imperial Defence as he had when out of office in 1923. In that year, he was a member of the Salisbury committee on co-ordination of defence and chairman of its special subcommittee on relations between the Navy and the Air Force.

For a brief period in 1923 the RAF's existence as an independent service was under threat but Balfour had seen its survival as a main priority, and indeed he had decided to back the RAF in its wish to continue to train and administer the Fleet Air Arm – an arrangement which was not to be reversed until 1937. At the Committee of Imperial Defence in 1926 Churchill's proposed Ministry of Defence met with Balfour's usual scepticism on this subject. In spite of a severe setback to his health in March 1928 Balfour, on his final appearance at the Committee in July, criticised as *dangerous* and *wholly impracticable* Churchill's move, as Chancellor, to place a ten-year rule on the extension of military expenditure. He also further advocated additional spending on naval anti-aircraft weapons ahead of expenditure on cruisers.

As Lord President, Balfour continued to take a close interest in scientific and technological developments, especially within the bodies for which he was responsible, namely the Department of Scientific and Industrial Research and the Medical Research Council; during both his periods as Lord President he was an assiduous attender at their meetings. It was said that the 'Lord Presidency used to be considered a general utility office. He [Balfour] converted it into a Ministry of Research'.[4] Always concerned about the future of the British

economy, he instituted a Committee of Civil Research which, with the Prime Minister sometimes in the chair, reported on 14 important subjects (such as overseas loans, the safeguarding of the iron and steel industry, and unemployment), before ill health in the autumn of 1928 finally removed him from active work. Out of courtesy and respect, Baldwin insisted on his retaining his office until the end of the government in May 1929.

In the opening months of 1925 Balfour toured the Middle East, attending in his robes as Chancellor of the University of Cambridge the opening of the Hebrew University in Jerusalem and being entertained by Chaim Weizmann, but Arab protests required him to cut short his tour. It was when he was in Palestine that Balfour was invited by Baldwin to replace the recently-deceased Curzon as Lord President and he took up the office on 29 April. His chief achievement during this last period of office was chairing (as a result of Baldwin's lumbago) the inter-imperial relations committee at the Imperial Conference in 1926. It was this Conference's report which was to lay the foundations for the Statute of Westminster of 1931 which was to define relations between dominions (of European settlement) within the Empire.

After 1923 Balfour ceased to play a continuous role in High Politics – he simply enjoyed the status of a respected and in some spheres revered elder statesman – although he occasionally played the part of a political *éminence grise*. His high public standing was not reflected in his private financial status. He and his brother Gerald had invested heavily, before the war, with what his second biographer, Young, describes as manic intensity, in an enterprise aiming to produce a supply of industrial fuel from processed peat. After the war they persisted with this loss-making venture by financing a company called Peco, which went bankrupt. By 1922 Balfour,

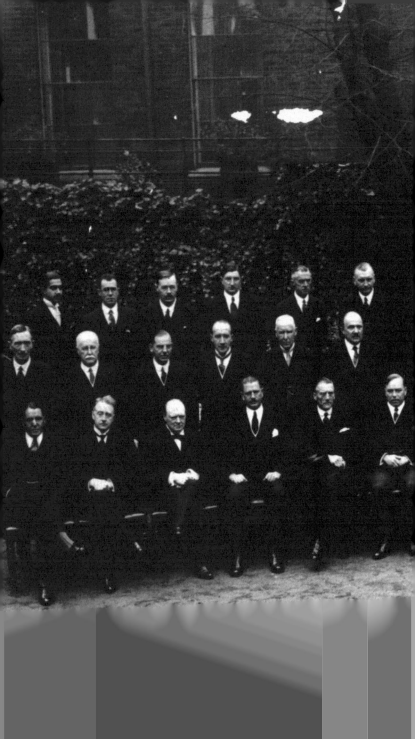

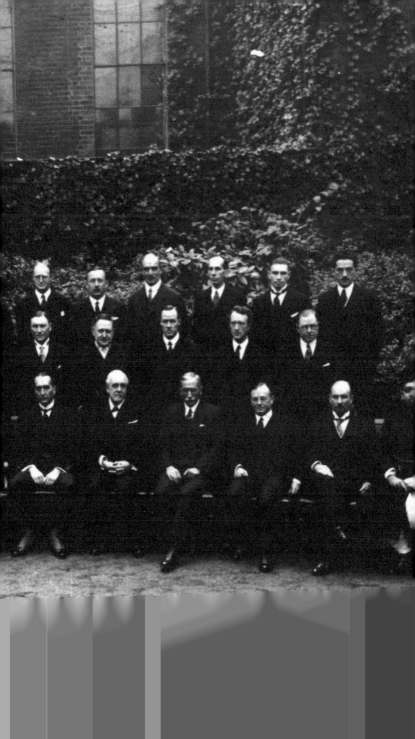

who had, until then, never had to worry about money, was having overdraft problems; and in 1928 he was working on his *Chapters of Autobiography* (not completed; published posthumously in 1930, edited by Mrs Dugdale) with an eye to the royalties. But he never freed himself from debt and his family could not, as he had hoped, live at Whittingehame House after him.

In spite of his financial ailments Balfour in the 1920s maintained an energetic level of non-political activities. He had been made a member of the Order of Merit in 1916. In 1919 he became Chancellor of the University of Cambridge, an office which he was to hold until his death. He was an active Chancellor, and played a part in the raising of money from Rockefeller for the new university library in 1928. On the death of H M Butler in 1918, there was some suggestion that he might become Master of Trinity College, but nothing came of this. One of the founding fellows of the British Academy, he was its president from 1921 until 1928, the longest tenure of the office in its history – 'a strangely inactive' period, according to Mortimer Wheeler, during which Balfour 'lent the majesty of his name for no less than seven years without imperilling it by the utterance of an annual address'.[5] While President, however, Balfour gave his second series of Gifford lectures, and in 1923 the published version of these appeared as *Theism and Thought*. It was to the academy that he delivered his final reflections on philosophy, 'Familiar Beliefs and Transcendent Reason', in 1925. He declined the presidency of the Royal Society in 1920, thus turning down what would have been a unique double. He wrote an introduction to *Science, Religion and Reality*, edited by Joseph Needham in 1925.

On 25 July 1928, his 80th birthday, Balfour was presented at Westminster with a tribute from both Houses of Parliament – a Rolls-Royce. He had for long been a motoring enthusiast.

In her biography Blanche Dugdale noticed how Balfour, in responding, addressed his earlier remarks 'almost personally to Lloyd George'.[6] Apart from colds and occasional influenza, Balfour enjoyed good health until 1928, and he remained a regular tennis player. However, at the end of that year most of his teeth had to be removed and he began to suffer from unremitting circulatory trouble which ultimately was to cause his death. Late in January 1929 Balfour was conveyed from Whittingehame to Fisher's Hill, his brother Gerald's home near Woking, Surrey. In the past he had suffered from occasional bouts of phlebitis and by the autumn of 1929 he was immobilized. Finally, soon after receiving a visit from Weizmann, Balfour died at Fisher's Hill on 19 March 1930. At his own request a public funeral was declined and he was buried privately on 22 March.

Chapter 8: Living his Politics

Balfour died, as he had lived, a confirmed bachelor. Although he had enjoyed close friendships with a number of women, perhaps most notably Mary Elcho and Etty Desborough, there is no evidence of any romantic linkages in his life. His life was politics.

Balfour's career as a Prime Minister and party leader seem at first glance to have been disasters. He fought three General Elections and lost all of them, and he has the unenviable distinction of being the only prime minister to have lost his own seat at an election. To some extent Balfour's failure can be seen as in large part his own responsibility. From mid-1903 to the end of his Premiership his political life was marred by divisions in his own Party over tariff reform. Yet perhaps Balfour could have avoided this. After all, he had manoeuvred, with Machiavellian subtlety, in the autumn of 1902 to create the space for a debate over British trade policy, and yet in the spring of 1903 he allowed his Chancellor of the Exchequer, C T Ritchie, to blackmail the government into accepting a budget that repealed the duties on imported corn under the implicit threat of his resignation. Arguably Balfour should have called his bluff. To begin with, he could have taken a leaf out of his uncle's book, for Lord Salisbury had called Lord Randolph Churchill's bluff in 1887 with the result that the latter had resigned as Chancellor, and Churchill was a far more

politically dangerous animal than Ritchie. Furthermore, in the early 1880s Ritchie had been one of the leading advocates of Fair Trade and hence his 'devotion' to Free Trade in 1903 was a perfect target for an accusation of personal, political inconsistency. If Ritchie and the other opponents of the corn duties had been allowed to resign in the spring of 1903, Balfour would still have had four years before he would have needed to call a General Election and the extended, reasoned, balanced debate which he clearly wished to have over British trade policy could perhaps have taken place, without the dramatic intervention of Chamberlain's soon to be famous (or notorious) Birmingham declaration of 15 May 1903. Also, had the corn duties been in place for longer it would have provided a clearer indication as to whether they would, as their opponents claimed, have caused a rise in the working-class costs of living – the 'food tax' bogey could possibly have been laid to rest.

This is perhaps to engage in an exercise in what Niall Ferguson would call 'virtual history', but not excessively so given that Balfour clearly wanted such a debate and had manoeuvred with some care and no little controversy to engineer the circumstances in which one could take place in the autumn of 1902. Ultimately, however, Balfour seems to have funked and lapsed into indecisiveness.

Indecisiveness was arguably also Balfour's major failing in 1910 over the House of Lords controversy and the Parliament Bill. It is doubtful if any Tory leader could have calmed the incensed 'backwoods' Peers who vetoed the Budget, but alternatives emerged in the aftermath. In the so-called 'Truce of God', brought about by the death of King Edward VII, Balfour could perhaps have pursued the reforms of the House of Lords advocated by members of his own Shadow Cabinet with greater vigour. Selborne's proposals, for example, put forward

the idea that part of the House of Lords should be elected, which would have diluted the strength of the Liberals' 'Peers versus the People' cry. Given that the Irish Nationalist contingent in the Commons simply wished to see the Lords' veto abolished, and that the Liberals depended upon the Irish for their majority, it is true that it is unlikely that a Conservative reform would have been acceptable or politically workable. However, there is perhaps an element here of George Bernard Shaw's view about Christianity, namely that it had 'not been tried and found difficult, but found difficult and not tried'. The House of Lords issue and the advantages the Liberals enjoyed were probably intractable, but it is difficult to avoid concluding that Balfour funked again. This was certainly the view of many in his own Party, both Diehard 'Ditchers' and some more moderate voices, and his absence from the country on the day the final Lords' vote was taken seems to confirm that Balfour really did lack the stomach for a fight.

'If you wanted nothing done, Arthur Balfour was the best man for the task. There was no equal to him.'

WINSTON CHURCHILL

At another level it is possible to defend Balfour's position. With regard to his electoral failures he, as noted above, did not inherit anything like as favourable a position as might at first seem the case. Salisbury may have gained the reputation of being what his latest biographer, Andrew Roberts, has called a Victorian Titan, but one of his greatest political skills had been postponing rather than confronting difficult positions. For example, Salisbury's first government in 1885 had contained nearly 60 Fair Traders and the Royal Commission on the Depression of Trade and Industry that he called in that year provided ample evidence that sentiments hostile to Free Trade were commonplace. But Salisbury, perhaps rightly anxious about this controversial question, used the

Premiership

There is no written constitution and therefore there is no definition of the role and the powers of the Prime Minister. What is
clear is that the office has evolved over time and has been shaped
by each individual holder. Some would argue that the early 20th
century Prime Ministers acted as *primus inter pares* amongst their
Cabinet colleagues and that as the years passed the leadership-style
became more autocratic, culminating at the end of the century in a
Prime Minister who acts more like an American president. Others,
however, would dispute this point and assert that changes to the
premiership have not occurred one after the other, that the evolu-
tion was not along a neat chronological line, but that some of the
20 Prime Ministers of the 20th century left a stronger impression,
changed the rules and procedures more than others. One thing is
certain: It depended on the character and the inclination of the
individual, whether they would be more or less willing to throw
out the rule-book. And therefore there will be a text box such as
this one in each of the 20 volumes of this series, pointing towards
a change to the role of the Prime Minister.

'[A] Balfourian innovation, the Committee of Imperial Defence,
whose secretariat was created by Treasury minute in May 1904, re-
affirmed, as Anthony Eden said later, that "Defence is very much a
Prime Minister's special subject." As John Ehrman has noted, "It is
... no accident that the Committee of Imperial Defence should be
peculiarly Balfour's monument. He was himself well aware of its
dependence upon him; he took care to be present at every one of the
meetings held during his premiership," and it was the main reason
why he stayed in office during the fractious year of 1905, because
he and the Committee of Imperial Defence were deeply involved
with the Anglo-Japanese Treaty. Planning for the contingency of
war is not the same as waging it but, to a large extent, the linkage
– like a Prime Minister's overall responsibilities for both – is complete. It was in this sense that Eden wrote as he did.'

[Peter Hennessy, *The Prime Minister: The Office and its Holders
since 1945* (Penguin Books, London: 2000) p 49.]

Royal Commission to postpone confronting the question and instead focussed his Party's attention on Ireland. This may have been an astute political move at the time but it could not but store up trouble for the future as the question of Britain's 'declining' economic position became more prominent. Intriguingly Joseph Chamberlain stated in 1892 that an apparently positive hint about Fair Trade by Salisbury had cost the Conservatives and Liberal Unionists 20 seats, so perhaps Salisbury's caution may have been justified. But the fact remains that Salisbury postponed the evil day and it was his nephew who was to confront it in no uncertain terms.

Likewise, with regard to the House of Lords issue in 1909–10, Balfour has been criticised for having allowed the Peers, and especially the 'backswoodsmen', to veto the People's Budget. But it is difficult to see how any Conservative leader could have controlled such a vitriolically-minded group. In this context it is only fair to point out that Balfour's successor, Bonar Law, was also to face continual sniping at his leadership between 1911 and the outbreak of the Great War, and there were at least two occasions on which he considered resigning his position. The Edwardian Conservative Party was in large part splintered and frequently uncontrollable, and being its leader was a task that could only have been enjoyable to a political masochist.

But if Balfour's career as a Prime Minister and Party Leader seems at best a failure and at worst a disaster, there are some positive features of his 1902–6 administration and also of his post-1911 career. One scholar of Balfour, Ruddock Mackay, has labelled him an international statesman, and in the sphere of foreign relations Balfour did cement the Anglo-Japanese alliance and also presided over the Entente Cordiale, with the latter being a cause of much centenary celebration in both Britain and France in 2004. Likewise Balfour was a

successful and subtle Foreign Secretary, tried hard to soften the blows levelled against Germany by the Versailles settlement, produced the subtle and influential Balfour Declaration (which was unfortunately not fully acted upon), worked hard and with commitment to make the League of Nations a genuine force for the preservation of international law, and at the Inter-Imperial Conference of 1926 laid the foundations of the crucial Treaty of Westminster of 1932. The foreign policy successes of Balfour's premiership and his activities as Foreign Secretary and within the foreign sphere as Lord President perhaps lead one to the conclusion that he should never have been Prime Minister, and that his strengths really made him a natural and effective 'second-in-command' or *éminence grise*. Certainly it is largely for his achievements after he left the leadership of the Conservative Party that he will be best remembered and for his diplomatic rather than his domestic achievements as Prime Minister.

Throughout his career, when he was presented with a specific topic or subject area, Balfour could be effective, efficient, even ruthless. Good examples of this were his shaping of local government reform in the 1880s and his constructive but equally severe regime in Ireland when he was Chief Secretary between 1887 and 1891. Likewise in foreign affairs he pursued the Entente with genuine commitment and vigour, and he appreciated the nuances of the situation in Palestine and in many ways his grasp of the complexity of Jewish-Arab relations still echoes in the 21st century.

That Balfour possessed a subtle intellect was a source for him of some self-satisfaction, and there were occasions when he deployed it to good effect. But it is also probably true that his love of sceptical examination of all problems was a source of great frustration to many colleagues and, as many in his Party suggested in the Edwardian period, rendered

him somewhat unapproachable or misunderstood both by his backbenchers and the electorate. He was not effective in the demotic arts of the demagogue, and in the age of mass politics this was a fatal flaw.

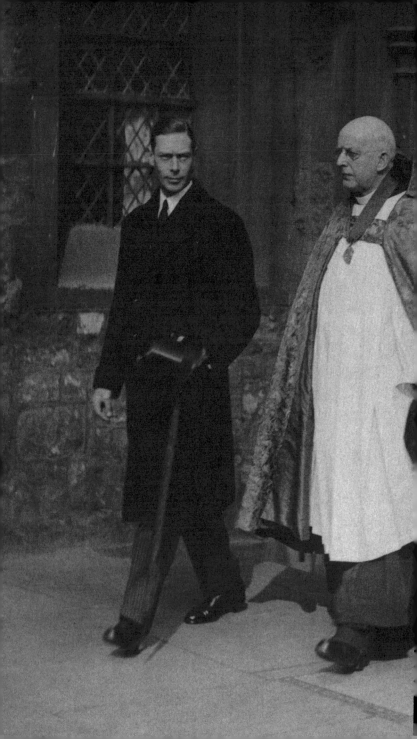

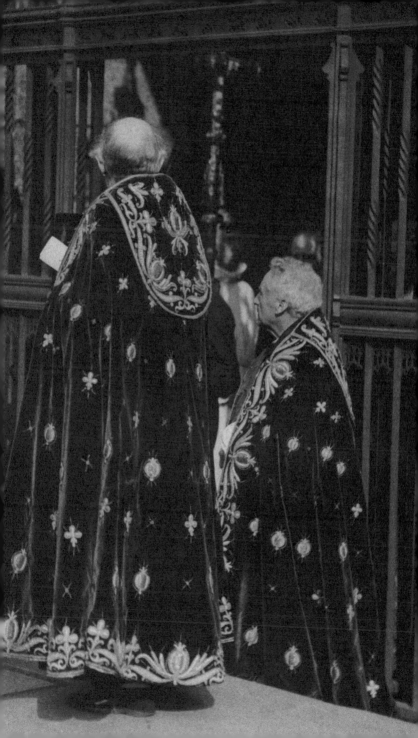

NOTES

Chapter 1: A Man Born to Rule

1. Cranborne to A Akers-Douglas, 26 July 1886, Akers-Douglas papers, Kent County Record Office, Maidstone ADP U564 C. 20/1.
2. Balfour to Akers-Douglas, 2 January 1888, Akers-Douglas papers, Kent County Record Office, Maidstone ADP U564 C.22/3.
3. Balfour to Salisbury, 27 August 1891, Salisbury papers, Hatfield House.

Chapter 2: Ruling Scotland and Ireland

1. G P Gooch, *The Life of Lord Courtney* (Macmillan, London: 1920) p 296.
2. J Ridley and C Percy (eds), *The Letters of Arthur Balfour and Lady Elcho* (Hamish Hamilton, London: 1992) pp 28–30.

Chapter 3: Prime Minister

1. See B E C Dugdale, *Arthur James Balfour* 2 vols (Hutchinson, London: 1939) Vol I, pp 168–81.
2. For bimetallism's particular appeal to the cotton industry and Lancashire see E H H Green, '*Rentiers* versus Producers? The Political Economy of the Bimetallic Controversy, 1890-98', *English Historical Review*, cii (1988).
3. Chalmers to Farrer, 19 November 1898, T H Farrer papers, London School of Economics Library, vol. 1, fo. 28.

4. A J Balfour, 'Politics and Political Economy', *National Review*, May 1885, reprinted in Balfour, *Essays and Addresses* (Edinburgh:1893) p 232.

5. Balfour, 'Politics and Political Economy' in *Essays and Addresses*, pp 229, 233–4.

6. A J Balfour, unpublished drafts of a manuscript on political economy, n.d. 1907–11?, Balfour papers, British Library, Add. MSS 49948, fos. 106–7.

7. Balfour Papers, British Library, Add. MSS 49950, fos. 10–14.

8. For full discussions of the historical school see G M Koot, *English Historical Economics* (Cambridge University Press, Cambridge: 1988), J Burrow, S Collini & D Winch, *That Noble Science of Politics* (Cambridge University Press, Cambridge: 1985), Ch 7, and E H H Green, *The Crisis of Conservatism: The Politics, Economics and Ideology of the British Conservative Party, 1880-1914* (Routledge, London: 1995) Ch 5.

9. W Cunningham, 'A Plea for Pure Theory', *Economic Review*, ii (Jan. 1892) p 34.

10. W Cunningham, *Politics and Economics* (1885), p 3.

11. W Cunningham, 'The Progress of Economic Doctrine in England in the Eighteenth Century', *Economic Journal*, i (March 1891) pp 73–94.

12. Cunningham, *Politics and Economics*, p vii.

13. Cunningham, *Politics and Economics*, p 87.

14. W Cunningham, *The Wisdom of the Wise* (1904) p 61, as the basis of economic action and nations as 'non-competing groups'. L L Price, 'Economic Theory and Fiscal Policy', *Economic Journal*, xiv (Sept. 1904) p 379.

15. W Cunningham, *The Alternative to Socialism in England* (Cambridge: 1885) pp 1–2.

16. Price, 'Economic Theory and Fiscal Policy', p 384.

17. See W J Ashley, *The Tariff Problem* (1903), pp 212–15;
    W Cunningham, *The Case Against Free Trade* (London:
    1911) p 37.

18. W J Ashley, *The Economic Organisation of England*
    (Longmans, Green, London: 1914) p 91.

19. Green, *The Crisis of Conservatism*, pp 169–71.

20. For the historical economists' support for bimetallism
    and tariffs, see Green, "*Rentiers* versus Producers?', and
    Green, *The Crisis of Conservatism*, pp 41–6, 169–71,
    176–83.

21. Balfour, unpublished treatise, Balfour Papers, British
    Library, Add. MSS 49945, fo. 185

22. Balfour Papers, British Library, Add. MSS 49948, fo. 1

23. Balfour, *Economic Notes on Insular Free Trade* (London:
    1903), p. 5

24. Balfour, Treatise, Balfour papers, British Library, Add.
    MSS 49946, fo. 36.

25. Balfour, Treatise, Balfour papers, British Library, Add.
    MSS 49946, fos 120-4

26. Balfour, *Economic Notes on Insular Free Trade*, p 15.

27. Balfour in Parliament, 22 April 1902, in A J Balfour,
    Fiscal Reform (Longmans, London: 1906) p 11.

28. Cunningham, *Politics and Economics*, p 16.

29. Balfour in Parliament, 28 May 1903, in Balfour, *Fiscal
    Reform*, pp 30, 36.

30. Balfour, *Economic Notes on Insular Free Trade*, p 8.

31. Balfour at the Constitutional Club, 26 June 1903, in
    Balfour, *Fiscal Reform*, p 61.

32. W Cunningham, *The Rise and Decline of the Free Trade
    Movement* (Cambridge University Press, Cambridge:
    1904) p 126.

33. Balfour at the Constitutional Club, 26 June 1903, in
    Balfour, *Fiscal Reform*, p 61.

34. Balfour, *Economic Notes on Insular Free Trade*, pp 24–5.

Chapter 4: Balfour the Enigma

1. For the most detailed description of the Cabinet discussions see J L Garvin and L S Amery, *The Life of Joseph Chamberlain*, 6 vols (Macmillan, London: 1932–65) Vol V, pp 109–61.
2. Balfour to Edward VII, 12 May 1903, in Garvin and Amery, *Joseph Chamberlain*, Vol V, p 82.
3. Balfour at Westminster Hall, 15 May 1903, in Balfour, *Fiscal Reform*, pp 26–7.
4. E Hamilton, Diary entry, 15 May 1903, Hamilton papers, British Library, Add. MSS 48680 .
5. Balfour to Devonshire, 28 August 1903, in Garvin and Amery, *Joseph Chamberlain*, Vol V, p 82.
6. For Hamilton's and Ritchie's position on the 'Blue Paper' see A M Gollin, *Balfour's Burden* (Anthony Blond, London: 1965) pp 97–8.
7. Balfour to Chamberlain, 16 September 1903, in Balfour, *Fiscal Reform*, p 69.
8. Balfour at Sheffield, 1 October 1903, in Balfour, *Fiscal Reform*, p 99.
9. Balfour at Manchester, 11 January 1904, in Balfour, *Fiscal Reform*, p 131.
10. Balfour at Manchester, 12 January 1904, in Balfour, *Fiscal Reform*, p 143.
11. Balfour at Edinburgh, 3 October 1904, in Balfour, *Fiscal Reform*, p 200.
12. Balfour to H Cecil, 16 July 1903, Balfour Papers, British Library, Add. MSS 49759.
13. J Chamberlain at Birmingham, 15 May 1903, in C Boyd (ed), *Speeches of the Right Honourable Joseph Chamberlain* 2 Vols (1914) Vol II, p 128.

14. Balfour, Memorandum to the Cabinet, 1 August 1903, Public Record Office, CAB 37/73/149.
15. Balfour to H Cecil, 2 December 1904, Balfour Papers, British Library, Add. MSS 49759, fos. 55–61.
16. Balfour at Edinburgh, 3 October 1904, in Balfour, *Fiscal Reform*, p 197.
17. Balfour at Manchester, 2 July 1892, in Balfour, *Fiscal Reform*, p 5.
18. Balfour at Westminster Hall, 15 May 1903, in Balfour, *Fiscal Reform*, p 27.
19. See F Trentmann, 'The Strange Death of Free Trade' in E Biagini (ed), *Citizenship and Community* (Cambridge University Press, Cambridge: 1996).

Chapter 5: Leader of the Opposition

1. Note of Balfour's position, taken by the Earl Crawford and Balcarres, 1 August 1911, in J Vincent (ed), *The Papers of the 4th Earl Crawford and Balcarres* (Manchester University Press, Manchester: 1984) pp 208–9.

Chapter 6: War in Europe and Westminster

1. Dugdale, *Arthur James Balfour*, Vol II, pp 113–14.
2. Sidney Zebel, *Arthur James Balfour: a political biography* (Cambridge University Press, Cambridge: 1973) p 202.
3. Lloyd George, *War Memoirs* (Odhams Press, London: 1938) Vol 2, p 1014.
4. Ruddock Mackay, *Balfour, Intellectual Statesman* (Oxford University Press, Oxford: 1985) p 313.
5. Zebel, *Arthur James Balfour*, p 241.
6. Zebel, *Arthur James Balfour*, p 244.

Chapter 7: Elder Statesman

1. Zebel, *Arthur James Balfour*, p 255.

2. Mackay, *Balfour, Intellectual Statesman*, p 328.
3. Churchill, 287.
4. Sir Frank Heath, quoted in Rayleigh, 46.
5. M. Wheeler, *The British Academy, 1949–1968* (Oxford University Press, Oxford: 1970).
6. Dugdale, *Arthur James Balfour*, Vol II, p 397.

CHRONOLOGY

Year	Premiership

1902   12 July: 13 days before his 54th birthday, Arthur James Balfour
 succeeds his uncle, Lord Salisbury, as Prime Minister.

The Imperial Colonial Conference, held in London, rejects
 Chamberlain's proposal that an Imperial Council be founded, but
 does pass a resolution endorsing Imperial Preference.

The Education Act sees the introduction of the first truly national
 education system in Britain. Local Education Authorities assume
 the duties of the school boards (created under the 1870 Education
 Act), which are abolished. The Liberal and Labour Parties, as well
 as the Nonconformists, oppose the Act. The National Passive
 Resistance Committee is formed in opposition, many members of
 which went to prison for refusing to pay the new school tax.

1903   The Tariff Reform campaign begins with a speech by Joseph
 Chamberlain at Birmingham Town Hall, eventually prompting
 a unionist split and allowing the Liberals to re-unite under the
 free-trade banner. Despite the strength of the Tariff movement
 Balfour was reluctant to go further than cautious protectionism,
 and hoped to stem debate by not publicly endorsing either
 free-trade of tariff reform. Five Cabinet Ministers, including
 Chamberlain, resign over the proposed tariff reforms, leaving the
 Conservatives bereft of several of its leading figures.

The Wyndham Land Act, allows tenants in Ireland – so long as
 they support the British government – to purchase their land,
 paying the exchequer over an extended period by staggered
 payment. More than a quarter of a million tenants bought out
 their holdings.

Employment of Children Act. The employment of children,
 properly regulated for the first time, is brought under the control
 of Local Authorities.

1904   Lord Lansdowne and the French Ambassador Paul Cambon sign
 the Entente Cordiale. It aimed to resolve issues of influence and
 control in Morocco, Egypt, Newfoundland, Siam and West and
 Central Africa, as well as ensuring free passage through the Suez
 Canal.

History	Culture
Triple Alliance between Austria, Germany and Italy renewed for another six years. USA acquires perpetual control over Panama Canal.	Claude Monet, *Waterloo Bridge.* Gauguin, *Riders by the Sea.* Joseph Conrad, *Heart of Darkness.* Gustav Mahler, *Symphony No. 5.* Arthur Conan Doyle, *The Hound of the Baskervilles.* Rudyard Kipling, *Just So Stories.* Scott Joplin, *The Entertainer*
British complete conquest of Northern Nigeria. King Alexander I of Serbia murdered. At its London Congress, the Russian Social Democratic Party splits into Mensheviks (led by Plechanoff) and Bolsheviks (led by Lenin and Trotsky). First flight of Wright Brothers.	Henry James, *The Ambassadors.* G E Moore, *Principia Ethica.* George Bernard Shaw, *Man and Superman.* Jack London, *The Call of the Wild.* Bruckner, *Symphony No. 9.* Film: *The Great Train Robbery.*
Start of Russo-Japanese War in February, Japanese defeat Russians in September. Britain recognises Suez Canal Convention and surrenders its claim to Madagascar. Roosevelt wins US Presidential election. Photoelectric cell is invented.	J M Barrie, *Peter Pan.* Puccini, *Madame Butterfly.* Thomas Hardy, *The Dynasts.* Anton Chekhov, *The Cherry Orchard.* Henri Rousseau, *The Wedding.* Freud, *The Psychopathology of Everyday Life.*

1905   The Unemployed Workmen's Act permits local authorities to engage in public works to provide employment for workers rendered 'idle' by seasonal or other forms of trade dislocation.

The Aliens Act was a result of the investigation of a Royal Commission set up in 1902 to look at immigration. It is the first major attempt by a British government to control, and even prevent, certain groups from gaining entry into the country. It granted the right to refuse entry to paupers unless they were fleeing political or religious persecution.

Anglo-Japanese Alliance; a renewal of the alliance signed in 1902 to safeguard against the perceived threat of Russia, is revised in the wake of Japan's victory.

Hampered by the party split over Tariff Reform, Balfour loses his seat in East Manchester, the only Prime Minister ever to suffer such a defeat.

4 December: Balfour leaves office, having served three years and 145 days as premier.

History	Culture
Port Arthur surrenders to Japanese.	George Santayana, *The Life of Reason*.
'Bloody Sunday' – Russian demonstration broken-up by police. Sailor's mutiny on the battleship *Potemkin*. Tsar Nicholas II issues the 'October Manifesto'.	'Les Fauves' christened by Louis Vauxcelles.
	Picasso begins 'Pink Period'.
Sinn Fein Party founded in Dublin.	Oscar Wilde, '*De Profundis*'.
	Hermann Hesse, *Unterm Rad*
	E M Forster, *Where Angels Fear to Tread*.
	Edith Wharton, *House of Mirth*.
	'Die Bruecke' artist group formed in Dresden.
	Strauss, *Salome*.
	Debussy, *La Mer*.

FURTHER READING

There is no 'full dress' modern biography of Balfour, although one is being prepared by R J Q Adams. The two-volume biography by his niece, Blanche Dugdale, B E C Dugdale, *Arthur James Balfour* (Hutchinson, London: 1939) is a useful introduction, although marked by familial loyalty. Dugdale also edited Balfour's *Chapters of Autobiography* (Cassell & Co, London: 1930) which are useful.

Lord Blake, *The Conservative Party From Peel to Major* (Heinemann, London: 1997) provides an introduction. The entry on Balfour in the *New Dictionary of National Biography* is serviceable, but disappointing. Sidney Zebel, *Arthur James Balfour: a political biography* (Cambridge University Press, Cambridge: 1973) is a good introduction, although historiographically dated. Ruddock Mackay, *Balfour, Intellectual Statesman* (Oxford University Press, Oxford: 1985) is a good analysis of his foreign policy interests.

On his Irish policies, Roy Foster's *Modern Ireland* (Allen Lane, London: 1988) has a fine introductory section, and A Gailey, *Ireland the Death of Kindness* (Cork University Press, Cork: 1987) is full and very helpful. On the key issue of his Premiership, A Sykes, *Tariff Reform in British Politics, 1903–13* (Clarendon Press, Oxford: 1979) is a good survey. E H H Green, *The Crisis of Conservatism: The Politics, Economics and Ideology of the British Conservative Party, 1880–1914* (Routledge, London: 1995) looks at the party as a whole and places Balfour's early career and the causes of his downfall as party leader in its broad context. On the politics of the People's Budget Neal Blewett, *The Peers, the Parties and the*

People (Macmillan, London: 1972) is excellent. Matthew Fforde's *Conservatism and Collectivism* (Edinburgh University Press, Edinburgh: 1990) is good on the land question, but has some eccentricities. A Adonis, *Making Aristocracy Work* (Clarendon Press, Oxford: 1993) is a superb study of Salisbury's management of the Lords and the reasons why Balfour was unable to pursue the same strategies in wholly different circumstances, when the Peers' resentments were uncontrollable.

PICTURE SOURCES

Page vi. A cartoon of Balfour from *The Saturday Review*.
(Mary Evans Picture Library)

Page 5. A photograph of the young Arthur Balfour.
(Topham Picturepoint)

Pages 12–13. A cartoon of Randolph Churchill speaking
while Balfour, Gorst and Wolff listen or sleep. (Mary Evans
Picture Library)

Page 20. A satirical cartoon of Balfour as Struwwelpeter.
(akg Images)

Page 27. A cartoon from *Punch* of Balfour and Salisbury's
attempts at reform in Ireland. (Topham Picturepoint)

Page 30. Balfour's passion for golf is caricatured in *Punch*,
18 May 1899. (Topham Picturepoint)

Pages 80–1. Winston Churchill, Balfour and Lord Morley
watching naval manoeuvres, 1911. (Topham Picturepoint)

Page 88. Arthur Balfour, circa. 1900. (Topham
Picturepoint)

Pages 98–9. Chaim Weizmann and Lord Montagu of the
Zionist Commision, 1917. (Topham Picturepoint)

Page 101. Balfour's typed letter to Lord Rothschild that included the Balfour Declaration. (Topham Picturepoint)

Pages 102–3. Lord Rothschild's response to Balfour on his receipt of the declaration. (Topham Picturepoint)

Pages 108–9. Balfour at the Treaty of Versailles, January 1919. (Topham Picturepoint)

Pages 112–13. Balfour and General Haig sit in the grounds of the Trianon Palace, July 1918. (Topham Picturepoint)

Page 116. Balfour, Nancy Astor and Lloyd George. (Mary Evans Picture Library)

Pages 108–9. A hostile demonstration in Damascus, against Balfour's presence in the city, takes place in El Margi Square, 25 April 1925. (Topham Picturepoint)

Page 122–3. The Imperial Conference participants gather in the garden of 10 Downing Street, 1926. (akg Images)

Pages 134–5. King George VI, when Duke of York, leaves the memorial service for Lord Balfour at Westminster Abbey. (Mary Evans Picture Library)

INDEX

THE 20 BRITISH PRIME MINISTERS
OF THE 20TH CENTURY

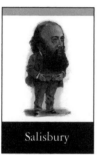

Salisbury

SALISBURY

Conservative politician, prime minister 1885–6, 1886–92 and 1895–1902, and the last to hold that office in the House of Lords.

by Eric Midwinter

Visiting Professor of Education at Exeter University

ISBN 1-904950-54-X (pb)

Balfour

BALFOUR

Balfour wrote that Britain favoured 'the establishment in Palestine of a national home for the Jewish people', the so-called 'Balfour Declaration'.

by Ewen Green

of Magdalen College Oxford

ISBN 1-904950-55-8 (pb)

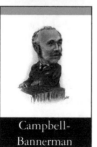

Campbell-
Bannerman

CAMPBELL-BANNERMAN

Liberal Prime Minister, who started the battle with the Conservative-dominated House of Lords.

by Lord Hattersley

former Deputy Leader of the Labour Party and Cabinet member in Wilson and Callaghan's governments.

ISBN 1-904950-56-6 (pb)

ASQUITH

His administration laid the foundation of Britain's welfare state, but he was plunged into a major power struggle with the House of Lords.

by Stephen Bates
a senior correspondent for the *Guardian*.
ISBN 1-904950-57-4 (pb)

LLOYD GEORGE

By the end of 1916 there was discontent with Asquith's management of the war, and Lloyd George schemed secretly with the Conservatives in the coalition government to take his place.

by Hugh Purcell
television documentary maker.
ISBN 1-904950-58-2 (pb)

BONAR LAW

In 1922 he was the moving spirit in the stormy meeting of Conservative MPs which ended the coalition, created the 1922 Committee and reinstated him as leader.

by Andrew Taylor
Professor of Politics at the University of Sheffield.
ISBN 1-904950-59-0 (pb)

BALDWIN

Baldwin's terms of office included two major political crises, the General Strike and the Abdication.

by Anne Perkins
a journalist, working mostly for the *Guardian*, as well as a historian of the British labour movement.
ISBN 1-904950-60-4 (pb)

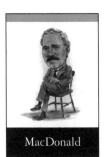

MacDonald

MACDONALD

In 1900 he was the first secretary of the newly formed Labour Representation Committee (the original name for the Labour party). Four years later he became the first Labour prime minister.

by Kevin Morgan

who teaches government and politics at Manchester University.

ISBN 1-904950-61-2 (pb)

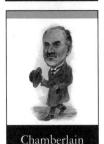

Chamberlain

CHAMBERLAIN

His name will forever be linked to the policy of appeasement and the Munich agreement he reached with Hitler.

by Graham Macklin

manager of the research service at the National Archives.

ISBN 1-904950-62-0 (pb)

Churchill

CHURCHILL

Perhaps the most determined and inspirational war leader in Britain's history.

by Chris Wrigley

who has written about David Lloyd George, Arthur Henderson and W E Gladstone.

ISBN 1-904950-63-9 (pb)

Attlee

ATTLEE

His post-war government enacted a broad programme of socialist legislation in spite of conditions of austerity. His legacy: the National Health Service.

by David Howell

Professor of Politics at the University of York and an expert in Labour's history.

ISBN 1-904950-64-7 (pb)

Eden

EDEN

His premiership will forever be linked to the fateful Suez Crisis.

by Peter Wilby

former editor of the *New Statesman*.

ISBN 1-904950-65-5 (pb)

Macmillan

MACMILLAN

He repaired the rift between the USA and Britain created by Suez and secured for Britain co-operation on issues of nuclear defence, but entry into the EEC was vetoed by de Gaulle in 1963.

by Francis Beckett

author of BEVAN, published by Haus in 2004.

ISBN 1-904950-66-3 (pb)

DOUGLAS-HOME

Conservative politician and prime minister 1963-4, with a complex career between the two Houses of Parliament.

by David Dutton

who teaches History at Liverpool University.

ISBN 1-904950-67-1 (pb)

Douglas-Home

Wilson

WILSON

He held out the promise progress, of 'the Britain that is going to be forged in the white heat of this revolution'. The forced devaluation of the pound in 1967 frustrated the fulfilment of his promises.

by Paul Routledge

The *Daily Mirror's* chief political commentator.

ISBN 1-904950-68-X (pb)

Heath

HEATH

A passionate European, he succeeded during his premiership in effecting Britain's entry to the EC.

by Denis MacShane

Minister for Europe in Tony Blair's first government.

ISBN 1-904950-69-8 (pb)

CALLAGHAN

His term in office was dominated by industrial unrest, culminating in the 'Winter of Discontent'.

by Harry Conroy

When James Callaghan was Prime Minister, Conroy was the Labour Party's press officer in Scotland, and he is now editor of the Scottish *Catholic Observer*.

ISBN 1-904950-70-1 (pb)

Callaghan

Thatcher

THATCHER

Britain's first woman prime minister and the
longest serving head of government in the
20th century (1979–90), but also the only
one to be removed from office in peacetime by
pressure from within her own party.

by Clare Beckett

teaches social policy at Bradford
University.
ISBN 1-904950-71-X (pb)

Major

MAJOR

He enjoyed great popularity in his early
months as prime minister, as he seemed more
caring than his iron predecessor, but by the end
of 1992 nothing seemed to go right.

by Robert Taylor

is Research Associate at the LSE's Centre
for Economic Performance.
ISBN 1-904950-72-8 (pb)

Blair

BLAIR

He is therefore the last prime minister
of the 20th century and one of the most
controversial ones, being frequently accused
of abandoning cabinet government and
introducing a presidential style of leadership.

by Mick Temple

is a senior lecturer in Politics and
Journalism at Staffordshire University.
ISBN 1-904950-73-6 (pb)

THE 20 BRITISH PRIME MINISTERS
OF THE 20TH CENTURY

www.hauspublishing.co.uk

History	Culture
Archduke Franz Ferdinand of Austria-Hungary and his wife are assassinated in Sarajevo. Outbreak of First World War.	James Joyce, *Dubliners.* Theodore Dreiser, *The Titan.* Gustav Holst, *The Planets.* Matisse, *The Red Studio.* Braque, *Music.* Film: Charlie Chaplin in *Making a Living.*
First World War. Germans sink the British liner *Lusitania,* killing 1,198. Germans execute British nurse Edith Cavell in Brussels for harbouring British prisoners and aiding escapes. Erich Münter plants bomb that destroys US Senate reception room	Joseph Conrad, *Victory.* John Buchan, *The Thirty-Nine Steps.* Ezra Pound, *Cathay.* Duchamp, *The Large Glass.* Pablo Picasso, *Harlequin.* Marc Chagall, *The Birthday.* Max Reger, *Mozart Variations.* Classic New Orleans jazz in full bloom. Film: *The Birth of a Nation.*
First World War. Western Front: Battle of Verdun, France. US President Woodrow Wilson is re-elected. US President Wilson issues Peace Note to belligerents in European war. Development and use of first effective tanks.	Lionel Curtis, *The Commonwealth of Nations.* James Joyce, *Portrait of an Artist as a Young Man.* Max Brod, *Tycho Brahe's Weg zu Gott.* Vicente Blasco Ibanez, *The Four Horsemen of the Apocalypse.* Matisse, *The Three Sisters.* Monet, *Waterlilies.* 'Dada' movement produces iconoclastic 'anti-art'. Richard Strauss, *Ariadne auf Naxos.* Ethel Smythe, *The Boatswain's Mate.* Film: *Intolerance*

FURTHER READING

H H Asquith

STEPHEN BATES

HAUS PUBLISHING · LONDON

First published in Great Britain in 2006 by
Haus Publishing Limited
26 Cadogan Court
Draycott Avenue
London SW3 3BX

www.hauspublishing.co.uk

A CIP catalogue record for this book is available from the British Library

ISBN 1-904950-57-4

Designed by BrillDesign
Typeset in Garamond 3 by MacGuru Ltd
info@macguru.org.uk

Printed and bound by Graphicom, Vicenza

Front cover: John Holder

Contents

Introduction: The Noblest Roman

Herbert Henry – H H – Asquith was the Liberal Prime Minister of Britain and Ireland for eight and a half years between 1908 and 1916 – the longest uninterrupted period of office for any premier in the 160 years between the administrations of Lord Liverpool and Margaret Thatcher (and, as I write this, Tony Blair). As he had been Chancellor of the Exchequer for two years before becoming Prime Minister, Asquith's continuous period in the two highest offices of government totalled very nearly 11 years.

During his premiership, the British Empire reached its zenith and, with the onset of the First World War, began its ultimate decline. It was a period in which the Prime Minister and his government faced a series of crises that would have rocked many administrations and confronted challenges, both domestic and international, that were as great as any faced by ministers at any time.

There was a lengthy constitutional confrontation with the House of Lords, after the government's introduction of the People's Budget which, with its inauguration of old age pensions, launched one of the most far-reaching social reforms of the 20th century. There was serious labour unrest, culminating in a series of major strikes, a flurry of anarchist terrorism, a mild but still shocking harbinger of what was to come later in the century, and the suffragettes' seething and increasingly

militant campaign to secure votes for women, which would also see echoes in later pressure groups. There was also an escalating crisis over Ireland and Home Rule, which briefly pitched the government against some of the officers in its own army and briefly created uncertainty about how far ministers could conduct the defence of the country. All this and then an expensive arms race against a background of intensifying international tension. And, ultimately, there was the outbreak of the First World War, the first continental conflict in which Britain had engaged for 100 years and one of the most devastating clashes that the world has ever seen.

The debate about how well Asquith and his government handled these crises has been controversial among historians. Indeed many of the issues these Edwardians had to address 100 years ago are still unresolved today, not least the problem of Ireland and Britain's long, slow, agonising disengagement from its troublesome neighbour.

To examine these events again is to enter a time that is both strikingly similar to and enormously different from our own. It was a country of great wealth, with the mightiest empire in the world and a huge, though slipping, industrial and trading base, but also great disparities of income, housing and education. It was a world in which a small civil service was beginning to direct widening areas of life but in which statesmen and politicians communicated through letters and telegrams, not telephones or, usually, personal meetings.

No American presidents had yet left the shores of their country during their terms in office, so British prime ministers never encountered them. Nor for that matter did Sir Edward Grey, Asquith's Foreign Secretary, who only ever went abroad once. When Mr Asquith went to meet the King on becoming Prime Minister, he caught the scheduled train on his own down to Biarritz where Edward VII was wintering, without

security guards or even a private secretary to accompany him. A few years later, when he was assaulted by militant suffragettes while playing golf on holiday at Lossiemouth in Scotland, he had to fend them off for himself with the aid of his daughter Violet.

It was an age moreover when the Prime Minister could take a taxi if he needed to go somewhere. Asquith was the first Prime Minister to be filmed and archive newsreel exists of him getting out of a cab in Downing Street and paying the driver. When he wanted to communicate in Parliament he made a speech and when he had something to say to his fellow countrymen he addressed a public meeting, often one attended by thousands of spectators, most of whom presumably could hardly hear him since he spoke without a microphone. The Prime Minister did experiment with at least one recorded speech: a three-and-a-half minute defence of the People's Budget, given in 1909, shows him to have had a strong and pleasant, accent-less voice, and an easy manner, to have spoken in sentences, using complicated words such as 'exigencies' – not a word you would hear many politicians using today. There were definitely no sound-bites.[1] Rather endearingly, at the end you can just hear him asking the sound engineer slightly impatiently: *Will that do?* Such a recording was rare, however. Presumably it would have had to have been bought as a gramophone record by those who wished to listen to it and would not have reached a wide national audience.

Many voters may have had only a hazy idea of what the Prime Minister looked like. In fact he was a handsome, authoritative-looking man, in his mid-50s when he took charge of the government, after 22 years in Parliament, with a full head of white hair, growing longer and more straggly the longer he remained in office, something a media consultant would not allow today. He became an increasingly portly figure in

office too, with a rubicund face, the result, so his enemies and sometimes his friends alleged, of good living and periodic heavy drinking. The alcohol was not usually incapacitating but it did earn him the private nickname of 'Squiff'. Such a habit would have been nearly insurmountable for a national leader in the intrusive world of today, but then the Prime Minister was not omni-present in the lives of his countrymen, nor did he seek to interfere or regulate much of what they did. He – and they – would have thought it both impertinent and unnecessary.

Asquith did not give interviews – like many prime ministers he despised the press, often with good reason, and he certainly did not cultivate it, though he occasionally dined with sympathetic editors such as C P Scott of the *Manchester Guardian* – nor did he employ a press officer or communications department, still less a spin doctor, had he or any one else in those days known who such a fellow was, or what he did.

He wrote copious letters, often several times a day, each up to a thousand words in length, and sometimes couched in the sort of intimate terms to women friends that would bring any politician's career to a grinding halt if they occurred today. With the postal service as it then was, he could post a letter in Downing Street in late afternoon and know it would arrive elsewhere in London that very evening.

He spent most weekends in the country, sometimes at his home outside Oxford, bought with the private assistance of the American banker J P Morgan who was at the same time commercially engaged with both the British and the US governments – something he did not think for a moment was potentially corrupting because he was not personally corrupted. But Asquith also often stayed at house parties attended not just by political allies but by opponents as well and he took long holidays, often abroad and sometimes out of touch with his colleagues and the government.

Such then was the world of Edwardian politicians and such were the crises which confronted Asquith and his government. It might be wondered that such serious events were surmounted for as long as they were. What is more remarkable is that for three-quarters of the duration of his administration, from 1910 onwards, the Liberal government did not have a parliamentary majority on its own but relied upon a series of coalitions to retain power. That it did so successfully was in no small measure due to the character and leadership skills of the Prime Minister.

Asquith – known as Herbert to his first wife, Henry to his second and, universally, as H H to his colleagues, friends and to contemporary newspapers – has often been called by his admirers the last, or noblest, of the Romans. It was a description that would have appealed to a man whose Victorian classical education and erudition led him to pepper his speeches and writings with classical allusions. To his followers it signified a political leader whose benign imperturbability transcended and scorned partisan politics and low quest for advantage over his opponents and the men of his own government who eventually schemed to bring him down. His enemies called it indolence and complacency. Such loftiness came at a price: Asquith was the penultimate Liberal prime minister and Liberalism's descent from the heights of power to the status of a distant third party throughout the last 80 years was at least partly his responsibility.

But there is much truth in the view that Asquith did indeed define the national interest for a prolonged period, in idealistic rather than partisan or self-interested terms. He was impervious to the manoeuvrings that accompany high office, in a way that does indeed seem old-fashioned today.

He certainly did not see the need to engage in frenzied activity, or change for change's sake, as proof of his govern-

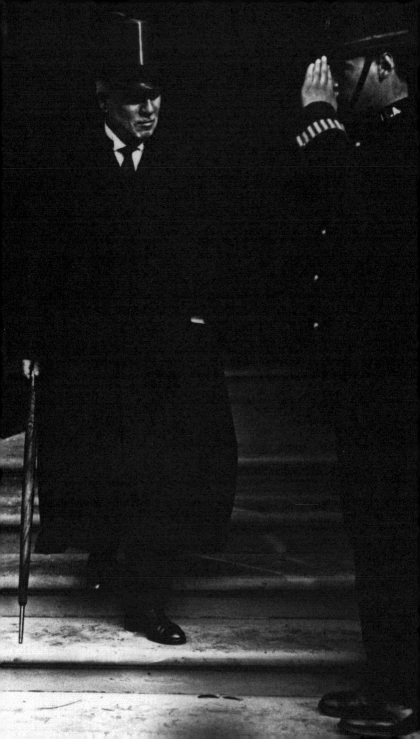

ment's existence and vitality. Quite the reverse: in office his most famous and enduring maxim was *wait and see*, which eventually, as the First World War became bogged down, increasingly disturbed his friends, aggravated his enemies and annoyed and antagonised the press. His leadership was certainly neither dynamic nor charismatic at a time when something of that sort was needed.

But despite this quaintness to modern eyes, it would perhaps be truer to see Asquith as the first of a new breed of 20th-century politician: the first prime minister to enter politics not out of a sense of noble obligation, or dynastic inheritance, or because he had time on his hands or money to spare for an occupation, but because he viewed it as a professional career.

Asquith did not come from a particularly wealthy or metropolitan background (though his family was much more comfortably off than that of his successor Lloyd George), nor did he have an influential patron to set him on the road to success at Westminster. He had to make his own way on his own efforts and talents. Moreover, he had been a successful lawyer and his need to earn money to maintain his family (and an extravagant wife) delayed his political advancement and provided a continuing source of insecurity.

Even when he was Prime Minister, King George V thought him 'not quite a gentleman',[2] although they actually got on well together. The writer Hilaire Belloc talked of people jeering behind his back and spoke of his 'ridiculous middle-class manner',[3] opinions undoubtedly shared by many of those with whom Asquith had to deal in office. They thought it was astonishing that he had come so far – or that he lasted so long as he did. But they underestimated his capacity, authority and resilience.

Part One

THE LIFE

Chapter 1: The Means of Ascent

H H Asquith was born on 12 September 1852 in Morley, near Leeds, the second son of Joseph Dixon Asquith, a 27-year-old wool merchant and his wife Emily. The family seems to have been long-established in Yorkshire – the surname may derive from Viking roots – and had a lengthy association with both religious nonconformity as Congregationalists and political liberalism. The Asquiths were loyal attenders at the local Reheboth Chapel and if in later years Asquith himself was not a regular church, or chapel, goer, his background remained both Nonconformist and beyond the established pale, unlike almost all his predecessors (and most of his successors) in Downing Street.

There were three children in the family: Herbert Henry himself, an older brother William Willans, named after their mother's father, who was crippled and had his growth stunted in a childhood sporting accident and spent his entire career as a public school master at Clifton College, and a younger sister Eva (as well as one other sister who died in infancy).

The Asquiths appear to have been well-off without being affluent but their life together was shattered when the father, Joseph, twisted a gut while playing cricket in the summer of 1860 and died. Thereafter his widow and three young children had to throw themselves on the charity and aid of relatives, first Emily Asquith's father William,

a successful Huddersfield businessman and former stalwart of the Corn Law reform movement, then, three years later when he died, on her brothers. The children received their early education from their mother and then the boys were sent to the Moravian School at Fulneck. By the time her father died in 1863 Mrs Asquith was an invalid, suffering from chronic bronchitis, and she then moved south, to St Leonards near Hastings in Sussex, for the benefit of her health. The family never thereafter returned to live in Yorkshire and Asquith would later describe himself as *to all intents and purposes a Londoner*. Instead, the two boys, aged 10 and 11, were sent to lodge with John Willans, their mother's oldest brother, who lived in Canonbury, north London and were enrolled to be educated at the City of London School. When their uncle moved back north to open a carpet factory, the two boys were farmed out as lodgers to a succession of Congregationalist families in Islington and Pimlico.

From an early age therefore, the Asquith boys were cast adrift both from their parents and their family roots and had to acquire self-sufficiency and self-reliance. Asquith himself, while a genial man and a loving father, remained both reserved, self-contained and vulnerable and it is not hard to sense that, in his clear craving for the companionship of young women, he was a man needing emotional support. He found his escape at least initially through education. The City of London Boys' School was a training-ground for city clerks but it had a dynamic new young headmaster, the Rev. Edwin Abbott, who encouraged his bright pupil and nurtured him to study outside the normal curriculum.

Young Bertie, as he was then still known to his family, studied English and the Classics, haunted the Guildhall Library and became a pillar of the school debating society.

He visited the public gallery of the House of Commons with his uncle John, studied the sermon oratory of the great preachers of the day, went with the crowds to watch the arrival of the Italian liberator Garibaldi and was eventually made captain of the school 'for keeping up the tone as well as the intellectual standard of the higher classes'[1] by his grateful headmaster. In 1870 he graduated, not to a high stool in a City counting house, but to a classics scholarship at Balliol College, Oxford.

Balliol suited the young Asquith and indeed Oxford University became his spiritual home for the next 55 years of his life, perhaps until it spurned the chance to make him its Chancellor in 1925 (even then, Oxford provided the title for his earldom). Here too, Asquith fell under the shadow of one of the great Victorian educators, the redoubtable Benjamin Jowett, newly appointed Master of Balliol, who was just embarking upon his great self-appointed project to train and civilise the future administrators of the Empire and to instil his college's undergraduates with what Asquith himself described many years later as their *tranquil consciousness of effortless superiority*.[2]

As an undergraduate, the young Asquith may have been less aware of this effortlessness however. Not for him the affluent and gilded life of his public school colleagues, or indeed of his sons a generation later. He worked hard at his books and shared a room with his brother for economy's sake when William came up to Balliol a year after him. The college was breaking loose from the intellectual slothfulness of mid-Victorian Oxford though and, although Asquith himself was probably too lowly and middle-class to be close to the great master – he had more affinity with Jowett's rival among the dons, the stern philosopher T H Green – he certainly imbibed Balliol's work ethic. The London day-boy scholar obtained a

first class degree in Moderations (the first university examination) and came close to winning several of the university's top undergraduate prizes ('a reason more for congratulation than for disappointment' in Asquith's biographer and fellow Balliol graduate Roy Jenkins's characteristically condescending estimation[3]).

But, almost as importantly for his future career, the serious young man also excelled at the Oxford Union debating society, that mark of Oxford student politicians' self-regard. He became the union's treasurer and then, at his second attempt and in his last term, while taking his final examinations, its president. At Oxford too, Asquith made life-time acquaintance with other high-achievers: Alfred Milner, the future Imperialist, A C Bradley, the Shakespeare scholar, and Charles Gore, later a bishop. He was learning, in his future Liberal colleague Herbert Samuel's phrase, that 'life is one Balliol man after another'.[4] Inevitably, Samuel was one of those Balliol men as were, slightly later, Edward Grey, Asquith's future Foreign Secretary, and one of his Tory opponents Lord Curzon.

In 1874, Asquith duly took a First Class degree in Greats (Oxford-speak for Literae Humaniores or Classics) and was elected to a Balliol junior fellowship, a post which would help to subsidise his career for seven years to come, while he started to make his way in the outside world. But he already knew that his career would not be an obscure one: he seems to have been too ambitious for that and perhaps realised he was not quite academically distinguished enough.

He spent a summer tutoring the sons of the Earl of Portsmouth and thereby acquiring a first taste of the agreeable life to be had in grand country houses – *I thus obtained a glimpse of a kind of life which was new to me*, he later recorded[5] – and, after one more year's residence at Oxford, decided to follow

the career path of the upwardly-mobile Victorian professional by becoming a lawyer. At the age of 24 Asquith became a student at Lincoln's Inn in order to train to be a barrister in the chambers of Charles Bowen, a future Lord Chief Justice, who also had the advantage of being yet another Balliol man and former president of the Union.

The congruence of that connection was scarcely a coincidence and can have done the young man no harm at all, but it was nevertheless a struggle for him to become established as a lawyer. For several years after he was called to the Bar in 1876 briefs were hard to come by and irregular and he supplemented his income by giving training lectures to aspiring solicitors at the Law Society, marking examination papers for the Oxford and Cambridge board at public schools (among the exams he marked were those of Curzon and Austen Chamberlain) and writing occasional leaders for *The Economist* and, more regularly, articles for the *Spectator*, getting them in usually when the editors were on holiday. There were 39 such articles in all, displaying his earliest recorded political opinions and showing that the essence of his beliefs was already formed: anti-Tory, cautiously radical but realist, an opponent of factionalism or extremism and supportive of *party spirit ... the product of a very complex sentiment which is slow to grow and hard to sustain and which thrives best where it can be nourished by historic memories* as he wrote in his first article entitled 'The English Extreme Left' in the magazine on 12 August 1876. He argued that Liberals should oppose fair (as opposed to free) trade but must be responsible in their opposition to the Disraeli government's foreign policy, since they should not allow the Conservatives to play the patriotic card against them.

An ambitious, serious young man then, maybe a little bumptious and frustrated, with time on his hands, trying to

draw attention to himself and make a name. He wrote a few years later to a friend: *I belonged to the very middle classes then ... I was young and callow and self-confident and ambitious, if possibly rather repellent ... Every day I went by the train to the Temple and sat and worked and dreamed in my chambers and listened with feverish expectation for a knock at the door, hoping it might be a client with a brief. But years passed on and he hardly ever came ... of all human troubles the most hurtful is to feel you have the capacity for power and yet that you have no field to exercise it. That was for years my case and no one who has not been through it can know the chilling, paralysing, deadening, depression of hope deferred and energy wasted and vitality run to seed.*[6]

While Asquith was never penurious during this time – he initially maintained rooms in Mount Street, Mayfair – he was certainly not creating a splash as a lawyer. He was however securing one valuable and lasting friendship with a fellow barrister and eventual cabinet colleague, Richard Burdon Haldane, a man who shared his Nonconformist background and Liberal political instincts and already had contacts within the party. Asquith 'from the beginning ... meant to be Prime Minister', Haldane wrote in his memoirs.[7] And, more importantly still, he got married.

Of all human troubles the most hurtful is to feel you have the capacity for power and yet that you have no field to exercise it.

ASQUITH

His wife was Helen Melland, pretty, gentle and retiring in character, the daughter of a Manchester doctor, whom he had met when he was 18 while staying with his mother at St Leonards. She was three years younger than him and they shared a common interest in literature and poetry. For six years they courted quietly and occasionally, becoming secretly engaged after his graduation in 1874. Their friendship clearly developed into a match of great mutual affection, but it was

not until he had been called to the Bar that Asquith plucked up the courage to ask Helen's father for her hand in marriage. Helen was a good catch for a young barrister – she had a private income of several hundred pounds a year – and it probably helped that her family were also Congregationalists. Dr Melland gave his consent in a formal letter to his prospective son-in-law: 'I have the fullest conviction that your industry and ability will procure for you in due time that success in your profession which has attended you in your past career.'[8]

Helen worried that she was not accomplished enough for her brilliant, ambitious young husband, but they were married in Rusholme Congregational Church in August 1877. The marriage was, Asquith wrote later, *a great success, from first to last it was never troubled by any kind of sorrow or dissension.*[9]

The couple moved to Hampstead, to a house opposite Keats's old home. Clearly their poverty was relative for before too long Asquith was blowing his savings to buy Helen a £300 diamond necklace, they regularly took holidays abroad and they also soon began a family. Their first child Raymond was born in November 1878, Herbert, known as Beb, followed in 1881, then Arthur, called Oc, in 1883, then Violet in 1887 and finally Cyril, or Cys, in 1889. Such family nicknames were a visible sign of affection and closeness and in due course Asquith himself became known to his sons and daughter as Old Boy.

The children were a huge and constant source of delight to both parents. Asquith was by no means a remote or stern Victorian paterfamilias. He played regularly and exuberantly with them and sat listening to their bedtime stories when he came home. His relish for family life may well have been caused by the lack of one of his own in his childhood. The

constraints of his Congregationalist upbringing were also lifted: there were regular trips to the theatre for melodramas and Gilbert and Sullivan and fireworks in the garden on bonfire night – 'nominally for his children' as Beb later recalled, 'but he was fond of playing with them himself and certainly discharged his fair proportion'.[10]

In 1883 Asquith's legal career finally began to take off when he was asked to devil for R S Wright (also Balliol) who succeeded Bowen as Junior Treasury Counsel. This, at last, gave the future Prime Minister, now aged 30, a proper opening into the political world. His talents of diligence, fluency and enthusiasm were noticed by the Attorney General Sir Henry James who asked him to draw up a private report on ways of finding a solution to a long drawn-out and seemingly intractable constitutional problem.

William Ewart Gladstone (1809–98) was the outstanding Liberal statesman of the 19th century (the 'Grand Old Man'). Originally a Tory, he had split from his party over the Corn Laws, and became a Liberal in 1859. Leader of the party from 1866, he was Prime Minister four times (1868–74, 1880–5, 1886 and 1892–4). His third term saw the British intervention in Egypt and the Sudan, while his later career was dominated by the issue of Home Rule for Ireland, which split the Liberal Party in 1886.

This was what to do about Charles Bradlaugh, the free-thinking Radical MP who refused to take a Christian oath to sit in the Commons and whose constituents in Northampton repeatedly re-elected him every time he was slung out of Parliament by the rules of the House. Asquith's elegant paper on the legal and constitutional significance of the Parliamentary oath did not solve the problem – that was eventually to be achieved by allowing non-believing MPs to affirm, by which time Bradlaugh had opted to take the oath

anyway – but it did draw him to the notice of the Prime Minister, Mr Gladstone.

Clearly such a parliamentary and political puzzle was right up Asquith's street. *From that time onwards I was a frequent visitor and worker at the Attorney General's room in the Law Courts*, he wrote later.[11] The next year, increasingly moving in the milieu of Liberal politics, he produced a legal guide for election agents to the new Corrupt Practices Act, which limited candidates' expenses for the first time and, following the general election of 1885, he was able to put his expertise to good and lucrative use in representing Liberal candidates whose returns had been disputed. He was becoming known at last in the party and his legal practice was now earning him reasonable money.

In that December 1885 election, Asquith's friend Haldane had been elected for East Lothian, where his family had business interests and a landed estate to assist his candidacy. But the Parliament was short-lived. Within six months Gladstone's Liberal government had split asunder on the issue of Irish Home Rule – the first attempt to introduce a Government of Ireland Bill – and a new election was called in the summer.

Joseph Chamberlain (1836–1914) made a fortune as a screw manufacturer in Birmingham, then turned to politics, becoming mayor of the city from 1873–6. Entering Parliament in 1876, he was on the social reforming wing of Gladstone's party, but the real conflict between them was over Home Rule for Ireland and Chamberlain lead the Liberals who spilt with Gladstone in 1886. His other interest was the Empire, and he was Colonial Secretary from 1895. Later he was involved in the campaign for tariff reform.

This time Haldane suggested that Asquith might try for the neighbouring seat to his of East Fife, where the Liberal

MP, J Boyd-Kinnear, a local laird, had refused to back the government and was instead supporting the Unionist faction led by Joseph Chamberlain. Asquith was accordingly chosen as the Gladstone-loyalist Liberal candidate by the desperate members of the local association only a fortnight before the election, even though he was effectively a carpet-bagging Englishman with no Scottish connections whatsoever.

It was a remote and insular constituency, incorporating the rural part of Fife, though not the area's largest centre St Andrews, and it had been Liberal since the Great Reform Act. As it happened, Boyd-Kinnear's apostasy was held against him, not least because he sought Tory voters' support, with no Conservative candidate being put up for the seat by agreement, just a few months after they had voted against him at the previous election. It was therefore a straight inter-necine Liberal fight. Mr Gladstone himself was standing in Midlothian only a few miles away. And, perhaps on his leader's coat-tails, the barrister from London found himself narrowly elected. He won by 375 votes: 2,862 to 2,487.

Asquith was to hold East Fife for the next 32 years but it was never a safe seat and he was not a particularly assiduous courter of its loyalty (parliamentarians of his era by and large did not feel the need to be omnipresent in their constituencies). Nor perhaps did he have a natural spiritual affinity or affection for his rural Scottish constituents, except possibly for their local golf courses, on which he became an enthusiastic though apparently largely talentless player. When in 1918 they threw him out, by 2,000 votes, they did so following a campaign in which he was pursued by raucous jeers.

That, however, was a third of a century away. In the summer of 1886, at the age of 34, H H Asquith had arrived as an MP. His career had changed course at short notice and he was entering Parliament for a party whose leader had just been

heavily defeated. His political destiny was to be in opposition for most of the next 20 years. But if that caused frustrations, it also created opportunities for a bright, ambitious and able man, to rise in his party and to build a career out of its wreckage.

Chapter 2: The Coming Man

The new member for East Fife had few of the means of his successors a century later at his disposal to make a name for himself, especially in a House of Commons as raucous and unruly as that of the late 19th century. He was part of a distinctly minority party. The Gladstonian Liberals had 191 seats and Chamberlain's Liberal Unionists 78 – groupings which fundamentally disagreed with each other even though they sat on the same benches side by side – and there were also 85 Irish Nationalists compared with 316 Conservatives. The party was led by a messianic but septuagenarian leader whose interest both in the succession and in young pretenders half his age was understandably limited. Asquith's career at the Bar had been just taking off and might now need to be curtailed and furthermore his wife Helen, though loyal, was distinctly unenthusiastic about his new life. She would stay increasingly at home in Hampstead while her husband attempted to make contacts among the dining clubs and society hostesses of Westminster and the West End.

As it happened, however, because of his seriousness, intelligence and ambition and also precisely because he did not draw particularly ostentatious attention to himself, Asquith was soon noticed as part of a talented coterie of new parliamentarians. Among the Liberals there were also Haldane and Edward Grey, with whom Asquith formed a long-standing

triumvirate, Tom Ellis, who would be Asquith's Chief Whip, and a number of others who together formed the Articles dining club, named after the founding formularies of the Church of England, so-called because, like the church statutes, there were 39 members drawn from both main parties.

These were gatherings of men who would shape British politics for 40 years to come, often fighting fiercely in public, but who were privately good friends, who visited each other and who dined together. Asquith himself was very close to A J Balfour, the future Conservative leader and later to the Tories Curzon and Alfred Lyttelton. He even retained a soft spot for Joseph Chamberlain, the man who had split his party, but who made a point of coming up to Asquith to praise his maiden speech.

These ties were strained later by the fierce quarrels over the constitutional crisis during Asquith's first government, after a new, more polemical, generation of politicians came into the Commons, but they remained largely intact even then. Asquith fitted clubbably into the scene.

Arthur James Balfour (1848–1930), was Lord Salisbury's nephew and his successor as Prime Minister. A brilliant intellectual, with interests in science and philosophy, he entered Parliament in 1874 and was his uncle's private secretary. In 1887 he was Chief Secretary for Ireland, where his strict suppression of disorder earned him the nickname 'Bloody Balfour'. When Salisbury resigned in 1902, Balfour became Prime Minister, but was decisively defeated in the General Election in 1905. He continued in politics, however, serving in the First World War coalition government as Foreign Secretary and held further offices up until the 1920s. (See *Balfour* by Ewen Green, in this series.)

Asquith did not make his maiden speech in the Commons for nine months, but when he finally did so in March 1887,

his loyal eloquence and seemingly instinctive magisterial authoritativeness were noticed. He sounded almost as if he was already on the front benches. Asquith pronounced himself *a loyal member of my party and a faithful follower of my leader* and went on to defend Mr Gladstone against a Tory attack over Ireland. *I was listened to very well and everyone said it was a great success*, he reported to Helen who, characteristically, was not present for the landmark occasion.[1] A few months later he was chosen to deliver a keynote speech at the National Liberal Federation meeting in Nottingham, which had formerly been a bastion of Chamberlain's supporters, known as 'Joe's Caucus', and there he delivered both a warning against making any more concessions to Joe's anti-Home Rulers and a fulsome endorsement of Gladstone who, usefully, was sitting on the platform and listened to himself being described as a leader *whose presence at our head is worth a hundred battalions. To the youngest it is an inspiration, to the oldest an example, to one and all a living lesson of devotion, hopefulness and vitality.*[2]

The Grand Old Man could not help noticing such loyalty and promise and not only invited Asquith to dinner after his maiden speech, but also offered him kindly advice which was remembered 50 years later when he came to write his memoirs: 'If ever you have to form a Government, you must steel your nerves and act the butcher.'[3] In the meantime, apart from Haldane and Grey, Asquith also offered his allegiance to John Morley, the former journalist and now an influential MP, who was Gladstone's acolyte and future official biographer, and to the Marquess of Rosebery, who at 39 was only a few years older than he was but was already a former Foreign Secretary and was clearly the rising force in the party. The loyalty Asquith showed grated occasionally even among his friends. Haldane suggested his reluctance to rebel was occa-

sioned because 'he had fewer views of his own than most of us'.[4]

Beyond the chamber and the smoking rooms of Westminster, Asquith was also able to make a name for himself as junior counsel to the eminent barrister Sir Charles Russell in 1888 at the Parnell Commission. This proved to be an extremely important opportunity to demonstrate his forensic and rhetorical skills to his colleagues.

The commission arose after the *Times* newspaper attempted to smear Charles Stewart Parnell, the Irish Nationalist leader, by accusing him of complicity in the 1882 Phoenix Park murders, an early Irish terrorist assassination, when the new Chief Secretary to Ireland Lord Frederick Cavendish and his Under-Secretary Thomas Burke were hacked to death while taking a stroll in Phoenix Park, Dublin.

The *Times*'s evidence, published under the headline 'Parnellism and Crime', took the form of a letter, subsequently proved to be forged, in which Parnell appeared privately to condone the murders, which he had publicly denounced. Other similar letters were also later released during the course of a court case. Convinced he would not obtain justice through the English courts, the Irish MP appealed for a Commons select committee to assess the evidence, but the Conservative government with no pretence at even-handedness eventually set up a statutory commission of three judges, who were all Unionists – hence political opponents of Parnell – to hear the complaint and also to investigate more widely the activities of Irish nationalists in recent years. Even more bizarrely to modern eyes, the *Times* was represented by the Attorney-General, as government law officers were at that time allowed to take private clients, while Russell and Asquith were engaged by Parnell, who had been impressed by the young MP's attack on the composition of the commission during a

Commons debate. The hearings dragged on for the best part of six months but came clattering to a halt when Richard Pigott, the man who had sold the incriminating letter to the *Times*, was finally called to the witness box, and revealed as a forger. He subsequently fled abroad, sensationally to shoot himself in a Madrid hotel.

Asquith's incisiveness was revealed not by this however but by his cross-examination at short notice of C J Macdonald, the *Times* manager who had authorised the purchase of the letters without taking the trouble to ascertain their authenticity first. More than 120 years later, wishful thinking still remains common and all-too frequently disastrous journalistic failing. As Asquith told it, his senior, Russell, suddenly turned to him and said: 'I am tired: you must take charge of this fellow.' This left him *never more surprised in my life*[5] but he performed the task so ably as to demolish the newspaper's defence and dent its reputation for probity so severely that some malign folk have even asserted it has never recovered. *I got on to what proved to be an effective and even a destructive line of attack and in the course of a couple of hours or so made the largest step in advance that I ever took in my forensic career ... It was a moment that will never fade from my memory*, he recorded in his memoirs.[6]

The vindication of Parnell and the demolition of the *Times*'s integrity had a startling effect on Asquith's legal career, which now burgeoned just as his interest in it declined. He was financially successful at last, earning in excess of £5,000 a year, to support both his family and his unpaid political career (payment of MPs, a cause which he supported, did not become a reality until his own government introduced a salary of £400 a year for MPs in the Budget of 1911). He became a Queen's Counsel, specialising in civil cases, but he left much of the work to his juniors, though it would not be until 1905 that he felt himself to be sufficiently secure to give up his

legal practice altogether in pursuit of his ambition to lead his party. As the 1890s dawned, however, he was beginning to think that a new Liberal administration was in the offing, one in which he might expect to be a minister.

It was at this moment that Asquith and his young family suffered the severest loss of their lives. In the summer of 1891 the Asquiths took their children to the Scottish Isle of Arran for a holiday in a handsome sandstone house with views across the bay where they could watch the Royal Navy's finest warships steaming past each day. One night 10-year-old Beb Asquith was taken ill with fever and his mother moved in to his bedroom to look after him. The next day she too fell sick, but insisted it was only trivial and that she must have caught flu from the child. Beb recovered but it was five days before a doctor was called to examine his mother and when he arrived he diagnosed not a feverish cold but typhoid, presumably contracted from the holiday home's drains. Helen Asquith appeared to be recovering but, three weeks after the illness first appeared, she suffered a relapse and died, aged 37.

Asquith was heart-broken. He would later describe his wife as *an angel from heaven and God took her back from this noisy world with unstained feet and an unspotted heart.* Meanwhile he wrote to a friend: *She died at nine this morning. So end 20 years of love and 14 of unclouded union. I was not worthy of it and God has taken her. Pray for me.*[7]

The recipient of that letter was Margot Tennant, a high-spirited, fiercely-intelligent young society woman who Asquith had already met on the dinner party circuit. She was the antithesis of Helen and she would become Asquith's second wife, as well as one of the most dynamic – some would say interfering – prime ministerial spouses ever to move into Downing Street.

Margot, the daughter of a Liberal MP who was one of the richest men in Scotland, with family wealth founded on the manufacture of bleach for cloth, was undoubtedly a fascinating and vivacious woman, educated and liberated to an unusual degree for Victorian society, while at the same time being constricted and frustrated by that society's expectations of what a young lady should anticipate from life. She was a keen horsewoman, extravagent and chic in dress, interested and opinionated in the arts and politics and happily flirtatious with the older men who practised it. She captivated Mr Gladstone when she sat beside him at dinner, flattered A J Balfour and had already won the attention of Asquith a few months before his first wife had died, though only in a platonic way.

Of their first dinner party meeting, Margot wrote later characteristically about the considerable charm and geniality that Asquith was effortlessly able to deploy towards herself and others: 'I was deeply impressed by his conversation and his clear Cromwellian face. I thought then, as I do now, that he had a way of putting you not only at your ease but at your best when talking to him which is given to few men of note. He was different to the others and although unfashionably dressed had so much personality that I made up my mind at once that this was a man who could help me and would understand everything.'[8]

'He {Asquith} was different to the others and although unfashionably dressed had so much personality that I made up my mind at once that this was a man who could help me and would understand everything.'

MARGOT TENNANT

Margot had met Helen socially without being particularly struck by her: 'no wife for him. She lives in Hampstead and has no clothes', but she now found herself being remorselessly pursued by the lovelorn widower. Even though she had

plenty of other suitors, not least of them Alfred Milner, and no particular wish to be tied down by a middle-ranking MP 12 years her senior in age, however promising, he was soon writing to her obsessively.

He quickly convinced himself that Helen had blessed the potential union: 'My love for you is not disloyalty to her,' Asquith wrote three week's after his wife's death. *As she lay dying, with the intuition that often comes then, she divined (I am certain) that it was to be ... but I am not going to force it upon you. It will keep. You know that it is always there, waiting if the time shall ever come when it can give rest and shelter and protection to that storm-tossed little heart ...*[9] Four days later he sent Margot Helen's photograph with a letter adding: *I am yours – and perhaps you somehow some day – but I can't finish the sentence.*

Such effusive, self-absorbed letters are not unknown from men who have been bereaved and feel lonely after a happy marriage, but Asquith certainly made a habit of them. Asquith himself had never had a relationship with any woman other than his wife, although strains had been showing in their relationship, between her homeliness and his ambition. His later letters when he was Prime Minister to a succession of young women correspondents have a similar sentimental, cajoling and manipulative tone as those to Margot. From the point of view of his reputation, he was unfortunate that his most intimate, eloquent and pathetic thoughts were only too well preserved for posterity.

Asquith continued the pursuit. A few months later, after 13-year-old Raymond came home from Winchester laden with prizes, *about 2,000 marks ahead of any other boy*, Asquith was asking Margot: *Wouldn't you like to be the mother of a really clever son?* The following June, when Margot had told him she would never marry him, he was begging her: *Upon my knees*

which I bend too rarely to God, I implore you to think twice and thrice before you shut the door ... For your love is life and its loss black darkness and despair.

Eventually he wore her down, but it took more than two years. She consulted other friends, including his political opponents, the Tories Balfour and Curzon, who assured her he would bring 'devotion, strength, influence, a great position – things that last and grow'.[10] She finally agreed to marry him in January 1894. Asquith told her: *The thing has come which I have most longed for, waited for, prayed for, willed as I never did with any other aim or object in my life. I swear you shall never repent it. Whatever happiness the will, the tenderness and the worship of a man can bring shall encircle you. To that I pledge my soul and devote my life.*

It was a grand society wedding, at St George's Hanover Square, the following May. Haldane was best man, the Bishop of Rochester officiated and no fewer than four past and future Prime Ministers attended: Gladstone, Rosebery, Balfour and Asquith himself. It was all a far cry from his obscure first wedding at Rusholme Congregational Church nearly 17 years before. Margot wept at the reception on Balfour and Curzon's shoulders.

This is worth dwelling on because of the influence of Margot on Asquith's future career and her fierce defence of her husband and his reputation both at the time in office and after his death. Despite the one-sided nature of the courtship, she proved to be a loyal, loving, if occasionally maddening, wife and tried hard to be a good though sometimes overbearing step-mother to his growing and occasionally obstreperous children. In due course, she bore two children herself – a daughter Elizabeth in 1897 and son Anthony, always known as Puffin, in 1902 – as well as suffering three miscarriages. Asquith remained devoted to her and she provided

something Helen would never have done, constant political advice, which he sometimes took.

During all this time, Asquith's political and legal careers continued to prosper and in 1892 he found himself in government at last after a general election which narrowly returned Mr Gladstone to power for the fourth and final time. Both Asquith and the Grand Old Man suffered reduced majorities and the Liberals could take power only with the support of the Irish Nationalists, whose support was dependent on the octogenarian Prime Minister's continuing commitment to Home Rule.

Lord Salisbury, the Prime Minister, did not resign at once but had to be prised out by a Parliamentary vote. Asquith was entrusted to move the successful motion of no confidence on 8 August 1894, in the last speech he would ever make from the Commons back benches. The old Queen petulantly received her Tory Prime Minister's resignation 'with great regret' and within the week Mr Gladstone was forming his government.

Asquith expected to be part of it and had hoped to be made Home Secretary – a tribute to his legal skills but an ambitious target for someone who was still a month short of his 40th birthday, who furthermore had risen without connections or inherited wealth, who had never held ministerial office before, had only been in the Commons six years and remained relatively junior in the party. He was in Brooks's Club when he received the Prime Minister's letter:

'My dear Asquith,
I have the pleasure of writing to propose that you should allow me to submit your name to Her Majesty for the office of Home Secretary.
I have understood that you are willing to quit your

practice at the bar and in consequence I find myself able to offer this just and I think signal tribute to your character, abilities and eloquence.

Believe me
Very faithfully yours,
W E Gladstone'[11]

When I was a boy, Asquith later wrote to a friend, *I used to think that to get into the Cabinet before one was 40 was for an Englishman who had to start on the level of the crowd, the highest height of achievement.*[12]

Asquith had told colleagues insouciantly that he would only accept office if other *new blood* was promoted as well, but in the event he did not hesitate. He was by far the most highly promoted of his generation – others received much more junior offices outside the Cabinet – and a few days later he and other senior ministers proceeded down to Osborne, the Queen's residence on the Isle of Wight, to kiss hands with the sovereign, receive their seals of office and be sworn in. Asquith was one of four to be made a privy councillor. Not a word was said, but the new young minister nevertheless made an impression: Queen Victoria noted that he was 'an intelligent, rather good-looking man'.

A week later she was sufficiently struck to invite him back to dine and sleep over on the island and confided her continuing favourable impressions in her journal: 'had a conversation with Mr Asquith whom I thought pleasant, straightforward and sensible … He is a very clever lawyer.'[13]

That was just what the new administration required him to be. With the 85-year-old Prime Minister devoting all his waning energies to Ireland, it was left to Asquith and his deputy, Gladstone's son Herbert, to take charge of the gov-

ernment's programme of domestic legislation. This was going to be more than usually tricky since the Conservatives made clear that not only would they fight Home Rule but they would also use their majority in the Lords to block all other measures of which they disapproved. This was an arrogant and unscrupulous – but successful – tactic against an elected government and one that would bedevil Asquith's own administration 15 years later. The Home Secretary borrowed a phrase from the Roman poet Juvenal to describe what they were doing: *ploughing the sands*, he called it.[14]

Nevertheless, Asquith went determinedly to work on an in-tray of a sort his successors a century later would recognise, containing issues and crises both slight and important, national and local. He always was a speedy and efficient dispatcher of ministerial business. His first decision was to establish procedures for the organisation of public meetings in Trafalgar Square, to ensure they did not descend as occasionally in the past into riots. The police's recent practice had been to ban demonstrations in the square altogether (a strategy the Queen favoured), but Asquith decided on the compromise of allowing meetings there at weekends and on bank holidays, thus permitting free speech but not disrupting weekday (or Parliamentary) traffic. It was an arrangement that worked so well that the regulations remained in force for a century.

Rather more courageously, given the government's need to placate the Irish MPs, Asquith set another precedent by refusing to pardon or release a group of Irish terrorists who had waged a dynamiting campaign on the mainland and had been in prison for more than a decade. He resolutely declined to differentiate between political and non-political offences in dealing with the prisoners – a practice also followed by his successors – and robustly defended his decision in the Commons.

Then during a coal strike in West Yorkshire he showed himself prepared to send 400 members of the Metropolitan Police to assist the local authorities in quelling disorder in the town of Featherstone. When that failed to work troops were also deployed to impose order. But when a demonstration grew menacing magistrates read the Riot Act and the soldiers opened fire, killing two men on the fringes. Asquith appointed a commission of inquiry which showed a willingness to investigate the authorities' handling of the matter, but then appointed both the former head of his legal chambers and his best friend Haldane as two of the three investigators. This certainly called into question the commission's independence though it is an open question whether the upright Home Secretary realised that the appointments would be seen as compromising its – and his – integrity. In the end, perhaps inevitably, the inquiry cleared those responsible for the shootings but Asquith would be followed by taunts of 'Remember Featherstone' at public meetings for many years afterwards. This clearly irked him and perhaps it is a measure of his punctilliousness or exasperation that, as his biographer and successor as Home Secretary Roy Jenkins relates, when decades later someone shouted out at a meeting: 'Why did you murder those miners at Featherstone in '92?' he pedantically retorted: *It wasn't '92, it was '93.*[15]

Clearly Asquith was not personally responsible for what had happened in Featherstone and there is some evidence of his private anguish when, as Home Secretary, his duties included confirming death sentences, though he did it. More positively in the coal dispute, he helped persuade Gladstone to appoint Lord Rosebery to arbitrate between the mine owners and the Miners' Federation to resolve the strike – an early government intervention in an industrial dispute. Asquith was also responsible for legislative proposals intended to

improve working conditions. The Employers' Liability Bill of 1893 was designed to make owners responsible for accidents to their employees and force them to take out insurance, but was wrecked by vested interests in the Lords. A follow-up Factory Bill to strengthen the factory inspection service was also pushed forward, though it was eventually to be formally passed by the incoming Conservative government, at Asquith's persuasion.

And there was Welsh Disestablishment, an issue almost forgotten now, at least until the Church of England is one day disestablished, a piece of legislation that took decades to pass and was only finally accomplished in the 1920s, long after Asquith himself had eventually left office. It was an issue which the Liberal government supported in order to shore up its Welsh and Chapel vote, but the measure bored the Home Secretary – though he defended it stoutly enough in the Commons – not least when he had to receive voluble delegations of Welsh Nonconformists demanding that the Anglican Church in Wales should lose its official status now that it represented only a small minority, largely from the Anglo-Welsh squirearchy. *As you know, I am not* passion-ately *fond of the Welsh*, Asquith would write years later. He privately described them as *moutons enragés*. For the time being the measure ran into the sand, defeated in committee with the assistance of radical Liberal MPs from the Principal-ity who wanted to make it a more generally devolutionary measure. In doing so, one of them, David Lloyd George, came to Asquith's notice for the first time, three years after his first election to the Commons.

These were mainly liberalising and progressive measures, both moderate and cautious in nature and, where they were allowed to be, effective in operation. They won Asquith an unusual degree of cross-party praise for what a later historian

called his 'prodigious efficiency' and a reputation for Parliamentary and ministerial competence, that was at odds with what was happening almost everywhere else in the administration. That they were also introduced and steered through by a man whose private life was in some turmoil and whose concentration was clearly at least partially elsewhere was even more remarkable.

By early 1894 the Gladstone administration was faltering. Although he was a loyal supporter of Home Rule, Asquith was not alone in questioning whether it was practicable to force the measure through or whether it should absorb the Prime Minister's entire, obsessive, interest. In March Gladstone was forced to step down – his Cabinet 'blubbing' obsequiously at their last meeting as he recalled it – and he was succeeded by Lord Rosebery, not without a struggle with the veteran Liberal Chancellor of the Exchequer Sir William Harcourt.

Asquith was instinctively a Rosebery man even though on policy issues he probably sided more often with Harcourt, who sat in the Commons and was popular with MPs, but was an obstreperous and difficult person to deal with, a trait not unknown in Chancellors: *to tell the naked truth*, Asquith later wrote, [He] *was an almost impossible colleague and would have been a wholly impossible chief*.[16]

Rosebery, the Foreign Secretary and Liberal leader in the Lords (where he led a small minority rump of Liberal peers) was young, hugely rich, charismatic and popular in the country and appeared destined by birth, wealth and upbringing to lead the nation. In office however he was also neurotic, indecisive and listless, disengaged from the business of government, perhaps because of his chronic insomnia. He was also completely at odds with Harcourt, his Chancellor, over both foreign and budgetary policy.

In such circumstances the Cabinet fell apart in rancour

and recrimination, with the Prime Minister all-but openly opposing the Chancellor over his plan to introduce death duties. 'As you know,' Harcourt wrote blandly to a colleague, 'I am not a supporter of the present government.'[17] When the administration was defeated on a minor matter in the Commons, it resigned with some relief and, in the ensuing election in the summer of 1895 was soundly beaten by the Conservatives. Rosebery, nominally the Liberal leader, was precluded as a peer from campaigning and took himself off in a yacht to sail round the north of Scotland instead.

Asquith was one of only six members of the Liberal Cabinet to survive the election undefeated and, out of the wreckage of the government, was practically the only person to emerge with his reputation enhanced and his friendships intact. It was by now clear that, if he wanted it, he would be leader of his party one day. Mr Gladstone had written fulsomely to him on his retirement the previous year: 'Great problems are before us: and I know no one more likely to face them, as I hope and believe, not only with a manly strength, but with a determined integrity of mind. I most earnestly hope that you may be enabled to fulfil your part, which will certainly be an arduous one.' Harcourt, who would now himself finally become party leader, told Margot Asquith: 'You need not mind any of the quarrels, your man is the man of the future.'[18]

The next decade, however, was to be one of deferred ambition and delayed advance for Asquith. The Liberals spent much of the time in internal faction-fighting and leadership intrigues. They provided inadequate opposition to Lord Salisbury's Conservative government, often seeming to be on the wrong side of every argument. As the 20th century broke upon the world, a new generation of politicians was emerging to develop new policies for continuing problems. And, as they did so, Asquith moved discreetly from being a

sleek young man on the rise to becoming a more rounded and senior figure, now red-faced, plump and even a little scruffy in middle-age. Unlike his wife, he took little interest in what he wore or how he looked.

His legal practice prospered in the civil courts, but it needed to, to attempt to meet the demands of his growing family and his wife's extravagence. In 1894 the family had moved into 20 Cavendish Square, where they would live with the exception of the Downing Street years until 1919, a fashionable address at which they frequently entertained but an inconvenient home and one that required a household of 14 servants to maintain. Asquith was probably earning about £10,000 a year by now and his wife had her own allowance from her father of £5,000, but it was not enough. When Harcourt resigned as Liberal leader in December 1898, Asquith was urged by his friends to stand, but he could not afford to give up his outside work in order to do so. Perhaps he also realised that electoral victory was still a distant prospect. Sir Henry Campbell-Bannerman, 16 years older than Asquith, 30 years a genial, shrewd, privately-wealthy, Scottish Liberal MP and former war minister, was elected instead, seemingly as a temporary measure.

Parliament did not really engage Asquith in these years. He was instinctively a ministerial type, not attracted to the frustrations and polemics of opposition or to contrariness for its own sake. In 1896 he spoke 18 times in the Commons but turned up to vote in only 124 divisions out of 419 and the following year he likewise voted only 124 times out of a possible 375. This was not necessarily unusual for MPs in those days, but it was hardly a demonstration of assiduousness. Nor did he stalk the country making major speeches or setting out radical manifestoes. That was never his style. Instead he chose his moments to contribute, mainly on high-

profile Parliamentary occasions, and colleagues grumbled about his failure to pull his weight for the party. One, Arthur Acland, wrote to Asquith in 1899 that he hoped he might do a good bit in the Commons 'if you have time to spare from law and society'.

The late 1890s though was a period of Imperial obsession: the Queen's Diamond Jubilee in 1897 was swiftly followed by the build-up to the imbroglio of the Boer War and, while Lord Salisbury's government may have faltered, the Liberal opposition did not benefit from any resulting public discontent. Instead, rather like the Labour Party over the Falklands War 80 years later, it was itself divided between its imperialist wing and its Gladstonian Little Englanders, over whether to embrace the Empire and the military adventures and costs it brought, or not. All the while, in the wings and almost unnoticed, its eventual nemesis, the Labour Party, was coming into existence, focusing on the ills of British society and shortcomings at home.

These great issues did not particularly engage Asquith. He wasn't much interested in the Empire as a patriotic construct, or indeed in foreign policy generally. But when the Boer War broke out he saw the political need to support the government in an unbroken front at a time of conflict and this drive for national – and party – unity against a perceived external threat eventually placed him, as a senior party figure, inevitably at the head of the Liberal Imperialist faction. The Liberals were hopelessly and irredeemably split in their attitudes to the war however and the Conservatives moved ruthlessly – as soon as they had the good news of the relief of Mafeking – to distract attention from military defeats elsewhere and to call a 'khaki' election to renew their mandate in the autumn of 1900. Joe Chamberlain, by now thoroughly in the Conservative camp, campaigned on the slogan that 'a seat lost to the

Government is a seat gained (or sold) to the Boers'. Asquith was returned but many of his colleagues were not.

After the campaign was lost and as the military conflict wound down, the internecine party struggle continued, with Campbell-Bannerman eventually coming out decisively against the war with a speech at a dinner in London: 'One is told that no war is going on, that it is not war. When is a war not a war? When it is carried on by methods of barbarism in South Africa.' Shades of Iraq, 102 years later. Such an outrageous slur on the decency of British troops, as it was depicted by the press, provoked Asquith to reply at another dinner shortly afterwards, that he had not changed his support (for the war), did not repent and would not recant. It was largely an irrelevance, even to the party's electoral fortunes: 'the hot bloods of the party are for war to the knife – and fork', one commentator noted sardonically.[19]

The party's divisions continued even after the war was finally over with a split over the 1902 Education Bill, which removed schools from boards to local authority control, in the process giving state funding to Anglican and Catholic church schools. This caused stirrings for almost the only time in his political life to Asquith's Nonconformist soul, leading him to oppose the measure like many of his colleagues.

Then, suddenly, on a very precise date, 16 May 1903, there was a glimmer of light and the dimmest prospect at last of future electoral victory. Margot Asquith recollected the moment quite well: 'My husband came into my bedroom at 20 Cavendish Square with the *Times* in his hand. "Wonderful news today," he said, "And it is only a question of time when we shall sweep the country."'[20]

The wonderful news was that Chamberlain, who had divided the Liberal Party and broken with it over Irish Home Rule in the 1880s was now set fair to do something similar

to the Conservatives. He had broken the long-standing cross-party consensus on the merits of free trade to British industry by broaching his idea for the introduction of protective tariffs on imported goods from outside the Empire. For the first time in years therefore there was an issue that could unite the Liberal Party in traditional support for a universal and high-principled free trading system and, equally to the point, rekindle Asquith's enthusiasm and zeal for political debate. Chamberlain resigned from the government and stumped the country arguing his case and doggedly behind him followed Asquith cogently rebutting his arguments one by one. As his biographer, Stephen Koss, has noted, the imperialist made his mark as a critic of a scheme meant to unify the Empire.

It was a good time to be doing it. The Conservative government was tiring in office but Campbell-Bannerman also seemed to many on his own side to be tiring out of it. He was in his late 60s and his health and that of his wife was waning. He was admitting to colleagues that 'he did not think that he would be able to take any part which involved heavy and responsible work' and Asquith and his friends such as Grey and Haldane, ambitious and hungry for office, thought so too. 'I long for my husband to have his chance while he is young and keen,' Margot Asquith wrote privately to the editor of the *Spectator* in January 1905.

With the prospect of winning an election so close, the circling round the party leader continued all year, trying to persuade him into semi-retirement in the House of Lords. In September, the Liberal Imperialist plotters, Haldane and Asquith, gathered at a country house the Asquiths were renting in the north of Scotland and drew in Grey who happened fortuitously to be fishing at a nearby village called Relugas. They divvied up the prospective Cabinet posts between them – Campbell-Bannerman, Prime Minister in name only, to go

to the Lords, Asquith to be leader of the Commons and Chancellor of the Exchequer, Haldane to become Lord Chancellor and Grey Foreign Secretary – and agreed that while Haldane would approach the King to let him know, Asquith would inform their leader what they proposed. To make sure they got their way they all agreed to accept no less and pledged to refuse to serve unless they got what they wanted.

However, the so-called Relugas Compact lasted only as long as it took Campbell-Bannerman to refuse to be ennobled and to offer Asquith the Exchequer, which he promptly accepted without consulting his friends. Lord Shaw wrote: 'C.B. said with a laugh, "Do you know it was the comicality of it that I could hardly get over. They were to serve *under* me but on condition that they were not to be *with* me ... I let it go on for three days and then I said to each and all of them, 'Now look here, I have been playing up until now ... But now let me just say – that it is I who am head of the government; it is I who have the King's Command; I am on horseback and you will be all pleased to understand that I will not go to the House of Lords, that I will not have any condition of the kind imposed upon me". So, says C.B., they all came in – no conditions and no nothing and there they are.'[21] Margot said that Campbell-Bannerman had merely remarked to Asquith: 'What would you like? The Exchequer I suppose.' Her husband had not even delivered his ultimatum, nor had he stuck by his friends. In the event, Grey did get the Foreign Office, but Haldane had to make do with the War Office.

The performance undoubtedly had its ludicrous side. It was little wonder the Liberal Imperialists were known as 'Limps'. Campbell-Bannerman had easily and shrewdly seen off the stirrings in the ranks, had achieved his purpose and made the appointments he wished to make. Asquith was said to have wailed: *See what a position I am in: if I refuse and go to*

my constituents they will ask why, was it on policy? I must say no. Were you not offered a good post? I must say, 'the best', then it was on personal grounds that you stood out and were prepared to break the party? What answer have I?[22]

Although the plotters thereafter sought to play down the significance of their compact, there was no doubt that they had been shown up. It left Asquith in particular with a slippery reputation. Just as 14 years earlier he had said he would hold out for new blood in the Gladstone Cabinet, but did not, this time he had not only conspired against his party leader, but also left his friends and co-conspirators in the lurch. However at least if Asquith was not leader of the Commons, he was clearly now heir-presumptive to an ailing and ageing Prime Minister. As it happened, the ministerial manoeuvrings all occurred before the general election even took place. The Conservative leader Arthur Balfour resigned in December 1905 hoping to exploit Liberal splits by not calling an election himself but giving way to allow the opposition to form an administration and then to bear the responsibility of appealing to the electorate.

Asquith himself spent part of the pre-election period while the new government was being formed at Hatfield House of all places, home of the Salisbury family and hence of the hereditary scions of the Conservative Party – a remarkable country retreat for one of the leaders of the opposition to choose in the run-up to an election, but then the Asquiths had all been invited to a weekend break and a ball there. 'My husband looked worn out and I admired him more than I could say for throwing himself into the social atmosphere of a fancy ball with his usual simplicity and unselfcentredness,' wrote Margot.[23]

Campbell-Bannerman saw off one last attempt to bounce him into the Lords by the *Times* and the new government

duly assembled at Buckingham Palace to accept their seals of office from King Edward VII. It is a metaphor too ironic to be overlooked that they did so on the morning of a pea-souper London fog so thick that several of them were unable to find their way back down the Mall to their offices half a mile away in Whitehall afterwards

The election campaign began after Christmas, for polling in January 1906. In anticipation of office, Asquith at last wound up his legal practice, telling Haldane it meant surrendering a brief worth £10,000 to defend the Khedive's property that very week. His annual salary as Chancellor would be half that amount. By way of preparatory belt-tightening, Margot Asquith finally gave up fox hunting and disposed of her horses. 'If Mrs Asquith can be prevailed upon to release her husband from the treadmill of society, Mr Asquith may have enough energy left in two years' time to lead the House of Commons,' the journalist W T Stead commented caustically.[24]

Instead, for now, Asquith stumped the country, inveighing compellingly on the evils of protectionism and the concomittant increase in the price of food if the Conservatives won the election and the evil prospect of 'Chinese slavery' – the importation of cheap Chinese labour to work the mines in South Africa – unless they could be stopped.

They were: even Balfour lost his seat in the landslide. The new Liberal government could rely on 400 members of its own, plus the support of 83 Irish Nationalists and 30 Independent Labour MPs, while the Conservatives were reduced to a rump of just 157. It was a huge defeat. Asquith was confirmed as Chancellor of the Exchequer but he and his family decided not to move into 11 Downing Street, the traditional home accompanying the office, as they thought it too small. At the age of 53, he was about to begin nearly 11 years of continuous ministerial office.

Chapter 3: Into Office

The Liberal government found itself in office but not in power almost as soon as it took over in the early months of 1906. It might have a majority of 350 over the Conservatives in the Commons, but the Conservatives had a majority of at least 400 peers in the Lords. The Conservative Party quickly made clear that it intended to frustrate the elected government in the upper house, a tactic it had employed whenever it lost power since the 1880s. It did so because it could and it scarcely bothered to make even the most perfunctory justification for its actions as being in the public interest. The party that considered itself 'born to rule' (as did many of its working-class supporters) clearly could not conceive of anyone else doing so.

Against this rock of imperturbable, seemingly unembarrassable and certainly indiscriminate obduracy the government faltered and gradually over the next four years frittered away the public support with which it had entered office. It announced that it planned to introduce 22 bills but many of these were emasculated or abandoned in the upper house. Mr Campbell-Bannerman might favour the option of 'send for the sledge hammer' to batter down the peers' resistance by threatening constitutional reform but by and large his administration backed away from confrontation. It was in any event inexperienced in power – only one minister had sat in a

majority government before and that had been more than 20 years earlier – and it had its own internal divisions and those of its Parliamentary allies to overcome on policy issues.

The composition of Parliament was changing with new types of career politicians coming in: working-class Labour men, middle-class careerists, ruthless young men on the make and in a hurry, impatient with the old conventions, such as F E Smith on the Conservative side, businessmen and, above all, lawyers: 64 barristers on the Liberal benches alone.

More than a third of Liberal MPs had been educated at Oxbridge. They instinctively understood the rules and tactics of the university union debating societies. Asquith fitted this milieu with comfort and ease. Not only was he heir apparent, but he was by far the most accomplished performer on the front bench. According to his Permanent Secretary he spoke 'with such lucidity and fluency as if he had been making budget speeches all his life.' Stephen Koss says: 'His speeches, while rarely startlingly original or especially eloquent, were invariably succinct, incisive and to the point.'[1] He goes on to quote Balfour as noting tartly: 'Asquith's lucidity of style is a positive disadvantage when he has nothing to say.'

Furthermore, he was the master of his brief as Chancellor of the Exchequer, telling Labour's own first Chancellor Philip Snowden years later that the job was *the easiest one in government*.[2] As in his previous job as Home Secretary years before, he acted cautiously – Asquith described himself later as *a financier of a respectable and more or less cautious type* – but this is not quite the whole story. He was also determined to effect social and fiscal change. In only two years in post he introduced three Budgets. The first, three months after taking office, abolished coal tax and reduced the tax on tea – measures designed to help the less well-off (sugar tax followed the next year) – and also reduced expenditure on

the navy by £1.5 million. The second budget a year later went further, giving indications of a minister turning his mind to longer-term planning beyond the annual time span. It contained provisions for the first time for a graduated income tax, reducing taxation on earned incomes less than £2,000 from a shilling to 9d in the pound – a differentiated system that has prevailed ever since – and also foreshadowed a more constructive use of the national surplus – a whopping £5 million that year – than handing it back in tax cuts to the rich. Most of this money was to be set aside to provide for the first time for a non-contributory old-age pension. Although his successor Lloyd George has always gained the credit for introducing the pension, it was actually Asquith who developed and first proposed it.

This was a near-revolutionary change and a positive social good, to save the impoverished elderly over the age of 70 from the dire choice of working until they dropped or entering the workhouse, separated from their spouses, without hope of remission until death. The measure was furthermore introduced altruistically as a recognition for the first time of the state's duty of care to its elderly, not for any ulterior, calculated motive. When it was finally introduced by Asquith in 1908 in a budget which he delivered shortly after becoming Prime Minister, it was modest enough: five shillings a week for those over the age of 70 whose income did not otherwise exceed 10 shillings a week: the equivalent of £13 a year each for half a million people.

The Chancellor erroneously believed the money could be found without increasing taxation. He was not, he informed the Commons, *what is called a Socialist*, but *there is nothing that calls so loudly or imperiously as the possibilities of social reform*. Ultimately the pension would not be introduced (in an amended form) until after Lloyd George's People's Budget in 1909, for

which Asquith was happy to give his Chancellor both full credit and firm backing. But the initial impetus was his.

Nevertheless the pension idea aroused strong opposition both from Conservatives representing the wealthy, outraged that their taxes should be spent in such a philanthropic way, from the armed services which wanted the money spent on armaments, particularly battleships, but also from some Liberals, of whom the plutocratic Lord Rosebery was most prominent, who believed that such largesse would encourage indolence and undermine thrift. The Radicals of course thought the measure did not go far enough. Some Tories were not at all averse to the principle of a pension, they just did not like the Liberals doing it and they certainly did not mind defeating the measure in the upper house.

These were solid achievements but elsewhere the government's programme was floundering. Its education bill, intended to extend the Tory 1902 act to give state payment to Nonconformist schools as well as Anglican ones, was effectively killed off in the Lords and had to be ignominiously dropped. The same fate befell the plural voting bill and bills for English, Irish and Scottish land reform and a licensing bill, designed to reduce the number of pubs (the brewers were traditionally Tory and Opposition MPs were not slow in pointing out that Liberal drinking clubs would be unaffected). The Tory peers let through the Trade Disputes bill but only because they saw the electoral advantage that the government was itself split over the measure.

It was no wonder that Liberal supporters were growing frustrated. The government's strategy of 'filling the cup' – introducing so many measures that the Lords could not block them all without incurring public odium – was not working, nor could it yet develop a coherent strategy for tackling the upper house. Meanwhile, Campbell-Bannerman, now aged

71, was distracted by the prolonged illness and slow death of his wife, whom he had nursed devotedly. Shortly after she died in August 1906, the Prime Minister himself suffered a severe heart attack. More followed at increasingly regular intervals. After the latest in November 1907, the Prime Minister spent two months abroad convalescing at a hotel in Paris (the government did not even send a doctor with him) and returned in January 1908, only to suffer another heart attack within a fortnight.[3] It was evident that the Prime Minister was dying but still he would not leave Downing Street, or resign.

When Asquith went to see him on 27 March, the Prime Minister praised his 'wonderful' colleague, 'so loyal, so disinterested, so able' and added earnestly: 'You are the greatest gentleman I ever met,' and, as the Chancellor was leaving: 'This is not the last of me. We will meet again Asquith.'[4]

They never did. A week earlier, the wonderful colleague had already written to the King's private secretary: *The status quo cannot go on ... there is absolutely no hope of a return to public life and the prolongation of the present uncertainty is having very demoralising results.*[5] The news was kept from the patient for fear of killing him off completely and it was not until 1 April that Campbell-Bannerman finally offered his resignation. He died, still in his bedroom in Downing Street, three weeks later.

No sooner had he received the resignation than the King, who was wintering in Biarritz and showing no sign of coming home early, had sent for Asquith to form a new government. There was some murmuring about other possible candidates, but none had remotely Asquith's standing: the main fear was that he would merely be offering more of the same frustrating and timid government as his predecessor. So it was that on Monday 6 April Asquith quietly left Cavendish Square after dinner to catch the 9 p.m. Continental boat train from Charing

Cross, *en route* to see Edward VII. The departure was unannounced, there were no crowds and the new Prime Minister travelled alone, without a secretary or bodyguard. *The Times* reported that he wore a thick overcoat and had a travelling cap pulled low over his eyes. He travelled by scheduled services, through Paris and then south to Biarritz, arriving late the following evening. On the Wednesday morning, he dressed in a frock coat and paid a visit to see Edward VII in his suite – appropriately enough – at the Hotel du Palais.

As Asquith wrote that night to his wife: *I presented him with a written resignation of the office of Chr. Of the Exr. And he then said: 'I appoint you PM and First Lord of the Treasury,' whereupon I knelt down and kissed his hand. Voila tout!*

He then asked me to come into the next room and breakfast with him. We were quite alone for an hour and I went over all the appointments with him. He made no objection to any of them and discussed the various men very freely and with a good deal of shrewdness ... The weather here is vile beyond description ... I leave at 12 noon tomorrow and arrive at Charing Cross 5.12 Friday afternoon. You will no doubt arrange about dinner that evening – Love, ever yours.[6]

After being out of touch with England and the government for five days, Asquith duly arrived back home – there were cheering crowds this time – and arranged the disposition of his Cabinet. Though he was not formally to be elected Liberal Party leader until the end of the month, after Campbell-Bannerman's death, never was a leadership election more certain.

The Cabinet was carefully balanced between the various party factions, Whigs and Radicals, and would hold together with very little change and no reshuffles for the next seven years. Most significant however, was the injection of two determined and radical young men to crucial and strategic posts.

Lloyd George became Chancellor and Winston Churchill, only four years after his defection from the Conservatives, entered the Cabinet for the first time, aged 33, as President of the Board of Trade. These men meant business.

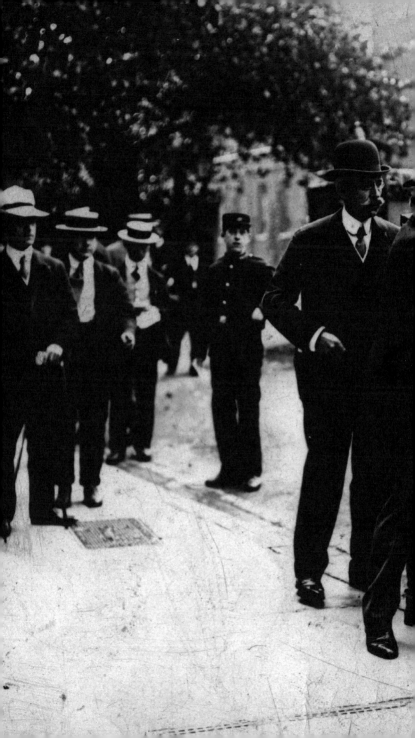

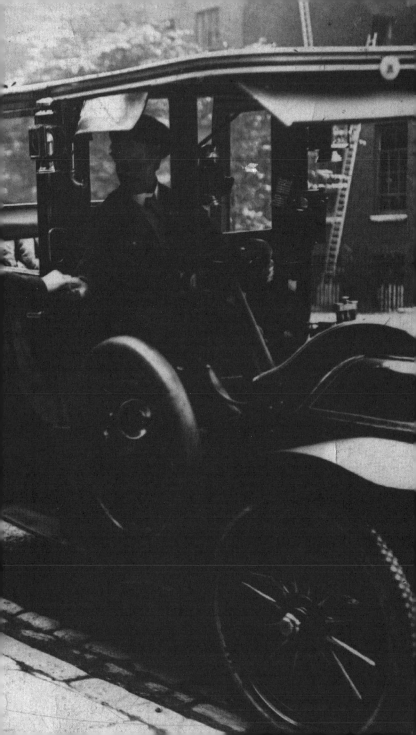

Part Two

THE LEADERSHIP

Chapter 4: Prime Minister

H H Asquith was aged 55 when he became Prime Minister and was perceived despite his years in Parliament and his ministerial career to be a new sort of politician, a man of the middle classes who had risen because of intellectual talent, ambition and agreeableness, not private wealth or hereditary status.

He was the first lawyer in 100 years to become first minister and he would adopt a congenial mode of working that would have startled his more Stakhanovite successors a century later. He enjoyed a rich social life, with stimulating political and literary chat and gossip, often with his children's friends or young women of his acquaintance, drink and bridge after dinner – he grumbled if he missed cards in the evening – regular nights out at the theatre (Gilbert and Sullivan for preference) and long weekends in the country and at house parties. There were regular golf excursions with Arthur Balfour, the Leader of the Opposition and latterly with the Labour leader Ramsay MacDonald and breaks and holidays lasting many weeks in Scotland, north Wales and on the Continent each year.

Every evening too, the Prime Minister would read for at least an hour, not the papers from ministerial red boxes but more improving literature: his diary for 1914 includes as his bedtime reading: Gosse on Ibsen, Fabre on spiders, Dean

Stanley's *Annals of Westminster Abbey*, *for some strange reason* a history of the Wars of the Roses, *a book by a Jew called Hirsch about the fortunes of his race in the Middle Ages*, his old tutor T H Green's *Prolegomena to Ethics*, two volumes of Kant (translated from the German), *Our Mutual Friend* and a number of other Dickens novels. During the First World War he would occasionally retire to the library of the Athenaeum in the afternoon to read, not official papers but novels and other books that took his fancy: *I walked across after 6 ... and took up a novel, 'Sir Perryworm's Wife'(a good title), wh. with judicious skipping I read from cover to cover ... I found it readable & rather soothing.* Do modern Prime Ministers enjoy such eclectic reading matter? Of course, they also have television to entertain them.

Britain as a country in 1908 was sublimely self-confident in its own power and righteousness, at the head of what it liked to call the greatest Empire the world had ever seen, an imperial reach stretching from Australia and New Zealand, across India, down through Africa, almost from Cairo to the Cape, into the Caribbean and across the prairies and tundra wastes of Canada, encompassing more than a quarter of the world's population. Explorers and adventurers were heroes, adding to the imperial lustre even if they occasionally came to grief as Captain Scott and his companions would do in the Antarctic in 1912. The country was still, just, the mightiest industrial nation in the world in terms of coal and cotton – currently enjoying boom years, hence the continuing popularity of free trade – but it had already been overtaken, scarcely noticed, by Germany and the United States in the production of manufactured goods and new vital commodities such as steel and chemicals. Its business and working practices would soon become outmoded, but such was the country's wealth that it would eventually be able to pay most of its own bill for the First World War from its own resources. It would be a

blow to prestige as well as a tragedy that the supreme symbol of the nation's technological self-confidence and prestige, the *Titanic*, should hit an iceberg and sink on her maiden voyage, also in 1912.

Britain's former policy of splendid isolation from Continental alliances was already challenged by the rising power of Germany which was openly competing against the Royal Navy's century-long supremacy of the seas with a battleship construction programme. Germany wanted its own imperial place in the sun and Britain was now finding itself forced into ententes with France and Russia to discourage the challenge. Constraints to Britain's national autonomy were becoming evident even though they were largely unacknowledged.

The country remained a nation of vast disparities of wealth and class and of a rigid social structure which only an able few – like Asquith – could penetrate. It was a society controlled by both deference and hierarchy, but one in which resentment was also gathering. Only now were governments beginning to consider paying for the education of the masses, or provision for the elderly. The landed gentry and aristocracy jealously retained their wealth and guarded their acres. They still employed large numbers of domestic servants and saw little need to ameliorate their conditions, or those of the factory workers, toiling for long hours in harsh conditions. For the middle classes too life was relatively sweet and becoming sweeter and more prosperous, as clean and relatively spacious suburban villas and garden suburbs began to spread out from urban centres. They too could afford cheap domestic servants and the modern inventions and appliances that were beginning to lift life's drudgery – safety razors, gas stoves, electric lights – and they also had the leisure and wealth to enjoy themselves, visit sporting events, go to the theatre and the music hall, the church and the chapel, using

cheap and regular public transport. An army of male clerks and female 'type-writers' was playing its part in servicing the nation and its empire. But 20 per cent of the population still lived below subsistence leve, a prey to squalid housing conditions, stunting diseases, poor diets and short life spans. Divisions therefore between plutocratic or even just comfortable lifestyles and abject poverty were vast and, if Britain was perhaps better at addressing some of these conditions than the other advanced industrial nations, it had as yet made only small, piecemeal, efforts to do so.

In part this was because political pressure for change was limited. Britain was already a mature parliamentary democracy but the female half of the nation did not have the vote – some were soon to make belligerent noise about this – nor did many men from the most impoverished classes. They had to make their views known through industrial action, which was usually ineffective and often degenerated into violence. If politicians could still rely on deference, the police and troops to maintain order, they feared that anarchy was only just around the corner.

Asquith did not believe it was his duty to disturb or reform much of this. He believed his job was to manage the government with as light a hand as possible, prudently directing the public finances, ameliorating abuses if strictly necessary for social benefit and ensuring the smooth conduct of the nation's affairs. He did not favour reform for its own sake, or as an example of ministerial vigour and activity. In this he did not differ greatly from his Conservative opponents, except that he had a slightly different view of the common good than they did.

Asquith saw himself as a facilitator and chairman and allowed his ministerial colleagues great leeway to devise and carry out policy. If that implies a certain detachment and

reticence about leadership, he also gave firm and loyal backing once collective Cabinet decisions had been made, to those such as Lloyd George with a more radical agenda than his own, however exasperated he might be with them privately. He certainly did not see it as his business to place his personal stamp on every government policy. His performance and leadership skills in a House of Commons increasingly made up of men like him was paramount, but he also had to keep a cabinet together, made up of strong and sometimes untrustworthy personalities such as Lloyd George and Churchill, ambitious just as he had been to reach the top.

The journalist A G Gardiner in a profile in the *Daily News* at this time described him in this way: 'He is the constructive engineer of politics, not a man of vision. He leaves the pioneering work to others and follows after with his levels and compasses to lay out the new estate. No great cause will ever owe anything to him at its inception, but when he is convinced of its justice and practicability, he will take it up with a quiet, undemonstrative firmness that means success ... If he is wanting in any essential of statemanship, it is a strong impulse to action. He has patience rather than momentum.' He did not, the writer added, inspire men with great passions, or utter great thoughts. As with other Balliol men, 'We admire them, we respect them: we do not love them, for we feel that they would be insulted by the offer of so irrational a thing as love.'[1] Indeed, Asquith prided himself on his calmness and rationality and distrusted and despised emotion and passion. Decisions should not be rushed, but should wait on events, not be swayed by rhetorical excess or partisan clamour.

There was a less benign view, expressed by R C Munro-Ferguson, Viscount Novar, who had entered the Commons at the same time as Asquith in 1886, in a letter to Rosebery in December 1907 just as the succession was being settled:

'Asquith is at heart a raw English middle class radical, with a character deteriorated by a vulgar society of another sort and by a free use of wine which he cannot carry ... He has come to be quite unreliable, for he would accommodate himself to any line of policy to secure the enticements of office.' More benignly, young Winston Churchill, who still sought Asquith's patronage, wrote at the same time: 'No better workman will have been installed since the days of Sir Robert Peel.'[2] The Prime Minister remained a great dispatcher of business.

Asquith could exasperate his colleagues by his apparent imperturbability, inaction and placidity but Munro-Ferguson's disparaging remarks also show that the Prime Minister's drinking was indeed becoming noticed by colleagues even at this stage and would be more so over the coming years as stress and maybe depression occasionally overcame his emotional control.

It was a subject for veiled gossip in the press and less restrained comment among colleagues, but it does not appear to have been incapacitating or, accordingly, public knowledge. Some called him 'Squiff' or 'Squiffy' – Churchill, who knew a thing or two about drink himself, would eventually describe Asquith as 'sodden' – but the most that seems to have registered was a certain unsteadiness on his feet late at night. The Tory MP Arthur Lee recorded how, during an evening debate on the perennially-returning Welsh disestablishment bill, at about 10.00 p.m. when the government was represented in the chamber by the ministers Rufus Isaacs and Herbert Samuel, Asquith had come in from dinner 'very flushed and unsteady in gait, plumped himself down between

'No better workman will have been installed since the days of Sir Robert Peel.'

WINSTON CHURCHILL ON ASQUITH

them on the bench and promptly went to sleep'. Lee added that Arthur Balfour, the Tory leader and Asquith's friend, had turned to him and murmered: 'I am getting uneasy about this bill and don't at all like the idea of the fate of the Church being left in the hands of two Jews who are entirely sober and one Christian who is very patently drunk.'[3] An authentic whiff of the prejudice and snobbery of the Edwardian ruling class.

For the moment though, in the years before the war, the Prime Minister was in control. The first challenge was to see the Budget through. For 1909 Lloyd George, his successor, planned to expand the ideas that Asquith had put forward the year before. He also needed to raise more revenue to introduce the pension scheme but also because of the government's commitment in the face of public and military pressure to build more Dreadnoughts for the Royal Navy. The entire government budget was projected at £164 million, which would mean a deficit of £16 million on the year. This extra expenditure would be met through higher land taxes and death duties, the introduction of tobacco and alcohol excise duties and a super tax on incomes above £5,000. Because of the radical nature of the plans, the Cabinet discussed them thoroughly, through 14 meetings, before the Budget was to be delivered in the Commons.

The process tied the entire Cabinet into the Budget, which Asquith certainly saw as a way of re-energising the government and broadening its appeal. The aim said Lloyd George was 'to wage implacable warfare against poverty and squalidness.'[4]

The Conservatives did not see it that way. They saw no reason why the rich should be taxed to pay for increased defence – surely the cost could be met from greater efficiency? – nor why they should pay for pensions for the undeserving

and clearly feckless poor. Their solution to raise the money was tariff reform but they cloaked their opposition in concern for the common man. As F E Smith told his Liverpool constituents: 'Its mischievous consequences will fall mainly on the lower classes, because it will increase unemployment, penalise unduly your harmless relaxations and aggravate generally the evils with which your class is now afflicted.'[5]

The question was: how would the peers react? Throwing out domestic legislation such as the government's licensing bill was one thing but the House of Lords had not rejected a money bill for 250 years. Would they dare to do so this time and provoke a clear constitutional challenge? However, members of the upper house were furious about the impertinent impositions on their wealth implied by the budget and reacted with outrage and obtuseness. The Duke of Beaufort said he would 'like to see Winston Churchill and Lloyd George in the middle of 20 couple of dog hounds', the Duke of Buccleuch refused to make a guinea donation to the Dumfriesshire football club because he felt so hard done-by and the Duke of Somerset announced that he would have to sack his estate workers and reduce his gifts to charity. Lord Anglesey, who had just bought himself a new yacht costing £1,500 a month to run, announced that he would in consequence of the Budget be cutting his subscription to the London Hospital from £5 to £3 a month.[6] This was naturally all grist to the mill of Lloyd George and Churchill who stalked the country gleefully rubbing their lordships' noses in the Budget.

In a famous speech at a pub in Limehouse, East London that July, the Chancellor argued: 'We are placing the burdens on the broadest shoulders. Why should I put burdens on the people? I am one of the children of the people. God forbid that I should add one grain of trouble to the anxieties which they bear with pain and fortitude ... I made up my mind that

in framing my budget no cupboard should be barer, no lot should be harder to bear.'[7]

It was becoming clear that the House of Lords would indeed reject the measure. The alternative was to give way, surrendering control by an elected government to the unelected, minority party or, more radically, to swamp the Lords with new, amenable Liberal-voting peers to force the measure through – an enormous constitutional step, effectively fixing the second chamber by design as it had in the past been fixed by circumstance and heredity.

In September Asquith warned during a speech to 13,000 people in Birmingham that: *Amendment by the House of Lords is out of the question. Rejection ... is equally out of the question ... That way revolution lies.* Edward VII was persuaded to warn the Lords of 'grave consequences' though without specifying what they might be. The Cabinet decided not to retreat – to do so would have destroyed the government – and not to drop the Finance Bill, or establish alternative means of raising money should rejection take place. They relied, successfully apparently, on voluntary payments meanwhile and agreed that if the bill was turned down they would seek a dissolution and call a general election, only four years into what were then seven-year terms of office. The King's secretary meanwhile quietly informed the Prime Minister that creating a large number of peers to swamp the Conservative majority would be 'almost' an impossibility. Such a thing had not been done since the reign of Queen Anne 200 years before. The Commons passed the Budget after 42 days and nights of sittings, then on 30 November 1909 the Lords rejected it, almost contemptuously, by 370 votes to just 75. The government thereupon secured a Commons motion declaring the Lords' action 'a breach of constitution and a usurpation of the rights of the Commons'.

Another winter general election campaign commenced. Asquith told another mass meeting, this time in the Albert Hall, that he and his colleagues would not take office again unless *safeguards ... for the legislative utility and honour of the party of progress* could be secured, remarks interpreted erroneously as meaning that he had already obtained the King's assent to creating the necessary peers, though a few days later the King told him privately that he would not do so unless there was a second general election first.

Not surprisingly, the Prime Minister did not divulge this information. He knew that, whatever happened, the outcome of the election would not solve anything. It made him listless and disengaged throughout the campaign. By comparison, Lloyd George and Churchill went once more onto the attack – the former's speeches, Margot said distastefully, were 'a *disgrace,* vulgar, silly and infinitely bad for us ... I have given up reading them, they are so disgusting'.[8] His attacks on her landed friends, she believed, scared away the middle classes. More likely the voters were confused at being drawn into an abstruse constitutional wrangle over a budget that would cost them money, over the course of an eight-week campaign in the middle of winter.

The January 1910 election was a great disappointment for the Liberals, worse than they had expected. They nearly lost their clear majority: reduced to 275 MPs to the Conservatives' 273 and thus relying on the 82 Irish Home Rulers and 40 Labour members to continue in government. In fact the result was only bad compared with four years before: it was actually only the second time a sitting government had been re-elected since 1885 and the outcome represented the largest progressive majority in Parliament, except for 1906, since 1832.

But Asquith knew, as others did not, that the prospect

was not only for an even more prolonged confrontation with the Lords over the Budget but also for a new battle over Irish Home Rule, the price of the Irish nationalists' support to sustain his government in office. The result accordingly demoralised the Prime Minister who retreated immediately to the French Riviera for a fortnight's holiday 'completely knocked up'. On his return he finally admitted publicly in the Commons that he had no assurances over the peerages from the King: *I tell the House quite frankly that I have received no such guarantee and that I have asked for no such guarantee.*[9] The best he could offer was the first use of what would become his catchphrase: *Wait and see.*

The news demoralised the government. Should they resign or soldier on? Should they press for a new constitutional settle-ment, or just try to undermine the Lords' veto? 'We must stick tight to principles and not go a' whoring after false constitu-tions,' Sir William Harcourt's son Lewis, known as 'Loulou' and now an MP himself, advised Asquith, urging caution. After some debate, the Cabinet backed the Prime Minister to tough it out and even go on the offensive, either by asking the King to exercise prerogative powers and create more peers or seeking a referendum in the country to endorse the reform of the upper chamber.

Wait and see.

ASQUITH

Asquith gave a doughty performance in uncompromis-ingly telling the Commons so, as his Chief Whip Alexander Murray, the Scottish laird known as the Master of Elibank, recorded enthusiastically: 'He announced the decision of the Cabinet in that wonderful language of his and with a dignity that abashed some of the ruder spirits opposite ... It was a stirring scene ... Under that modest, unassuming, almost shy nature – so often mistaken for coldness – the Prime

Minister has a softness of character which attaches men to him humanly as firmly as his great intellectual gifts compel their admiration.'[10]

In April 1910 the government published its Parliament Bill with the threat that, after a further general election, it would indeed ask the Sovereign to create the necessary peers. The bill itself proposed depriving the House of Lords of all power of veto over money bills such as budgets and limiting its delaying power over other legislation to no more than two successive Parliamentary sessions. The bill also reduced the length of parliaments from seven to five years.

Sensing that it had perhaps gone as far as it could and that the January election had given the government a mandate for its budget, the House of Lords finally backed down over the finance measure. It meekly passed the re-presented Budget that had caused it so much outrage six months before without amendment or division. Now the decks were cleared for the battle over constitutional reform. In preparation, the House adjourned for a ten-day recess.

It was at this point that King Edward VII complicated matters by dying unexpectedly. The Prime Minister first heard the news that the King was sick while taking his break sailing on board the Admiralty yacht *Enchantress* in the company of Reginald McKenna, first Lord of the Admiralty, off the coast of Portugal. The ship was ordered to turn for Plymouth immediately and shortly afterwards the Prime Minister received a further message that the King was dead.

Asquith wrote: *I went up on deck and I remember well that the first sight that met my eyes in the twilight before dawn was Halley's Comet blazing in the sky ... I felt bewildered and indeed stunned. At a most anxious moment in the fortunes of the state, we had lost, without warning or preparation, the sovereign whose ripe experience, trained sagacity, equitable judgement and unvarying consideration*

counted for so much ... Now he had gone. His successor with all his fine and engaging qualities was without political experience. We were nearing the verge of a crisis almost without example in our constitutional history. What was the right thing to do? This was the question which absorbed my thoughts as we made our way ... through the Bay of Biscay.[11]

Asquith's previous tactic, which had come close to persuading Edward VII, was to demonstrate that their lordships' obstructiveness was unconstitutional and unacceptable. Now that argument had to be begun all over again with a new King, who clearly could not be harried at such a time. George V was politically and constitutionally inexperienced, but firmly conservative in principles and beliefs, suspicious of the radical, dangerous and parvenu ministers that he had inherited. He was surrounded by secretaries, advisers and courtiers who were at least disposed to caution if they were not openly partisan in favour of their friends in the House of Lords. The whole business of enlisting the crucial support of the monarch for reform would have to be conducted cautiously and slowly.

So the Prime Minister proposed a constitutional conference with the Conservative leaders to try and reach an agreement on the House of Lords without resorting to another general election. Talks continued throughout the summer in a desultory way – Lloyd George even suggested a way out of the impasse by the formation of a coalition government at one stage, much to Asquith's annoyance – before breaking up in disagreement in November. The Unionists had tried to insist that Irish Home Rule should be excluded from any agreement on limiting the Lords' veto, something that the government could never afford to accept while it remained dependent on Nationalist votes.

Finally, in November 1910, Asquith went once more

to Buckingham Palace to secure a dissolution and a fresh election. In the course of doing so he finally secured from George V a secret agreement that he would if necessary use prerogative powers to create the extra peers. 'After a long talk I agreed most reluctantly to give the Cabinet a secret undertaking that in the event of the government being returned with a majority ... I should use my prerogative to make peers if asked for. I disliked having to do this very much but agreed that this was the only alternative to the Cabinet resigning, which at this moment would be disastrous,' the King wrote in his diary.[12]

With this assurance that the logjam could eventually be broken, the Prime Minister led the campaign more vigorously than earlier in the year. The outcome was virtually the same – on a reduced turnout: Liberals and Conservatives 272 seats each, Irish 84, Labour 42, giving an anti-Conservative majority of 126. But Asquith had now effectively won three elections in succession – the Conservatives could scarcely have been asked to form a government – a feat otherwise unmatched between 1832 and Mrs Thatcher's third victory in 1987, and had secured a mandate for reform. *I think our election here has cleared the air*, Asquith wrote to the British ambassador in Washington.

The new Parliament Bill eventually passed the Commons in mid-May 1911 and entered its stages in the Lords. Asquith presented the King with a memorandum preparatory to asking him formally to create the requisite peerages and a prospective list of 249 names was accordingly drawn up.

The 'puppet peers' list included party hacks and elder statesmen, baronets and Army colonels, even an admiral, but also some eye-catching celebrities including General Robert Baden-Powell, the hero of Mafeking and founder of the Boy Scout movement, Gilbert Murray, the Regius Professor of

Greek at Oxford, Thomas Hardy, the novelist and J M Barrie, the playwright and author of *Peter Pan* – a wide assortment of Liberals but hardly a nest of revolutionaries.

However, Tories in both Commons and Lords did not take the hint from the election result and attempted to tear the bill to shreds, through a summer of baking heat and sweaty, bad-tempered sessions – temperatures in early August when the House was still sitting through what would normally have been its long summer recess topped 90 degrees F on nine successive days.

I think our election here has cleared the air.

H H ASQUITH

There was arm-twisting at the palace, aided by the King's secretary, the pragmatic Lord Knollys. He advised the reluctant King, erroneously, that the Tories would be unable to form a minority administration if the government fell and that the monarchy would thereby be thrown into the heart of the constitutional controversy, the latter part of which was at least true. Asquith was finally able to advise the Opposition leaders, Lord Lansdowne and Balfour, that 'His Majesty has been pleased to signify that he will consider it his duty to accept and act' on the government's advice to create the new peers. Their fox shot on the assurance of the unhappy King, the Tories in Parliament went berserk. As Asquith – who had been cheered all the way to the Commons – rose to speak four days later, he was howled down by a baying – but coldly organised – mob of Tory backbenchers.

He stood largely silently as they screamed abuse: 'Traitor!' and 'The King is in duress!' and yelled that he had killed the old King, while his old friend Balfour looked on regret-fully but without intervening from the Opposition front bench. Margot, watching from the Ladies' Gallery, sent a note down to the Foreign Secretary Grey urging him, for God's

sake, to defend her husband from 'the cats and the cads'.[13] Churchill – a close friend of the Tory backbench ringleaders F E Smith and Lord Hugh Cecil (who had been his best man) – denounced the scene as 'a squalid, frigid, organised attempt to insult the Prime Minister'. Eventually, after half an hour or so, Asquith sat down, unheard – itself an unprecedented event for a Prime Minister – murmuring that he was declining to degrade himself further. The sitting was eventually suspended. It had been, said F E Smith unrepentently 'a hateful necessity', the more cynical and ungrateful he might have added, since Asquith had recommended him only a few weeks before, and despite Balfour's opposition, for membership of the Privy Council.[14]

The scene did little to help their cause. The Tories dissolved into mutual recrimination between the so-called 'hedgers' willing now to compromise and 'ditchers' ready to die for the cause in the last ditch. The fastidious Balfour himself was also the target of their anger. They wanted more vigorous, less scrupulous leadership. Their leader took himself off on holiday abroad to recover.

The Parliament bill eventually passed the Lords, relatively narrowly, on 10 August, with Lord Curzon leading 37 Tory peers to vote with the government. It was enough for a majority of 137 to 114, to carry the measure. Most of the rest of the Tories abstained or voted against to the bitter end. The King had not had to create the extra peers after all: Hardy, Barrie and Baden-Powell remained unennobled for the rest of their lives. Change had been effected, to the Prime Minister's satisfaction, through existing procedures: not force-majeure but just the threat of it.

The long hot political summer was over, the constitutional crisis at an end. Victory over the Lords had been by no means certain but Asquith had cautiously held his course and, even-

tually, had won. It was the peak of his achievement in government and it altered for ever the constitutional balance of power between the two chambers.

Chapter 5: Local Difficulties

The constitutional crisis was not the only one with which the Asquith government had to deal at the same time. The years 1910 to 1912 saw an unprecedented outbreak of strikes in vital industries, a flurry of supposed anarchism, the increasing militancy of the Suffragettes' campaigning for votes for women, a ministerial scandal in the Marconi affair, Cabinet divisions over foreign policy and expenditure on armaments and a growing crisis over the government's attempts finally to legislate for Home Rule in Ireland.

Some of these crises happened simultaneously, others in sequence. Together they represented as daunting a series of challenges as can have confronted any 20th-century British government in peacetime. Indeed they have even given rise to the myth, first propounded in the seminal 1930s history *The Strange Death of Liberal England* by George Dangerfield, that the government and indeed Liberalism itself were in terminal decline by the time the First World War broke out in 1914. That is no longer regarded as the case by modern historians of the period. By that summer Asquith and his colleagues had surmounted many of these problems and could regard even the Home Rule question as at least provisionally settled. But they did make for a draining and exhausting few years, even for a Prime Minister who slept easily, took long holidays, did not work most weekends and was, in the words of his

colleague and friend Haldane, 'fortunately not afflicted with nerves'.[1]

Nevertheless, even by 1911, the Prime Minister was looking far from well. Constance Battersea, an old friend, wrote to her sister in October 1911 after having lunch with the Asquiths: 'The PM kind, extremely cordial – but how he is changed! Red and bloated – quite different from what he used to be. He gave me a shock. They all talk of his overeating and drinking too much. I am afraid there is no doubt about it.'[2] The following April, Asquith admitted to his wife that he had been suffering giddy spells for several weeks: 'I looked up and saw his tired eyes looking quietly at me and an expression of exhaustion written like a railway map over his whole powerful face,' she wrote.

'The PM kind, extremely cordial – but how he is changed! Red and bloated – quite different from what he used to be.'

CONSTANCE BATTERSEA

The Prime Minister was persuaded to cut back his food and alcohol consumption and within weeks was delivering a two-hour speech to introduce the Home Rule Bill. He was well aware that stress had killed Campbell-Bannerman and paralysed Joseph Chamberlain with a stroke, but he at least avoided that fate.

To add to his ministerial stress levels at this time the Asquiths were also moving house. Since 1907 they had used Archerfield House, up on the Firth of Forth, taken over from Margot's brother Frank, for their holidays. But now they were moving into The Wharf, a couple of large cottages next to a coal barn on the banks of the Thames at Sutton Courtenay, outside Oxford. This was much more congenial and convenient but it required £3,000 (on top of its £1,500 purchase price) to renovate and convert into a country house. Four years into his premiership, Asquith could not afford that sort

of money on top of all the other extravagances of his family life, so Margot blithely asked her friend, J P Morgan, the American financier and one of the richest men in the world, who willingly stumped up the cost.[3] The fact that Morgan had financial dealings with both the British and American governments never gave either Asquith or his wife – nor, it has to be said, anyone else – any pause at all. It was to be Asquith's country home for the rest of his life.

If on the surface the Prime Minister remained calm, even cold, and certainly imperturbable to colleagues, we do have the clearest possible indication of the seething and emotional – even sentimental – nature within, in the letters that he wrote to a series of young female friends during this entire period. The recipients were part of the Asquiths' social set, which always contained a high proportion of bright young things, many of them friends of the Prime Minister's dauntingly accomplished sons and daughter. It is one of Asquith's most attractive sides that he appears to have been so unstuffy in his private relations, as well as remaining close to all his children.

The letters however form one of the most extraordinary and intimate archives of any Prime Minister's thoughts and feelings and were written with an urgency and sometimes appalling candour even as events occurred, sometimes while Asquith was actually sitting in Cabinet apparently listening to his colleagues and taking decisions. Asquith wrote to a series of correspondents, especially young women, as well as to his wife and daughter Violet during the whole period. Margot was aware of at least some of this and the family referred to the recipients as the harem: they included Cynthia Charteris, his son Beb's wife; Pamela Jekyll, wife of his Cabinet colleague Reginald McKenna; Viola Tree, daughter of the actor Sir Herbert Beerbohm Tree; Dorothy Beresford, a vicar's wife; Lilian Tennant, Margot's niece; latterly Katherine Scott, the

widow of the Antarctic explorer and, most intimately of all, Venetia Stanley, a friend of Violet's.

Venetia became a special confidante over the three years between 1912, when she was 25 and the Prime Minister was 60, and her marriage in 1915 to Edwin Montagu, who had been Asquith's Parliamentary Private Secretary and would become Chancellor of the Duchy of Lancaster in the Cabinet. Addressed to *My Darling* or *Beloved* and signed *All my love*, the letters were written at an almost daily rate – sometimes several times a day – and revealed details of Cabinet discussions and divisions, even troop deployments once the war had started, as well as family news, political gossip and nicknames for colleagues (Montagu was called 'the Assyrian' or 'Shem' with insouciant anti-Semitism, because he was Jewish).

Although the archive (Asquith's letters survived while Venetia's did not) was made discreet use of by Roy Jenkins in the early 1960s for his biography, the letters were not published in all their grisly mawkishness until 1982, long after both participants were dead.

One example from August 1914, a fortnight after the outbreak of war, gives a flavour: *It was a great blow to get no letter this morning. I was afraid you might perhaps not be well – so I wired but I trust that it is no more than a delay in the post ... It will be 27 years tomorrow since you opened your eyes on this sinful world and not yet 3 since I made my great discovery of the real you ... I cannot tell you for you might think I was exaggerating, the length and breadth and depth of the difference it has made to me .*[4]

The consensus of opinion is that the relationship, as with all Asquith's other women friends, was platonic and that the correspondence served as a secret safety-valve to unburden pent-up emotions and frustrations, but the friendship must at least have had a preoccupying effect. What is more possible is that the Prime Minister was something of a groper – he

would not be the first or only politician to be so – though the evidence is fairly slight. Lytton Strachey, not necessarily the most reliable of second-hand witnesses, reported that Lady Ottoline Morrell, another member of the artistic Bloomsbury set, wife of an Oxford brewer and a near neighbour of the Asquiths at Garsington, had told him how the Prime Minister 'would take a lady's hand as she sat beside him on the sofa and make her feel his erected instrument under his trousers'.[5]

It is perhaps significant that this account was also never published until after all concerned – including Asquith's daughter and doughtiest defender Violet – were dead. In any event, the Prime Minister was extraordinarily fortunate in the discretion of all his lady friends, even in an age when kiss-and-tell memoirs would have been looked on with disdain and indeed revulsion as at the very least a social solecism.

Even as the constitutional crisis was reaching its climax, a wave of potentially crippling national strikes broke out. In August 1911 there was both a dock strike, which erupted into violence and a sudden rail strike, which threatened the whole transport network. Although Asquith was privately sympathetic to the railwaymen's case and met their represent-atives to offer them a royal commission to investigate their grievances, publicly he warned them that he would *employ all the forces of the Crown* to keep the railways open. This had the counter-productive outcome of precipitating the strike, not preventing it – it had not occurred to Asquith that he should let them know of his sympathies, or that he had also privately censured the employers' side – and Lloyd George was deputed to reach a settlement instead. In Jenkins's words: 'He employed all the cajolery, all the psychological insight, all the appeals to patriotism which Asquith had disdained to use'[6] and got the strike called off within two days, but not until there had been bloodshed.

'The men who have been shot down have been murdered by the government in the interests of the capitalist system,' exclaimed Keir Hardie, the Labour MP, during the course of a Parliamentary debate.[7] Socialism was indeed a fear, particularly of the King, at this time. To keep its coalition colleagues on side the government slowly sought to reverse the Osborne legal judgement of 1909 which had the effect of preventing trade unions from using their funds for political purposes, such as supporting the Labour Party, a move which had a critical effect on its viability. To offset this, a system of contracting out was introduced for individuals who did not wish to make contributions and the 1911 Budget introduced for the first time a wage for MPs, which had the effect of giving working-class Labour members at least some financial independence.

In February 1912, a national coal strike broke out in pursuit of '5 and 2': a minimum wage of five shillings a shift for men and two shillings for boys. Nearly two million men were out of work as a result: the miners and those in allied industries and factories dependent on coal. It was during this dispute that Churchill, now Home Secretary, sent

James Keir Hardie (1856–1915) was the first independent Labour Member of Parliament, winning West Ham (South) by a majority of 1,232 in 1892. A lifelong trades unionist, he was known as 'the Member for the Unemployed'. He was instrumental in the founding of the modern Labour Party, and in 1906 became first chairman of the 28-strong Parliamentary Labour Party. The best-known and most popular Labour figure of his day, as war approached in 1914 he attempted to organise the Socialist International to declare a general strike in all countries should war break out, but the failure of these plans, and the decision of the majority of the Labour Party to back the war when it came, deeply disillusioned him and he died a year later.

troops in to quell disturbances in Tonypandy, earning him the undying enmity of the South Wales miners. Again Asquith was privately sympathetic to the strikers but was unable forcefully, in an era when government intervention in industrial matters was cautious and unusual, either to persuade the employers to come to agreement or to negotiate a compromise.

In the end the government forced a Minimum Wage Bill through Commons and Lords (their Lordships saw no advantage in directly confronting the unions instead of the administration) which did not concede the miners' demands but at least set up compulsory machinery for discussion to take place and it was enough for the strike to be called off. The Prime Minister, choking with emotion, told the Commons: *We claim we have done our best in the public interest – with perfect fairness and impartiality.*[8] It was calculated that strikes in 1912 cost the loss of 40,890,000 working days, more than all the stoppages of the previous eight years.

Asquith showed much less sympathy with the Suffragettes, campaigning for votes for women, some of whom were changing their tactics and, out of frustration at the lack of progress towards winning the vote, increasingly resorting to violence. Extending the franchise was a long-standing issue which divided both Conservatives – aware perhaps that a majority of women would be likely to vote for them – and Liberals, not least within the Cabinet where a majority, including Lloyd George, Churchill, Grey and Haldane, favoured at least some reform of the franchise.

We claim we have done our best in the public interest – with perfect fairness and impartiality.

ASQUITH

The issue seems to have represented a legalistic blind-spot on Asquith's part – Jenkins says it was a failure of imagination – seeing reform not as an issue of fairness or equality,

or even pragmatically one which could produce political benefits at little cost, but merely as a utilitarian question of whether female suffrage would produce better government or whether there was evidence that women's views were not already taken into account by male MPs. He also questioned whether most women really wanted the vote – as opposed to the articulate, mainly middle-class women campaigning for it – though this position seems not to have been based on any objective assessment, merely the views of his closest circle of acquaintances, not least his daughter Violet, who was also at this stage vehemently anti. Asquith had been publicly opposed to extending the vote to women since at least the Third Reform Act of 1884, before he had ever entered Parliament and, having made up his mind, he declined to change it whatever the benefit.

The Suffragettes naturally targeted him as Prime Minister, not only scuffling with him on the golf links at Lossiemouth and Lympne but also assaulting him with a dog whip when they waylaid his car on the way to unveiling a memorial to Campbell-Bannerman at Stirling, interrupting his speeches and periodically breaking the windows in Downing Street. Such behaviour, together with less personal but high-profile events such as the slashing of the Rokeby Venus in the National Gallery and the death of the suffragette Emily Wilding Davison who threw herself in front of the runners in the 1913 Derby and succeeded in bringing down the King's horse, had the reverse effect on the Prime Minister to that intended by his shrill and angry protagonists.

As the campaign intensified Asquith dug his heels in even more. In the words of Roger Fulford, the historian of the movement: 'The idea of converting a human being's reason by parades, marches and fighting the police was incomprehensible to him. The more the women marched,

the less his reason marched with them. Therefore the work of the militants strengthened his opposition ... he remained like a rock.'[9]

The government made intermittent attempts to deal with the issue in other ways, including oppression. The Suffragettes' prison hunger strikes produced the coercive and counterproductive tactics of forceable feeding and the so-called 'Cat and Mouse Act' of 1913 which allowed the women to be freed on health grounds and then rearrested once they had recovered if they offended again. But there were also some efforts to deal with their grievances. In 1910 a Conciliation Bill offering a very limited franchise was tried and there were attempts over following years to introduce similar measures. In 1912 as part of a package of legislation, which included the abolition of plural voting rights, subsequently defeated in the Lords, the government launched a new reform bill which would have the effect of expanding the male franchise from 7.5 to 10 million.

It decided to allow a free vote for the first time on whether some women of property should also be admitted to the franchise, which might have produced a workable compromise except that the idea was scuppered unexpectedly by the Speaker of the Commons, James Lowther. He ruled that such a vote would so radically alter the nature of the bill as to make it necessary to withdraw it and reintroduce the measure again from scratch. Asquith wrote to the King: *This is a totally new view of the matter which appears to have occurred for the first time to the Speaker himself only two or three days ago and is in flat contradiction of the assumptions upon which all parties ... hitherto treated the bill ... .[It] is entirely wrong*, though he also admitted that *the Speaker's coup d'etat has bowled over the women for this session – a great relief*.[10]

The decision scuppered immediate hope of reform – the whole bill was dropped – and there the matter rested, with

Emmeline Pankhurst

Emmeline Pankhurst was a well brought-up woman, a person of middle-class morals, dress and tastes who could, however, still declare to a public meeting: 'We have blown up the Chancellor's house!'. For more than two years, from March 1912, sabotage tore across the country in the cause of Votes for Women. Historic houses and churches were burned and bombed, paintings slashed, and water mains, telegraph cables, sporting venues and letterboxes damaged. Hundreds of women were imprisoned for the cause. Many went on hunger strike and faced forcible feeding. Emmeline Pankhurst led from the front, undertaking not only repeated hunger strikes but also more serious hunger and thirst strikes.

Emmeline did not chain herself to the railings or disrupt any sporting events, nor did she undergo force-feeding, though she came to personify the suffrage campaign to such an extent that it was, and is, popularly assumed that she did all these. Her genius was to realise how far women would go in pursuit of the franchise and to encourage them to test their personal limits. She made individual sacrifice collective and the resulting collective struggle into a great theatrical public representation of Everywoman's fight for justice. The suffragettes' destructive phase covered only a small part of Emmeline Pankhurst's agitation for the vote, which started when she attended her first suffrage campaign meeting as a girl in 1872 and ended in 1914 when the policy of militancy was called off. Until 1909 even 'militant' actions were symbolic rather than actually violent. There was a militant truce for most of 1910 and 1911.

She was an odd leader for a movement calling for more democracy … When a group of supporters urged her to behave less autocratically she obliged them to leave. Even her daughter Sylvia was expelled for doctrinal failings and another daughter, Adela, was sent to Australia. It was this exiled daughter who gave one of the most penetrating critiques of her mother when she said: 'It was the family attitude – Cause First and human relations – nowhere … if [Emmeline] had been tolerant and broadminded, she would not have been the leader of the suffragettes.' [Jad Adams, *Pankhurst* (Haus Publishing, London: 2003)]

the Suffragettes themselves falling out over tactics and public sympathy waning as a result of the violence, until after the First World War, by which time Asquith himself had come to accept the inevitable. Women over the age of 30 were given the vote for the first time in 1918 and those over the age of 21 finally received parity with men in 1928, after his death.

This was indeed a time of social violence and unrest, prompting fears over the spread of anarchy. Just as a century later, popular hysteria would be whipped up about asylum seekers, so in Edwardian England, the press was concerned particularly about Jewish immigration from Russia and Eastern Europe and the possibility of revolutionary violence that it was thought they might bring with them. These fears were given potent force in a flurry of sensational activity in late 1910 and early 1911 when a small group of young Latvians – possibly anarchists but certainly criminals – briefly wrought havoc in the East End of London. This occurred during a series of bungled armed robbery attempts in which several policemen were shot – an especially shocking event in a society unused to such violence – before members of the desperate gang were cornered and killed in a house in Stepney, in the so-called siege of Sidney Street. The event was given notoriety by the presence, apparently personally directing events, of the excitable young Home Secretary Winston Churchill who not only authorised the deployment of armed Scots Guardsmen from the nearby Tower of London, but also gave orders that the house in which the would-be robbers were besieged should be allowed to burn down when it caught fire. Two charred corpses were eventually discovered in the rubble, though other members of the gang probably escaped.

This was a new sort of political stunt for a minister to indulge in – what would many decades later be called a

photo opportunity – and not one that Asquith would have approved. Churchill, summoned from his bath that morning by the news that the robbers had been run to ground, decided to go and see for himself what was happening. Dressed flamboyantly in top hat and overcoat with astrakhan collar, the Home Secretary featured prominently in the following day's newspaper pictures. 'I can understand what the photographer was doing, but what was the right honorable gentleman doing?' drawled Mr Balfour incredulously.

Churchill was not the only flamboyant member of the government, of course. There was also Lloyd George, the Chancellor of the Exchequer, who became embroiled with two other ministers and the Liberals' Chief Whip in 1912, in the midst of all the government's other crises, in what came to be known as the Marconi scandal. This too has a surprisingly modern whiff about it. The ministers, Lloyd George, Rufus Isaacs, the Attorney-General and, less heavily implicated, Herbert Samuel, the Postmaster General and the Master of Elibank, the Chief Whip, were accused of improperly buying shares on their own account (and also for the benefit of Liberal Party funds) in the Marconi company, at that stage bidding for a government contract, which it subsequently won, to build wireless telegraphy stations to connect Britain with the Empire. The conduit was said to have been Isaacs's brother, the company's managing director.

The accusations carried an anti-semitic subtext, of course – Isaacs and Samuel being Jewish – but the ministers were disingenuous in blandly informing the House when the matter was debated in October 1912 that they had no connection with the company. They were technically correct – in fact, the share dealing had been with Marconi's American subsidiary, which was not itself involved in the contract – so they had done nothing wrong, even if they had been imprudent.

But the ministers did not choose to reveal this until months later, by which time plenty of mud had been thrown and their admission could only serve to enhance accusations of slipperiness and what a much later minister would one day term 'economy with the actualité'.

The whole, complicated affair dragged on through a Commons select committee inquiry and a libel action (in which the ministers were represented by their Tory political opponents Sir Edward Carson and F E Smith in their private capacity as barristers) and ultimately the ministers were exonerated, but not without a tarnishing of their reputations. They had had a narrow scrape. Asquith himself was privately scathing about their conduct – it had been lamentable and difficult to defend, he said – but he publicly stood by them, refused their hesitantly proffered resignations and never made any capital, nor exacted any price, for his loyalty to colleagues in trouble. Lloyd George was not to be so loyal or grateful to him two years later.

Welsh disestablishment was another measure which made its tortuous way through the House once more, 20 years after the last Liberal government had attempted the reform. It was fought tooth and nail by the Tories, particularly and cynically by the likes of F E Smith, who had no interest in Welsh affairs, indeed no personal religious faith, but who sought whatever means of opposition was at hand to delay and frustrate the bill and accordingly the government. Smith's egregious hyperbole, when he claimed in May 1912 on Second Reading that the reform had 'shocked the conscience of every Christian community in Europe', eventually drew one of the most lethal poetic ripostes ever penned, on this occasion by G K Chesterton:

'Are they clinging to their crosses,

F.E. Smith,
Where the Breton boat-fleet tosses,
Are they Smith?
Do they fasting, trembling, bleeding,
Wait the news from this our city?
Groaning "That's the Second Reading!"
Hissing "There is still Committee!" ...
... Do they Smith?
... It would greatly, I must own,
Soothe me Smith,
If you left this theme alone,
Holy Smith!
... Talk about the pews and steeples,
And the cash that goes therewith!
But the souls of Christian peoples ...
Chuck it Smith!'

The government must have wished he would, for certainly it could produce no such effective response to the Conservatives' tactics. Ultimately the disruption did the clever barrister Smith no harm – a couple of years later he would enter Asquith's wartime coalition Cabinet – nor is there any evidence, unfortunately, that he ever knew of Chesterton's poem.[11] Disestablishment finally completed its parliamentary stages in September 1914, only to be suspended from enactment until after the war.

The obstructive Conservative tactics however also had a much more devastating and dangerous effect in their opposition to the infinitely more crucial Irish Home Rule legislation. Many Conservatives – members after all of the Unionist Party – were viscerally opposed to what they saw as the break-up of both the British Isles and its empire through the concession of Home Rule to Ireland, which had been sought by

Irish Nationalists for many years. The Irish MPs were now demanding their reward for sustaining Asquith's government in office, although Home Rule had anyway been a long-standing Liberal commitment since the days of Gladstone's third ministry in the 1880s. It was a measure that Asquith himself had always supported. He even saw it as a means of preserving the unity of the United Kingdom, by maintaining Ireland as part of the home countries.

A number of Conservatives had landed estates in Ireland – Lord Lansdowne, the leader in the Lords, owned part of Kerry – but their opposition was not particularly coherent. While they wanted the Union to remain, presumably with Irish MPs at Westminster, they objected to the influence those MPs wielded in pressing for Home Rule. In any event, the Conservatives, balked over the Parliament Act, now sought to frustrate the government over Home Rule and they were not fastidious about how they went about it. They also now had a new party leader, in the dour Scottish-Canadian Presbyterian Andrew Bonar Law, who had replaced the ineffectual Balfour in 1911. He had an affinity with the Ulster Protestants and was quite prepared to sanction extra-Parliamentary action to defeat Home Rule.

The government introduced its Government of Ireland Bill in April 1912. The measure did not propose complete independence but the establishment of a parliament in Dublin to decide and regulate the island's domestic affairs. But any such move was resolutely opposed by Protestants particularly in the northern parts of Ireland where they represented the majority of the population – a legacy of the 'plantation' of Scots loyalists in the 17th century intended precisely to anchor the island's loyalty and bolster British interests against the indigenous Catholic population. They had no wish to be subsumed into a Catholic-dominated South. Many Catholics

were themselves ambivalent, or indifferent, to the nationalist campaign for independence. The Conservatives determined to 'play the Orange Card', by giving the Ulster Protestants their absolute and unconditional backing, as they had before when Home Rule had been first proposed by Gladstone in the 1880s.

They did this not out of any particular sense of fellow-feeling or sympathy – apart perhaps from Bonar Law – rather the reverse. F E Smith, a Merseyside MP who ostentatiously waged war on their behalf, privately dismissed Home Rule as 'a dead quarrel for which neither the country nor the party cares a damn outside of Ulster and Liverpool'.[12] In a sense the opposition campaign was a continuation of the House of Lords battle by other means. Now they no longer had a veto in the upper house the Conservatives were quite prepared to appeal to a succession of outside forces to overcome the government's plans in whatever way they could, even at the cost of destabilising the country or resorting to extra-Parliamentary, even violent, tactics to get their way. They appealed to the King (who was privately sympathetic), they called in anti-Catholic bigotry to warn of Rome Rule, not Home Rule, their supporters started drilling militias in the North to protect Protestant 'rights' and they even urged revolt on the officers of the Army, pressing them not to intervene to enforce the law if called upon to do so by the government. It was not Conservative and Unionism's finest, or most democratic, hour.

The Tories clearly still resented the Liberals for being in power after an unprecedented three elections. Jenkins describes them as 'sick with office hunger'. Some of them were consumed with hatred and jealousy for the long-lived administration as well as frustrated ambition. Asquith, bland and apparently imperturbable, even a little smug, particularly irritated them. No-one reckoned on the imminence of

an international war, which would curtail the struggle, and no one on the Conservative benches seemed prepared openly to urge caution or restraint.

Asquith himself seems to have been slow to wake up to the threat, perhaps finding the Opposition's resort to extra-Parliamentary tactics either inconceivable or crass. His whole political career was predicated on constitutional settlements by constitutional means and any other tactics were anathema to his view of how politics should be conducted. In this, as a rationalist himself, he failed to appreciate the seething and profound passions being generated on both sides. However, he could not say that he had not been warned. As he and Bonar Law had strolled back to the Commons at the start of the Parliamentary session after the King's speech foreshadowing the Home Rule bill in February 1912, the Conservative leader had murmered to him: 'I am afraid I shall have to show myself very vicious, Mr Asquith, this session. I hope you will understand.'[13]

The bill passed its Commons stages easily enough by majorities of more than 90. It seems to have been almost automatically assumed that the island of Ireland formed an obvious political entity – that was certainly the Nationalists' assumption – and a compromise amendment to exclude the four most Protestant, Ulster, counties was defeated. This was eventually going to be a fallback position for the Unionists and the government, one it seized increasingly desperately later as the degree of Ulster obduracy became clear, but it was a solution it could expect the Nationalists to oppose.

So far, so constitutional, but the Tories were by now stalking both sides of the Irish Sea, raising the already heated level of confrontation by denouncing the legislation in the most overwrought and emotional terms. Bonar Law told the Protestants of Belfast that they were living in a besieged

city: 'The Government have erected by their Parliament Act a boom against you to shut you off from the British people ... You will burst that boom ... Help will come and when the crisis is over men will say to you in words not unlike those used by Pitt – you have saved yourselves by your exertions and you will save the Empire by your example.' At a rally in the grounds of Blenheim Palace in Oxfordshire in July 1912 the leader of the Conservative Party went further, accusing the government of being 'a revolutionary committee which has seized upon despotic power by fraud' – a novel, not to say unhinged, description of Mr Asquith and his administration – and adding ominously that he could 'imagine no length of resistance to which Ulster can go in which I should not be prepared to support them'.[14] Sir Edward Carson, the grim-featured Protestant lawyer who sat for Dublin University and who was willing to brook no compromise, did indeed go further, openly associating with the Protestant Ulster Volunteers paramilitary militias and inspecting their weapons as 7,000 of them paraded the following year. By his side in a three-piece suit and trilby hat pranced the distinctly unmilitary F E Smith who thereby gained the derisive nickname 'Galloper' – as in the subaltern deputed to jump to his master's command – from exasperated Liberals. With such incitements – not that they needed much encouragement – it was no wonder that nearly half a million Protestants queued up in Belfast City Hall in September 1912 to sign their names in blood – or ink – never to recognise a Dublin Parliament and to resist Home Rule and the subversion of their civil and religious liberty to the end.

In the circumstances, Asquith's equable assurance in a speech in Dublin in July 1912 that *I do not believe in the prospect of civil war, quite frankly ... Ireland is a nation, not two nations but one nation*, was hardly likely to pacify Orangemen

going quite puce with rage and betrayal. His perfectly sincere assurances would be misinterpreted by both sides in Ireland, leaving the Unionists angry that he was selling them out and the Nationalists frustrated by his equivocations.

The moderate Irish Nationalist leader John Redmond, who had announced in the Commons when the bill was introduced 'I personally thank God that I have lived to see this day', might threaten but would not vote against the Liberal government for fear of getting something worse, or less. But he himself was being outflanked by more militant Nationalists, who also began arming themselves in Ireland in response to the Unionists in preparation for the coming struggle.

> *Ireland is a nation, not two nations but one nation.*
>
> ASQUITH

In July 1913, the Home Rule Bill passed its final Commons stages but it was rebuffed by the Lords, whose leader Lord Lansdowne insisted that the peers would not consider it unless there was a general election first. The government prepared to invoke the Parliament Act to force the legislation through over the heads of the Lords who could now only hold the legislation up for two parliamentary sessions. Meanwhile the Unionists attempted to subvert George V, encouraging him to urge an election, or even a referendum on the government or, failing that, to sack it or veto the legislation altogether. When the King subsequently suggested to Asquith that he should indeed call an election, the Prime Minister told him bluntly that he risked making the Crown *the football of contending factions*.

Asquith's instead now began private discussions with the Unionist leadership, exploring the possibility of shaving Ulster off from the rest of Ireland, though this was still conceived of as only a temporary measure. The Conservatives

were openly opposing the whole bill but appeared willing privately to compromise over splitting the island. This took no account whatsoever of Nationalist sentiment and attempts to persuade the party's MPs to accept 26 counties rather than 32 broke down in January 1914. The Cabinet proposed allowing Ulster a veto on any legislation passed in Dublin that affected the province, but it was the King himself who told the Prime Minister that would be an insufficient safeguard for the Unionists. At the same time it would be too great a compromise for the constitutionalist nationalists to swallow if they were not to be outflanked by more militant extra-Parliamentary groups.

So the drilling of militias continued on both sides and violence seemed imminent. In Spring 1914, guns were being clandestinely unloaded by both sides in the ports of Ireland – first Larne in the North, then later in the summer, Howth in the South. The weapons were old and not very serviceable but by the outbreak of war as many as 250,000 Irishmen were members of militias. In preparation for the inevitable struggle, the government sanctioned the mobilisation of British troops from their training camp on the Curragh, the plain outside Dublin, to make ready to preserve the peace in Ulster. Their officers, many of them of Anglo-Irish, Protestant extraction and of Unionist

General Hubert de la Poer Gough (1870–1963). Despite his career almost being terminated by the Curragh Mutiny, Gough was in command of a cavalry brigade in the BEF in 1914. A protégé of Haig, who admired his professionalism, optimism and aggression, he rose through divisonal and corps commands to head the Fifth Army in 1916. He commanded the attack in Flanders in 1917 ('Passchendaele'), but his army's near-collapse in the face of the German March Offensive in 1918 made him the scapegoat for the crisis and he was relieved.

sympathies, had been happy enough in the past to coerce the local Catholic population, but they objected to being ordered to move against their own kin. About 57 cavalry officers were reported by their commanding officer, Brigadier General Hubert Gough, himself 'the hottest of Ulsterians', to be refusing the order and preferring resignation.

This 'Curragh Mutiny' was handled maladroitly by the Army, whose highest ranks were clearly sympathetic to the Ulster officers against what Lieutenant General Sir Arthur Paget, the Commander-in-Chief in Ireland, described as 'those swines of politicians'. But the government was also giving out mixed messages. J E B Seely, the Secretary of State for War, nearly surrendered the whole position by telling the Army that officers with direct family connections in Ulster would not be obliged to follow orders and could 'disappear' for the time being. Meanwhile Winston Churchill, who was by now First Lord of the Admiralty, was ordering the Third Battle Squadron to deploy in the Irish Sea.

Asquith was forced to intervene himself, against his normal instincts, over an affair he had previously thought would be *cleared up in a few hours* – as indeed it should have been. A new Army Order asserted civilian control over the military, the Curragh mutineers got away with their insubordination, the Navy was recalled, Seely resigned (as eventually did only two of the Curragh mutineers) and Asquith himself added the War Office to his ministerial responsibilities. For this, as with all politicians taking on Cabinet ministerial responsibility before 1918, he had to resign his seat and notionally fight a by-election, where he was returned unopposed. The government decided against bringing criminal prosecutions against the Ulster Volunteers parading ostentatiously around the province with their smuggled weapons, a clear indication of its uncertainty and lack of resolve in the face of the threat of

armed insurrection by groups claiming loyalty to the Crown. Carson crowed: 'Drilling is illegal. The volunteers are illegal and the Government know they are illegal and the Government dare not interfere.'

The message this gave to Nationalists was that the government was insincere in its intentions and therefore not to be trusted. It was perceived to be partial to the Unionists because it would not uphold its own laws. Under the threat from the North, the Nationalist militias' ranks started swelling. The Unionists took the message that the government was not sincere too. In May Asquith was again shouted down in the Commons, causing Margot to complain that she had 'never known the Tories so vile, so rude and so futile as now'.[15]

In June the government put forward a bill in the Lords to accompany the Home Rule measure, allowing a temporary opt-out for Ulster, only to see the peers fillet it in accordance with the most extreme Unionist demands. They wanted the creation of a separate nine-county province in perpetuity – not four as had been originally suggested, nor the six that they would eventually secure. With this, Lords and Commons were again in direct and deadlocked conflict.

The initial way out was the calling of a joint conference of all parties at Buckingham Palace in July 1914. Among those attending were the Ulster Unionists, an indication that they were prepared to settle for the partition of Ireland, even if the Nationalists were not. The conference broke up after three days without agreement. By now, the Nationalist Volunteers were parading with their own guns, landed in broad daylight outside Dublin with very little police intervention. There were outbreaks of sporadic violence. And it was at that point that events across the Channel finally forced themselves on the attention of the government.

Chapter 6: Wartime

One of the most remarkable features of Asquith's premiership in its first six, peacetime, years was how little he was actively engaged in dealing with foreign affairs. He had enough on his plate of course domestically but, given the international situation, his relative passivity even inside the Cabinet appears strange now. Although he regularly holidayed in France – usually on the Riviera – and occasionally in Germany (Margot, who had been partly educated in Berlin, was a strong Germanophile and the Asquiths employed a German governess) the Prime Minister did not go out of his way to meet his foreign counterparts. He left foreign relations firmly with his old friend Sir Edward Grey, the Foreign Secretary throughout the administration, who preferred to spend his holidays birdwatching on the family estates in Northumberland and Scotland. Grey, not the most communicative of men, rarely saw the need to discuss or explain policy to his Cabinet colleagues or consult them, or indeed talk with any of those outside his small circle of acquaintance within the Foreign Office.

In part the government's disengagement was a result of Britain's traditional caution about foreign entanglements beyond its empire and in particular a desire to remain aloof from European affairs, so long as the balance of power was maintained between its two greatest powers, Germany and

The Balkan Question

The most persistent and the most explosive of the great issues of that period was how to distribute the inheritance of the European part of the Turkish Empire, the so-called 'Balkan Question' ... The Balkan Question more than any other issue of that period was likely to lead to open conflict between the great powers – especially since the vital interests of one of them, Austria, were directly affected by the national aspirations of Serbia. It is, however, doubtful, that this outcome was inevitable.

When in July 1914 the German government promised to support whatever steps Austria decided to take against Serbia, it identified itself with the Austrian interest in the prostration of Serbia as though it was its own, while Russia identified itself with Serbia's defence of its independence. Thus a conflict at the periphery of the European state system transformed itself into a struggle that threatened to affect the over-all distribution of power within that system.

Bargaining had become impossible if it was not to be the bargaining away of one's own vital interests. Concessions at somebody else's expense could no longer be made, because identification of one's own interests with the interests of the smaller nations involved had turned concessions at the apparent expense of others into concessions at one's own expense. The conflict could not be postponed because most of the great powers feared that postponement would strengthen the other side for an armed conflict that was considered to be inevitable. For, once the issues had been brought from the periphery into the centre of the circle of the great powers, there was no way of side-stepping them: there was, as it were, no empty space into which to step in order to evade the issue. Russia had to face the Austro-German determination to settle the Serbian problem on Austria's terms. In consequence, France had to face the invocation of the Franco-Russian alliance by Russia, Germany had to face the activation of that alliance, and Great Britain had to face the threat to Belgium. There was no side-stepping these issues except at the price of yielding what each nation regarded as its vital interests. [Hans J Morgenthau, *Politics Among Nations* (A A Knopf, New York: 1978) pp 357–8]

France. But this policy, which had kept British troops away from Continental battlefields since Waterloo in 1815, was by now evolving due to the growing military and industrial power of Germany which by 1904 had become so alarming as to entice Britain into the Entente Cordiale with France, an agreement reached by the Conservative government and subsequently quietly endorsed by Campbell-Bannerman, Grey and Haldane, the Minister for War, apparently without discussion with the rest of the Cabinet. This was because it was regarded as a limited engagement rather than a military alliance involving a wartime commitment. So peripheral was the policy in fact to the government's strategic thinking that Asquith did not know that it had resulted in Anglo-French military 'conversations' since 1905 until 1911, three years after he had become Prime Minister. When the news was revealed in the Press and subsequently raised in Cabinet, Asquith ordered that any such discussions in future must remain non-committal (in which case what was the point of having them?) and any developments from them would require Cabinet approval. It was, he confided wonderingly later, *one of the most curious examples in his memory of a concurrence of untoward events working to a conclusion which no one intended and no one could defend.*[1]

But Asquith's caution about foreign involvement was also because of the strains both within the Cabinet and the Parliamentary Liberal Party over just how active Britain's role in the world should be and particularly how much should be spent on defence. This was a long-standing debate, most recently exemplified by the divisions between the Liberal Imperialists and the Little Englanders over the Boer War, but it became increasingly raw as pressure mounted to expand the Royal Navy in response to Germany's own warship building programme. Part of the difficulty over the People's Budget

was caused by the need to raise money not just for old age pensions but also for the requirement to build more Dreadnoughts, the mightiest and most technologically advanced battleships yet conceived. They were a much more congenial project as far as the Conservatives were concerned than providing pensions for the elderly poor.

Indeed the Dreadnought programme was initiated under Balfour's government although the first, eponymous, ship was not launched until 1907. Bearing ten 12-inch guns, more than double those of previous battleships, capable of firing a simultaneous broadside of 6,800 pounds of high explosive shells over 6,000 yards ('three bursting on board every minute would be HELL!' exulted Admiral Jackie Fisher, the First Sea Lord and chief proponent of the new vessels), weighing 15,000 tons and with a top speed verging on 21 knots, much faster than any other existing battleships, the Dreadnought was a formidable weapon to deploy to preserve Britain's century-old mastery of the high seas.[2]

But everyone was building them, especially since the Russo-Japanese War of 1904 had shown the vulnerability of the Tsar's older, smaller battleships and Britain's new ships accordingly had to be both the biggest and the best in the world. National prestige demanded it, but Germany was catching up fast. Its battlecruiser *Von der Tann*, launched in 1909, was 4,000 tons heavier and four knots faster than the first Dreadnoughts and that was followed on both sides by other ships larger still, some capable of reaching 27 knots. In 1905, the navy already absorbed more than £30 million a year, a fifth of the government's entire expenditure, and the Liberals coming into power found themselves committed to ever heavier spending. By 1909 Asquith was having to head off naval, newspaper and political pressure to maintain the programme while simultaneously reassuring doubters

within his own party who were either pro-German (a not inconsiderable element of political opinion) or pacifist and still hoped that the government might fulfil Campbell-Bannerman's aspiration to place Britain at the head of a league for peace. There was little hope of that. The compromise reached was to build four new Dreadnoughts at once and then another four the following year. In 1911 too, shortly after his Sidney Street adventure, Winston Churchill was moved to the Admiralty where he would become a strong advocate for Naval expansion.

Colleagues such as Lloyd George, who as Chancellor had to find the money to pay for the new ships, increasingly complained of being kept in the dark over foreign relations and had to be periodically mollified by being included in the Cabinet's foreign policy committee and its Committee on Imperial Defence, both of which met intermittently and sometimes without informing all their members. Churchill and Lloyd George, both friends and normally allies, fell out publicly as the Cabinet debated the Naval Estimates, with both threatening to resign at one period or another, though both were ambitious enough ultimately to stay. In the circumstances, Asquith was fortunate to keep the Cabinet together throughout the period.

But, as international tensions and flash-points increased, over Morocco in 1905, then six years later in the port of Agadir, also in Morocco, with stand-offs between the Germans and French, then in 1912 and 1913 as localised wars broke out in the Balkans, the British government found itself increasingly being pushed along inexorably in the European wake, towards what everyone eventually assumed would be a Continental war. The Agadir crisis in July 1911 – just as the government's constitutional row was reaching its peak – seemed for a time very likely to be the spark to set off the

conflagration. Germany claimed its interests in North Africa were threatened by French colonial expansion there and sent a gunboat to the port, which lay close to the British colony of Gibraltar. There were concerns that Germany would try to annexe the whole country and it was Lloyd George – by now alert to the dangers of war – who warned them off, in the course of a speech at the Mansion House in London, saying: 'If Britain were to be treated where her interests were vitally affected as of no account ... peace at that price would be a humiliation intolerable for a great country to endure.'[3]

The Germans backed off but it was only a temporary respite. The following year Haldane, the war minister, a fluent German speaker – having been to university in Berlin – and convinced Germanophile, was sent to the German capital, ostensibly to disuss university reform of all things, but actually in an attempt to negotiate a reduction in German naval expenditure, while reassuring them that Britain had no belligerent intentions towards them. He met with a complete lack of success. Asquith told Grey he thought negotiations were doomed: *I confess I am becoming more and more doubtful as to the wisdom of prolonging these discussions ... Nothing I believe will meet her purpose which falls short of a promise on our part of neutrality: a promise we cannot give. And she makes no firm or solid offer, even in exchange for that.*[4]

By 1914, absorbed in the Irish crisis, Asquith and his ministers believed there was no immediate likelihood of a European war – as the Balkan wars had not sparked a wider conflict it seemed less likely than for some time – and initially saw that summer's flurry of activity on the Continent as no more momentous than previous flashpoints. The Cabinet envisaged a prorogation of Parliament at the end of the year and was starting to discuss calling an election, preferably the following summer.

The First World War remains such a scar on the British psyche (and not only that of the British of course) and forms such a watershed in modern history, that it is sometimes hard to remember quite how unexpectedly its outbreak occurred in the late summer of 1914, when most of the staff of the chancelleries of Europe, to say nothing of its rulers and heads of government, were on holiday, taking their ease in the oppressive and dusty heat of July and early August. The British government did not even discuss the crisis until nearly a month after the assassination of the Austrian Archduke Franz Ferdinand and his wife in Sarajevo, by Bosnian nationalists equipped with Serb weaponry, on 28 June. As alliances were called in across Europe – Russia to the aid of Serbia in response to an ultimatum from Austria, Germany mobilising to get its long-prepared war plan under way, provoking France to come to the aid of Russia – Asquith saw no reason to intervene. Personally, he told the Archbishop of Canterbury, he thought the Serbs deserved a good thrashing.[5] *The curious thing is*, he wrote, *That on many if not most of the points Austria has a good and Servia [sic] a very bad case. But the Austrians are quite the stupidest people in Europe (as the Italians are the most perfidious) and there is a brutality about their mode of procedure which will make many people think that it is a case of a big power wantonly bullying a little one.*[6] The Prime Minister gradually came to the view towards the end of July that war was likely but he saw no reason for Britain to be embroiled, since it had no obligation to France or Russia. As late as 22 July he was writing: *Happily there seems to be no reason why we should be anything other than spectators.*

That changed suddenly in the first week of August as it became clear that the German war plan involved a violation of the neutrality of Belgium – across whose eastern plains the German Army intended to roll in order to sweep down on

Paris, behind the French forces massing further east along its border. Belgium's neutrality was guaranteed by the nearly-forgotten Treaty of London of 1839 which had been negotiated by Lord Palmerston to safeguard the independence of the new state. This sense of moral obligation to the

Happily there seems to be no reason why we should be anything other than spectators.

H H ASQUITH

small country (there was no legal obligation) was perhaps the strongest motive for Asquith's decision in favour of war, though even so he held back in Cabinet as the merits of intervention were lengthily discussed and the idea of calling for a congress of great powers was mooted.

The Cabinet was itself divided, with possibly half its members opposed to war. At one point or another during the discussions four members offered their resignations, fortunately none of them crucial to the government. Ultimately only two, John Burns of the Local Government Board and John Morley, Gladstone's biographer and self-appointed (and self-righteous) keeper of the flame of Liberalism, actually resigned. However, they did reflect a considerable strand of party feeling in the Commons which, with opposition to the war strong also among the government's minority party supporters, Labour and the Irish Nationalists made Asquith's task in keeping the government together by no means easy. That he managed to do so was a tribute to his continuing authority as well as a growing sense that war was inevitable.

By 2 August, the Prime Minister had listed six points to consider in relation to the crisis, which he shared with his colleagues, the King, the Opposition leadership and Miss Stanley, four of which came down in favour of intervention and the other two not against it. But it was actually Grey who announced the British ultimatum to the Commons the

day before war was declared. It was clear by then however that nothing could stop the drive to war. The expectation was inciting wildly-cheering crowds in the capitals of Europe, not least in London, egged on by expectations of martial glory and a quick victory promoted by the belligerent press. They were *a mob of loafers and holiday makers*, said the Prime Minister contemptuously. He reminded Venetia of his 18th-century predecessor Sir Robert Walpole's remark in similar circumstances: '*Now they are ringing their bells, in a few weeks they will be ringing their hands*'. *How one loathes such levity.*

The Catholic Belgians had felt sympathy for Austria after the assassination but that dissipated when their government received an ultimatum from Germany on 2 August giving them just 12 hours to agree free passage through their country, an impossible demand. As the German Army swept across the frontier into Belgium, Britain mobilised the Fleet, followed the next day, 3 August, by the British Expeditionary Force, the small professional army, to go to the assistance of the French. On the afternoon of 4 August the British ambassador in Berlin was told to deliver Britain's ultimatum and ask for the embassy staff's passports to be returned by midnight unless Germany withdrew. This time Asquith himself addressed the Commons, though he took a drive immediately afterwards to collect his thoughts. Back in Downing Street, Margot joined her husband, Grey and Lord Crewe, all smoking cigarettes, in the Cabinet Room while the minutes ticked away. As she left to go to bed after the ultimatum had expired, she passed Winston Churchill 'with a happy face' striding in.

Across St James's Park, the German ambassador Prince Lichnowsky, who had earlier burst into tears as he urged Asquith not to intervene, was roused from his bed in the embassy in Carlton House Terrace to be informed that war

was declared. He was handed his passport by the young British diplomat Harold Nicolson, despatched to deliver the message because he was the most junior official present in the Foreign Office that night. Outside, Nicolson recalled in a broadcast years later, the crowds could be heard cheering in the Mall.[7]

Asquith appears to have regarded the war as one more problem among many which had to be confronted and got over. It had, after all, been on the minds of the statesmen of Europe for at least a decade. He had no doubt that his government would surmount the crisis and that he would without question see it through as Prime Minister. But he did not imagine that it would be a brief or bloodless affair. *Speaking for myself personally*, he told the Commons three days later, *A crucial and almost governing consideration was the position of the small states.*

He told Venetia Stanley in a chatty letter on the day war was declared: *The whole thing fills me with sadness ... We are on the eve of horrible things. I wish you were nearer my darling: wouldn't it be a joy if we cd spend Sunday together? I love you more than I can say ...*[8] To his wife Margot, hugging him sadly in his office in Downing Street, Asquith, wan and grey with exhaustion, merely said, *Yes, it's all up.*

Professor H C G Matthew says in his account of Asquith for the *Dictionary of National Biography* (*DNB*) simply: 'Asquith's decision for war with Germany was the most important taken by a British prime minister in the 20th century and was more important than any prime ministerial decision of the 19th century. It not only dictated the involvement of the United *Yes, it's all up.* Kingdom in war but affected H H ASQUITH much of the pattern of imperial, foreign and economic history for the rest of the century.'[9]

Asquith remained supremely, indeed serenely, confident of his own abilities as leader and manager of the war effort. Tired as he was, he never considered doing anything else. He had led his Cabinet and party through the declaration of hostility without splitting it, he himself was in command at the age of 62 after more than six years as Prime Minister, with no challenger apparently in sight and he had an extremely able and experienced corps of ministers. Central to them were Lloyd George, the Chancellor, now wholeheartedly committed to the fight and Winston Churchill at the Admiralty fizzing with aggression and ideas. Even the Conservatives were supporting the struggle and promising no fractious opposition – there would be 'no jiggery-pokery' Bonar Law assured Asquith[10] – though that pledge did not extend to the Ulster question or Welsh disestablishment, where they continued to make trouble.

The Prime Minister however saw no reason to bring them into government for the duration of the crisis: Balfour, their former leader, was a member of the Imperial Defence Committee which seemed quite enough. After the troubles of the previous four years, unsurprisingly, he considered the other leading Tories ill-bred and unsuitable for inclusion in his government. That arrangement suited the Conservatives too as it left them free to criticise the government's conduct of the war without having to take any responsibility for the actions taken. They continued to attack the government viciously over Ireland and incited their friends in the Press to do the same over the war as well.

The first important decision Asquith took in the crisis was the appointment of Lord Kitchener, the Imperial hero of Khartoum and defeater of the Mahdi's army at Omdurman, possibly the most distinguished soldier the country had known since Wellington, as Minister of War. Kitchener was

no politician – indeed his politics were certainly not Liberal – but his appointment to the Cabinet was a reassuring and popular one, at least for those in the press and the Commons who feared for the government's zeal and efficiency in prosecuting the war. His face would soon adorn a million recruiting posters and although in time he would prove a difficult, inflexible and occasionally obtuse colleague – he was in Margot's view 'more of a great poster than a great man'[11] – for the moment he symbolised the government's commitment to the war effort. Within a very few months Kitchener would come to be seen as a liability by other ministers: unimaginitive, incompetent, secretive and contemptuous of his civilian colleagues. Though he and Asquith got on surprisingly well together, the Prime Minister was well aware of his shortcomings. But for the time being he became, in Leo Amery's words, the government's ' splendid Kitchener umbrella'.

The British Expeditionary Force, the bulk of Britain's standing professional army, was rapidly deployed to France and then over the Belgian border to the mining town of Mons, where it first encountered the on-rushing Germans on 23 August. The Kaiser memorably described the BEF as a 'contemptible little army' and it was heavily outnumbered, four infantry divisions against six. Indeed it was small and under-equipped in comparison to the vast citizen armies being assembled across Europe: Germany alone mobilised 715,000 conscripts in 1914. The British force was pushed back, in concert with the French, who had been nearly annihilated, almost to Paris, before the situation stabilised, the Germans were pushed back across northern France and both sides dug in in preparation for a long war of attrition.

In the circumstances, although the superb British professional troops acquitted themselves well in fighting successful rearguard actions, the retreat from Mons followed

by the late autumn stalemate, hardly represented the sort of glorious victory anticipated by the press. Kitchener had successfully appealed for 500,000 volunteers, rapidly followed in September by a further half-million, then a million in November and two million more in December, but it would be some time before they would be ready to fight. The men of the professional army who would have to train them were already dying in France and in the meantime the government was left looking for a knockout blow in an attempt to kickstart its offensive. 'Are there not other alternatives than sending our armies to chew barbed wire in Flanders?' demanded Churchill in a memorandum to the Prime Minister on 29 December 1914.[12]

In the Cabinet's discussions, Asquith maintained an extraordinarily passive role. As in peacetime he deferred to ministers in taking charge of their departments, so in war he deferred to the military men, pre-eminently Kitchener and Jackie Fisher, the First Sea Lord, who was erratic and soon at loggerheads with Churchill over how the navy should be deployed. Asquith, rather like Lincoln in the American Civil War, took time to settle into a quasi-military role and was inclined to take too much on trust from the military. A war committee was eventually set up in November 1914 to coordinate and direct the daily conduct of the war but it was large and unwieldy, most of its members had no military training or understanding, leaving decision-making ponderously diffuse and clouding the clear direction of operations.

The committee did not even take proper minutes – one confidential report of its proceedings to the King in 1916 reported blandly: 'Considerable discussion took place without

any definite conclusion being reached on a number of miscellaneous topics' – and in the circumstances it was no wonder that, in Curzon's words: 'The Cabinet often had the haziest notion as to what its decisions were ... Cases frequently arose when the matter was left so much in doubt that a minister went away and acted upon what he thought was a decision, which subsequently turned out to be no decision at all, or was repudiated by his colleagues.'[13]

Asquith must carry the responsibility for this laxness. If masterly inactivity or prudent delay, waiting upon events, had served relatively well during the constitutional and other crises of peacetime before the war, they were tactics which were entirely unsuitable to fighting a major continental conflict. But he was resistant to taking a more dynamic or intrusive leadership role than he had in peacetime, being content to be, as always, the efficient organiser and dispatcher of business.

Wartime to him, says H C G Matthew in his *DNB* biography, 'was an aberration not a virtue. In terms of the political style of Britain's conduct of the war, that was an important virtue, but it led Asquith to underestimate the extent to which 20th-century warfare was an all-embracing experience and his sometimes almost perverse personal reluctance to appear constantly busy and unceasingly active told against him in the political and press world generally.' Of course, there had never been a war so all-embracing before so perhaps this was understandable. Modern historians now recognise to a much greater extent than even a few years ago how far the groundwork for the successes at the end of the First World War was laid during the first two years of Asquith's administration, when gradually the expansion, training and gearing up of its citizens' army took place and the key appointments of its leadership were made. His trouble

was that he was not a natural rabble-rouser or willing and capable, as Churchill was 30 years later, of inspiring, harrying and leading the nation – that was the sort of behaviour that Asquith rather despised.

This made him an easy target for a press anxious for rapid success and it has also done much to undermine his historic reputation, overshadowed by his brash successor Lloyd George, who continued much the same policies but shouted rather louder about them, certainly in his self-serving post-war memoirs. It also made his leadership increasingly prey to ministerial intrigues, leaks, briefings and counter-briefings, leaving ambitious ministers mutually distrustful and privately at each other's throats – Lloyd George and Churchill seemingly the worst culprits – and the Prime Minister's authority and control increasingly undermined.

Asquith did not help his own case either by carrying on determinedly with much the same life as before, cards and parties in the evening, Friday afternoon drives with Venetia Stanley, weekends in the country, though now often at Walmer on the Kent coast, where he borrowed one of the castles used by Wardens of the Cinque Ports, rather than at the Wharf in Oxfordshire. No one could complain that the Asquiths were not doing their bit – all four of his adult sons enlisted – but the Prime Minister and his wife formed a soft target. Margot was thought to be a closet German agent – she won libel damages for this – and the Asquiths had to be reluctantly persuaded to get rid of their younger childrens' long-standing German governess Frau Meyer from Downing Street.[14] From an early stage in the war, accelerating as the months passed, the Prime Minister was subjected to relentless denigration in the Press, particularly Lord Northcliffe's papers and especially *The Times*, then the most authoritative of the lot. Northcliffe also owned the *Daily Mail* so the attack

came from both ends of the market. Supportive newspapers such as the *Manchester Guardian* were less shrill and were anyway opposed to the war.

As 1915 began, the government was looking hard for ways to break the deadlock of trench warfare on the Western Front and, in the words of a memo from Lloyd George, 'a clear definite victory somewhere ... visibly materialised in guns and prisoners ... in unmistakeable retreats of the enemy's armies and in large sections of enemy territory occupied',[15] even though it was generally recognised that ultimately victory in the war would have to be achieved in France. The First Sea Lord, Fisher, was anxious to use the navy to enable a landing on the Baltic coast of northern Germany. But increasingly the Cabinet was drawn to Churchill's passionate advocacy of a landing on the Gallipoli peninsula, commanding the Dardanelles passage between the Aegean and Black Sea, between Europe and Asia Minor, which would have the effect of knocking the Ottoman Empire out of the German side in the war, denying German access to the Middle Eastern oil fields, safeguarding India and, hopefully, giving the enemy a knockout blow. The Cabinet, especially its military advisers – Fisher was

Anti-German feeling in Britain reached fever-pitch during the First World War, forcing the resignation of Prince Louis of Battenberg as First Sea Lord and causing the Royal Family to change its name to Windsor (on hearing this, the Kaiser joked that he looked forward to the next production of 'The Merry Wives of Saxe-Coburg Gotha'!). As well as attacks on German-run (or even German-sounding) businesses, it is said that daschunds were stoned in the streets and outlandish rumours were spread about long-naturalised people of German extraction: one businessman's tennis court was said to be a concrete base for a German gun to shell London.

vociferously opposed – was never entirely convinced of the wisdom of an invasion so far from home and so distant from the main theatre of the war, but nevertheless gave the go-ahead for what was to become a fiasco.

It was a politician-imposed military strategy. In large part, the failure of the Dardanelles campaign, which dragged on through eight months of 1915 without coming close to achieving any of its objectives, was due to the hesitancy with which the scheme was put into operation. The attack was delayed and uncoordinated, between the navy's initial attempts to force the passage and its subsequent bombardment of the coastal defences and the army's landing two months later. While it is probable that a determined initial naval attack would have worked, the delay meant that the land assault on 25 April 1915 came up against determined and reinforced positions and stood no chance of success. This was indeed obvious from an early stage and the long drawn-out failure of what became a hellish campaign, fought on exposed and arid mountainsides, caused convulsions in the government.

At the same time, ministers took responsibility for a perceived shell shortage on the Western Front, which was blamed particularly by Field Marshal Sir John French, the commander of the army there, for the failure of several attacks. French and Kitchener were certainly mutually antagonistic but the appearance of the general's complaints in the *Times* in May 1915 exacerbated the public sense of failure.

It was true that Kitchener, who had made his reputation fighting colonial wars on a shoe-string, was parsimonious in husbanding resources for the long struggle ahead (which he estimated would last three years) and it was also true that the gearing-up of the war effort was still taking place. But the military shortcomings in France and Belgium were more

complicated than not having enough ammunition available – in fact the number of shells fired by the British at the Battle of Neuve Chapelle in March 1915 was greater than in the entire three years of the Boer War[16] – and the government was unfairly pilloried. Asquith was left particularly exposed by the row since, on Kitchener's advice that there was as much ammunition available as the army could possibly use, he had just told an audience of munitions workers in Newcastle that they were doing a splendid job. He appeared complacent and out of touch.

As if this was not bad enough, Admiral Fisher chose this point – the same day, 14 May, as the *Times* leak – to walk out of the government, following his umpteenth disagreement with Churchill over the Gallipoli campaign. This had been brewing for months

Field Marshal Sir John French (1852–1925) was the first commander of the British Expeditionary Force in the First World War. A successful cavalry commander in the Boer War (when Douglas Haig was his chief of staff), he rose to Chief of the Imperial General Staff but was forced to resign in 1914 over the Curragh Incident. Recalled to command the BEF on the outbreak of war, he commanded throughout the retreat from Mons and the first battles of trench warfare, but he was ill-equipped for the scale and nature of the war on the Western Front, and his mishandling of the Battle of Loos in 1915 cost him the confidence of his subordinates and he was replaced as commander of the BEF by Haig in December that year.

– *He is always threatening to resign and writes an almost daily letter to Winston expressing his desire to return to the cultivation of his roses at Richmond,* Asquith sighed[17] – but it precipitated the government's growing crisis. Now the Prime Minister seemed losing control. Fisher had to be winkled out of the Charing Cross Hotel where he had gone to ground after his

resignation. The admiral was ordered to return to work and then sacked, leaving him complaining that whereas Kitchener had got the Order to the Garter for his efforts, he had got the Order of the Boot.

What no one else knew was that Asquith had been badly affected by two personal events. The first was the death of the young poet Rupert Brooke, a friend of his son Raymond's, *en route* to the Dardanelles. But he was also privately devastated by the news that Venetia Stanley, his long-term confidante, had also told him that same week that she was going to marry 'the Assyrian', the Prime Minister's former private secretary and now Cabinet colleague, Edwin Montagu. It was an inevitable blow but one which Asquith had not seen coming – Venetia had turned the unprepossessing Montagu down once and would have to convert to Judaism, something Asquith thought inconceivable, if she married him in order to preserve his inheritance. Now she was depriving Asquith of her company and leaving him alone at a time when he needed her most. The extent of his dependency on a young woman, who was still only 28, had become quite extraordinary: in the first three months of 1915, Asquith had written her 141 letters, most of them hundreds of words long

> **The First World War** on the Western Front was dominated by artillery – the cause of the majority of casualties in that theatre. The British army went to war in 1914 principally equipped for a war of manouevre, so although well-equipped with shrapnel-firing field guns, it was critically short of the heavy howitzers firing high-explosive shell necessary for dealing with enemy trenches, dugouts and bunkers, which gravely handicapped the BEF in the first two years of the war. However, by 1918 advances in production, equipment and techniques put the British artillery in a position to play a vital role in finally breaking the trench deadlock.

– 3,000 words in one day once. Now he wrote to her: *This breaks my heart. I can only pray God to bless you – and help me.*[18] The Prime Minister paid several visits to Venetia's flat near Oxford Circus, walking home alone to Downing Street afterwards, and went to her family home in Cheshire, but came to realise the inevitable: *I thought once or twice yesterday for the first time in our intercourse, that I rather bored you.*[19] It was at this time that the first note of doubt about his continuance in office occurred: *I sometimes think that Northcliffe and his obscure crew may perhaps be right*, he wrote to her. Their correspondence ceased almost at once and was over by the time of her marriage in July.

With the Opposition threatening a vicious attack on the handling of the war and murmerings even within the ranks of the Cabinet, particularly by Lloyd George, Asquith now moved to deflect the crisis by inviting the Conservatives to join a coalition government. It was actually an astute move, lacing the Opposition directly into the war effort at a desperate time, but it was not a welcome one to the Prime Minister. The price of Conservative participation was the enforced departure of Churchill from the Admiralty (he was demoted to Chancellor of the Duchy of Lancaster instead) and the sacking from the government altogether of the Lord Chancellor, Lord Haldane, Asquith's oldest political friend. Haldane was being publicly and unjustly attacked for being pro-German, because of his long-standing links with that country (he had once, long before the war, injudiciously remarked that Germany was his 'spiritual home') and his suspicious fluency in its language. Tabloid unreason and xenophobia is by no means new. Asquith bowed to the pressure and ruthlessly, and almost without a word to his closest and loyalest ally, cast him out. Jenkins describes this as 'the most uncharacteristic fault of Asquith's whole career'.[20]

The Conservatives entered the government on 19 May 1915, within a few days of the crisis starting. They had proved surprisingly submissive in accepting posts in the reformed administration. In particular, Bonar Law, who might have expected one of the great offices but for his peripheral involvement in a family share scandal, was content to become colonial secretary instead. Liberal members retained their majority in Cabinet and their hold on the major jobs, with Lloyd George being moved to take charge of Munitions Production.

Asquith told the King that he had concluded that *for a successful prosecution of the war, the Govt. must be reconstructed on a broad and non-party basis*. Privately, he wrote: *To seem to welcome into the intimacy of the political household, strange, alien, hitherto hostile figures* [was] *a most intolerable task.*[21]

> *To seem to welcome into the intimacy of the political household, strange, alien, hitherto hostile figures {was} a most intolerable task.*
>
> ASQUITH

The Prime Minister generally invited in Tories like Curzon for whom he had some congeniality, but he still felt nothing but contempt for the Conservative leader, quoting the 18th-century Lord Bolingbroke's remarks about Bishop Warburton: 'Sir, I never wrestle with a chimney sweep' and adding: *A good saying, which I sometimes call to mind when I am confronting Bonar Law.* Churchill, one of the victims of the move, later described Asquith as 'a stern, ambitious, intellectually proud man fighting his way with all necessary ruthlessness ... These were the convulsive struggles of a man of action and of ambition at death grips with events.'[22]

Unfortunately, the reconstitution of the government did not alter the direction of the war, or improve its management and nor did it reduce the Cabinet intrigues. The wartime stalemate continued through the rest of 1915, with casualty

figures mounting and no sign of impending victory. There was a renewed attempt to force the Dardanelles but in December the government had to admit defeat and order the evacuation of the remaining 83,000 troops on the Peninsula: an operation that was ultimately carried out efficiently and with more skill than many that had preceded it, almost uniquely without casualties. But this private success was only perceived publicly as a defeat, not surprisingly as the Gallipoli campaign had cost the Allies 265,000 casualties (and 300,000 on the Turkish side) for no gain whatsoever. There was one casualty at home too as Churchill, regarded as the main architect of the debacle, was ejected from the Cabinet. Further east in Iraq, there was humiliation for a British force, beseiged at Kut and left to starve and die of disease while being taken into Turkish captivity. On the Western Front too the battles of Loos and Vimy Ridge caused massive casualties – 65,000 British, 165,000 French – which would only be overshadowed the following year at the Somme and Verdun. For all the fighting, the line of the Western Front moved only about three miles all year. – and mostly in the direction of the Allies.

Field Marshal French was replaced by Sir Douglas Haig in the wake of the battles of 1915 while Sir William Robertson, dour but competent, the only field marshal to have risen from the ranks, was made chief of the newly constituted and powerful Imperial General Staff. Both men would be resolute in pursuing victory over the next three years and unfortunately, but probably inevitably, both were convinced that the only way to do it was to erode the German forces by attrition.

Asquith, whose son Oc had served throughout the Gallipoli campaign and whose other sons Raymond and Beb were on the Western Front, was by now dealing with huge degrees of public venom in the Press and political circles. He and Margot

were accused, wrongly of course, of being German spies, having shares in the German arms manufacturers Krupps, even feeding German prisoners of war 'with every dainty and comestible' and playing tennis with them. Rumours of his drinking, and of his nickname, 'Squiffy', spread. Douglas Haig (a member of the whisky distilling family, of course) gives concrete evidence of this in his letters, though he was charitable enough when Asquith visited his headquarters in September 1916. He wrote to his wife: 'You would have been amused at the Prime Minister last night. He did himself fairly well — not more than most gentlemen used to drink when I was a boy, but in this abstemious age it is noticeable if an extra glass or two is taken by anyone!'

'The PM seemed to like our old brandy. He had a couple of glasses (big sherry glass size!) before I left the table at 9.30 and apparently he had several more before I saw him again. By that time his legs were unsteady, but his head was quite clear and he was able to read a map and discuss the situation with me. Indeed, he was most charming and quite alert in mind.'[23] It should be remembered that earlier that day the Prime Minister's party

Field Marshal Sir Douglas Haig (1861–1928), commander of the BEF in France from December 1915 to the end of the First World War. One of the most controversial military leaders of the 20th century, Haig has been damned by some as a 'butcher and bungler' for the bloody stalemates of the Somme and Passchendaele, and praised by others for winning the greatest land victories in British military history in the final offensives of 1918. An experienced, well-educated and thoughtful professional soldier, under his command the BEF endured the hell of the trenches and eventually emerged victorious. After the war, his concern for his men continued to be shown in his tireless work for the British Legion.

had come under German shellfire near the front line and that he had also met his eldest son Raymond, serving in the trenches, for what – although he could not have known this – was to be the last time. Raymond was killed a few days later. The visit would in any event have been a harrowing and distressing one for any man in his position, particularly as a father.

'I am told,' Margot wrote, 'that no greater campaign of calumny was ever conducted against one man than that which has been and is being conducted against my husband today ... Henry is as indifferent to the Press as St Paul's Cathedral is to midges, but I confess that I am not.'[24] In October 1915, it was perhaps unsurprising that the normally robust Asquith collapsed under the strain and was laid low for several weeks, probably a victim of depression and overwork.

> *'The PM seemed to like our old brandy. He had a couple of glasses (big sherry glass size!) before I left the table at 9.30 and apparently he had several more before I saw him again.'*
>
> FIELD MARSHAL SIR DOUGLAS HAIG

By now the War Cabinet was a nest of plotting, usually centred around ongoing demands for the sacking of Lord Kitchener, threats of resignation (by Lloyd George) unless he was removed, and devious behaviour from Bonar Law who first agreed to Asquith taking over from Kitchener at the War Office in addition to all his other duties and then opposed it. The Conservative leader disingenuously lectured Asquith, in a letter rather than to his face: 'As Prime Minister you have not devoted yourself absolutely to coordinating all the moves of the war because so much of your time and energy has been devoted to control of the political machine.' Asquith was reluctant to get rid of Kitchener, not least because, in Margot's words: 'there (will) be a scream all over, from the King to the Navvy ... when the public learn that K has gone.'[25] The

dithering however not only hindered the war effort, but also exacerbated the sense of government and prime ministerial drift – and gave ministers such as Lloyd George ample scope for intrigue.

In the end the problem of the War Minister was only solved when Kitchener was drowned at sea after the cruiser on which he was travelling to a meeting in Russia was struck a mine off the north of Scotland. But that was not until June 1916. Ironically, Lloyd George should have been accompanying him, but he had been diverted by Asquith to Ireland, to try and resolve the crisis there. Instead, he became Kitchener's successor as War Minister, but not before Asquith had considered appointing Bonar Law to the post.

Lloyd George and the Conservative leader had actually met privately to discuss which of them should take the job (they mutually agreed that, if offered it, Bonar Law would refuse) and the former then tried unsuccessfully to increase his powers before accepting the new post: an early indication of the battle for supremacy with the Prime Minister which would erupt again six months later.

As early as the formation of the Coalition, critics of the Prime Minister were already circling to replace him as well as Kitchener, even though there was no obvious alternative candidate to lead the country. 'I look round all the conceivable alternatives and I find him not!' wrote Balfour. It would almost certainly have to be a Liberal, since they were the majority party. For the moment Lloyd George was content to rule himself out, saying he would be 'too much exposed to jealousy and criticism' – but it was clear that he personally could think of no one better to take on the job.

The problem was given added point during the latter end of 1915 because of a growing and acrimonious debate about the introduction of conscription to supplement the forces at

the Front. Initially, Asquith was constitutionally opposed to the idea, as was Kitchener and older colleagues such as Grey, McKenna and Balfour, together with many Liberals, the entire Labour Party, the Irish and the Trades Union movement, while Lloyd George, Churchill (while he lasted), Curzon and F E Smith – mostly colleagues the Prime Minister distrusted – supported the move. But it was a decision that could not be indefinitely delayed as the Front continued to absorb casualties at a greater rate than men could be recruited or trained on a voluntary basis.

By now the war was forcing the government to take several measures its Liberal members disliked, including the introduction of import tariffs – the end of the shibboleth of free trade – and by the end of 1915, Asquith himself had come round to conscription. What was seen as his defection caused anguish to his most loyal supporters. The measure was presented as a means of managing the depletion of the industrial workforce and gaining greater control over the management of the war effort, but there is little doubt that the Prime Minister also saw it privately as a way of curtailing the manouevrings of Lloyd George against him. He even took his munitions minister to a conference in Rome with him, as a means, the secretary of the war committee Maurice Hankey wrote, of keeping 'Ll.G. out of mischief for a day or two.' It scarcely worked, as conscriptionists battled it out in the Commons with volunteerists, notwithstanding the Prime Minister's warnings that if there was no conscription there could be no summer offensive at the Front to break the stalemate.

It was understandably not a convincing or popular argument from a man who had until a few months before opposed compulsion in recruitment. Almost for the first time, the House greeted his announcement coldly. Furthermore,

the policy change made him appear even weaker, a man without a backbone as some in the Press said. 'There is a cabal every afternoon and a crisis every second day,' wrote H E Duke, the Conservative MP for Exeter.[26] Asquith himself thought he knew who was responsible for the crisis: *Of course Lloyd George is the villain of the piece. You know what I think of him*, he told Lady Scott, widow of the Antarctic explorer, his latest confidante.

Of course Lloyd George is the villain of the piece. You know what I think of him

ASQUITH

It was at this point, Easter 1916, that an armed rebellion broke out in Dublin, led by a handful of Sinn Fein nationalist militants dissatisfied with the delay in introducing Home Rule (which was being postponed with the agreement of the constitutional Nationalist MPs until a year after whenever the war finished). They seized the General Post Office and demanded immediate independence, seeing 'England's difficulty [as] Ireland's opportunity'. The rebellion was put down within a few days (as the rebels' leaders, concerned with making a blood sacrifice in a noble cause, knew it would be) to no little Irish popular acclaim – there were many thousands more Irish volunteers serving on the Western Front than shooting fellow Irishmen and women and English troops in the middle of Dublin – until the British authorities started fulfilling the rebels' expectations by shooting the ringleaders.

The reaction was understandable, given the state of the war, especially as the rebellion had caught the British by surprise. Asquith, absorbed in the conscription row, muttered imperturbably only: *Well, that's really something*, when told of the uprising and promptly went off to bed. Although the execution of 15 of the rebels substantially changed Irish opinion towards the rebellion and was clearly maladroitly handled, originally 90 had been sentenced to death and it

would have been hard at that stage in the war, after several hundred casualties and the devastation of central Dublin, to have expected a more lenient response. As it was, the remaining rebels were released after serving brief prison sentences and the government once again attempted to reach a constitutional settlement to the Irish question – its last opportunity to do so – only to be frustrated by the Conservatives, who once again played the Orange Card, seeing their opportunity in the government's difficulty. The rebellion had exposed serious shortcomings in the administration of Ireland and led to the resignation of Augustine Birrell, the Chief Secretary, another Asquith loyalist. As if he did not have enough to do already – or felt himself to be indispensible – Asquith took on the job himself.

The execution of the former British diplomat and Irish Nationalist Sir Roger Casement, arrested almost as he stepped ashore in Ireland from a German submarine after trying unsuccessfully to recruit Irish prisoners of war to the cause of rebellion, also caused the government anguish. Asquith had wanted Casement reprieved but he was hanged, following lengthy Cabinet discussions about the propriety of intervention, giving another martyr to the Irish cause.

There is no doubt that the Prime Minister's handling of the conscription issue, especially after he had made up his mind that it was essential, was hesitant and faltering – as Hankey said, he hated the job. Asquith tried delaying a decision by making another appeal to the dwindling pool of potential volunteers. He even contemplated resignation, though without acting on it. But finally the legislation could be delayed no longer. The war committee secretary wrote in his diary: 'The fact was, that the people who want compulsory service don't want Asquith while those who want Asquith don't want compulsory service.' It was an impossible dilemma. Koss quotes

Roger Casement

In early May 1916, awaiting trial for high treason as a prisoner in the Tower of London, Roger Casement dictated a brief autobiography to his solicitor. It was little more than a sketch that left considerable gaps in the narrative of an altogether extraordinary career spanning 20 years in Africa and seven in South America. It would end with his execution for his role in Ireland's 1916 Easter Rising in the midst of the First World War. When Casement dropped through the scaffold behind closed doors at Pentonville Prison on 3 August 1916, few contemporaries understood who he was or what he represented; those who did know preferred to forget. A biographical pamphlet, circulated before his execution, admitted that though Casement was 'in a certain sense the figurehead and original prime mover in the rebellion' of 1916, no one knew much about him.

This understanding was partly self-perpetuated and partly obscured by the culture of secrecy surrounding the two conflicting spheres that Casement had briefly dominated: British foreign diplomacy and Irish revolutionary activity. His intense involvement with both of these causes meant his life would remain shrouded by a veil of mystery and intrigue. While he was widely known for his humanitarian activities exposing the Imperial atrocities of Belgium's King Leopold II in the Congo, his consular work remained unknown beyond the level of his published reports and his treatment in the Imperial press. Although his pro-Irish views were public knowledge in England, they were considered an eccentric enthusiasm rather than a dangerous threat to the Empire that he served with distinction.

Following his resignation from the Foreign Office in 1913, Casement emerged as a pivotal figure in transforming the conversation amongst cultural nationalists in Ireland into a dialogue of colonial resistance. The Home Rule crisis forced Ireland's nationalist community to respond. Casement became the catalyst in the initial recruitment drive for the Volunteers and subsequently acted as the international emissary for the Irish independence movement in the US and Germany. [Angus Mitchell, *Casement* (Haus Publishing, London: 2003)]

Hankey's biographer, Stephen Roskill, as saying: 'For all his qualities Asquith's character was surely flawed by lack of the moral courage to adopt the course in military affairs in which he believed, because of the likely political consequences. And in the end that weakness destroyed both him and the Liberal Party.'[27]

The state of the war in the spring of 1916 made compulsory recruitment urgent. The government was coming under intense pressure from its French allies for a major summer offensive to relieve their troops from the German attack further along the Western Front, against the French defences at Verdun. Both sides were by now, literally, bleeding each other dry and seeking to do so as a strategic purpose. The result was to be the British attack on the Somme, starting on 1 July 1916, a day of high summer in which, on the first morning of the initial assaults 57,470 British troops became casualties, a third of them killed. What made the worst day in the country's military history even more bitter – and more resonant then and ever since – however, was the fact that the men who were wounded and killed were mostly the volunteer recruits who had flooded to answer Kitchener's call in 1914.

The Battle of the Somme in 1916, long seen as the epitome of the bloody, pointless slaughter on the Western Front in the First World War, was brought about by the need to relieve the pressure on the French at Verdun, which led to the expansion of the British role in the attack on the Somme, while reducing that of the more experienced and better-equipped French. Although Haig has been condemned for continuing the battle into November, the need to draw German reinforcements from Verdun made it essential.

They had enlisted together, served together in local regiments and now they died together. Whole towns,

especially in the industrial north of England, but also those of Ulster, found many of their young men would never be coming home. The misery was concentrated, not diffuse. Their deaths had come despite the most protracted and thorough military build-up and artillery assault in British military history. The battle dragged depressingly on and was only called off when late autumn rains made further attacks impossible in November, by which time there had been 415,000 British casualties and no appreciable break-through.

In September 1916, the war brought home its price directly to the Asquith family. Raymond, Asquith's oldest and most brilliant son, the one most like his father, the one thought most likely to emulate his achievements, was killed on the Somme. He had spurned the chance of a safe staff job in favour of serving with the Grenadier Guards in the front line, where he was shot, leading an attack over the top. It was a numbing, devastating shock and came only a week after the two had met during the Prime Minister's visit to the Front.

Asquith wept bitterly: *Oh! The awful waste of a man like Raymond – the best brain of his age in our time – any career he liked lying in front of him. I always felt it might happen – Oc* [third son, Arthur] *may get off but not Raymond.*

Margot recorded that some hours after the news had arrived she found her husband still sitting in the same chair,

Oh! The awful waste of a man like Raymond – the best brain of his age in our time – any career he liked lying in front of him.

H H ASQUITH

'his poor face set with tears but quite simple and natural – a wonderful exhibition of emotion, self-mastery and unself-consciousness ... I was never more struck by the size and depth of his nature, the absence of bitterness and largeness of his heart and purpose than that night'.[28] Asquith himself wrote three days later:

Whatever hope I had for the far future – by much the largest part ... was invested in him. Now all that is gone. It will take me a few days more to get back to my bearings. It is difficult to believe that some of the fight did not go out of Asquith from that time on.

Britain was by now in dire straits in its prosecution of the war and a general gloom had set in. The Tory leader in the Lords, Lord Lansdowne, recorded the sense of despair in a memorandum as the battle of the Somme drew to its close. By this stage of the war there had been 1.1 million casualties, including 15,000 officers killed. 'We are slowly but surely killing off the best of the male population of these islands. The financial burden which we have already accumulated is almost incalculable', he wrote that November.

The much vaunted British and German fleets on which so much money and energy had been expended, fought an inconclusive battle at Jutland but it was the German U-boats that were beginning to throttle trade and food supplies. In September 1916 alone 100,000 tons of shipping was lost; in December it was 180,000 tons. The potato crop failed in a wet summer, bread was in short supply, fish catches were halved. 'Generations will come and go before the country recovers from financial ruin and the destruction of the means of production that are taking place,' Lansdowne concluded pessimistically (and erroneously). 'All this is no doubt our duty to bear but only if it can be shown that the sacrifice will have its reward.'

It was at this point that Lloyd George screwed up the courage to challenge the Prime Minister. He wrote later: 'I thought, rightly or wrongly, that there was hesitation, vacillation and delay and that we were not waging this war with the determination, promptitude and relentlessness with which it must be waged. It is a national war, everyone must contribute

and it is on that basis alone that we shall be able to achieve a great triumph.'

Asquith's public imperturbability was certainly a handicap. It spelled complacency and apparent indolence. Even the music-hall comedian George Robey was satirising it in song:

'Just stem this tide of ignorant conjecture,
Remain inert and dormant just like me,
And cultivate spontaneous quiescence,
In other words: "Wait and See!"'[29]

Asquith did not see the coup coming. In November 1916, he asked colleagues to write memoranda on how they saw the coming year (Lansdowne's was one of these). The response of Lloyd George – who had consulted Bonar Law, as he was to do throughout the crisis of the next few weeks – was to call for a new, smaller war committee to coordinate the day to day conduct of operations, independent of the Cabinet. The present committee now had nine regular members – many mutually antagonistic and recriminatory – and was often bogged down in minutiae. He claimed the idea originally came from Hankey, during a chat at a conference in Paris. Bonar Law noted shrewdly that Lloyd George had by now become 'at the same time the right hand man to the Prime Minister and to the Leader of the Opposition'.[30]

Lloyd George proposed that he, rather than the Prime Minister, should take charge of it. Indeed, Asquith should not even serve on it, though he could be kept 'in close touch'. But the ministerial plotters themselves: Lloyd George, Bonar Law and Sir Edward Carson, the old Ulster rebel who had briefly been Attorney General in the Coalition government,

were mutually suspicious and initially by no means sure that they all wanted the same thing.

Lloyd George's plan, said Bonar Law, 'boiled down to one simple proposal – to put Asquith out and himself in', whereas he himself was worried that Carson might challenge him for the Tory leadership. Bonar Law acted, said Margot Asquith 'with the intrepidity of a rabbit and the slyness of a fox, determined to break the coalition … rather than let them [Carson and Lloyd George] break him'. Their alliance was however bolstered by the national Press whose attacks on the war effort were intensifying.

Such a proposal was clearly impossible for any Prime Minister to accept, but Asquith's initial response was far from dismissive. He wrote to Lloyd George: *Though I do not altogether share your dark estimate and forecast of the situation … I am in complete agreement that we have reached a critical situation in the war and that our methods of procedure … call for reconsideration and revision. The two main defects of the war committee, which has done excellent work, are (1) that its numbers are too large and (2) that there is delay, evasion and often obstruction on the part of the departments in giving effect to its decisions … it is overcharged with duties.*

I am clearly of the opinion that the war committee should be reconstituted and its relations to and authority over the departments should be clearly defined and more effectively asserted.

However he added: *In my opinion, whatever changes are made … the Prime Minister must be its chairman. He cannot be relegated to the position of an arbiter in the background or a referee in Cabinet.*[31]

While the plotters schemed over their next move – Lloyd George desperate to gain Bonar Law's agreement that the Prime Minister should be sidelined, the Tory leader considering whether he and his colleagues should resign from the

government – Asquith took himself off to Walmer for the weekend. On his return to Downing Street on Sunday he saw Lloyd George and agreed that the war committee could meet under the latter's chairmanship, so long as the Prime Minister was reported to daily, retained 'supreme and effective control' of war policy and could still attend meetings if he wished to do so. They appeared to reach agreement that the Cabinet should be re-formed and Lloyd George returned to his department that afternoon where his first visitor was Lord Northcliffe himself.

The following morning the *Times* carried a full, though not in the least impartial, account of the previous day's negotiations, suggesting that Asquith had accepted that he was an ineffective war leader and ceding his power for 'supreme direction of the war' to Lloyd George. An accompanying leader column asserted that the Prime Minister was 'disqualified from membership on the ground of temperament'.[32] An infuriated Asquith assumed not unreasonably that Lloyd George had given the proposal to the newspaper – it would not have been the first time – but it may have been Carson, passing on what he had been told. The Prime Minister promptly reversed his support for the previous day's compromise, writing to Lloyd George: *Unless the impression is at once corrected that I am being relegated to the position of an irresponsible spectator of the war, I cannot possibly go on.*

Lloyd George responded imperturbably: 'I have not seen the *Times* article, but I hope you will not attach undue importance to these effusions. I have had these misrepresentations to put up with for months. Northcliffe frankly wants a smash … I attach great importance to your retaining your present position.'[33] Clearly Lloyd George did not want to jeopardise the agreement he had previously reached. Asquith also met a group of his Liberal Cabinet colleagues who all offered him

their support and apparently also a delegation of Conservative ministers: Curzon, Cecil and Austen Chamberlain who pledged their loyalty as well and, thus fortified, he obtained the King's permission to form a new government.

Bonar Law now sought an audience with the Prime Minister and the pair met, first at the Commons and then Downing Street, where the Conservative leader insisted that unless the revised war council plan was adopted, he and his colleagues would not participate in a new coalition.

Unless the impression is at once corrected that I am being relegated to the position of an irresponsible spectator of the war, I cannot possibly go on.

H H ASQUITH

By now Asquith's mind was made up. He wrote to Lloyd George to tell him that the war committee could only be made workable and effective if the Prime Minister was in charge as chairman: *any other arrangement ... would be in my experience impracticable and incompatible with the Prime Minister's final and supreme control*. Furthermore, he insisted that membership of the committee would be for him to decide. He must have known that this decision must precipitate the resignation of either Lloyd George and Bonar Law, or himself, for they clearly could not continue to serve together.

Lloyd George offered his resignation the following, Tuesday, morning, but made clear he intended to fight his corner. They had worked together for 10 years, he said, without a quarrel, but now 'unity without action is nothing but futile carnage. Vigour and vision are the supreme need at this hour.' Now support began to peel away from the Prime Minister: first came Balfour who Asquith had thought the previous day was on his side but who now defected, sending a note from his sickbed saying he supported the new war committee idea. Balfour thus passed, wrote Churchill later, 'like a powerful, graceful

cat walking delicately and unsoiled across a rather muddy street'. Balfour, who had been First Lord of the Admiralty, was to become Foreign Secretary in the new administration. According to Lord Beaverbrook when offered the post he is said to have replied: 'Well, you hold a pistol to my head – I must accept.'

Next to see Asquith was a delegation of Liberal ministers who thought he should resign in order to face down the challenge, then a group of Conservatives who told him they were not prepared to serve in a government without Lloyd George and Bonar Law: 'this was evidently a great blow for him,' said Chamberlain, one of the leaders of the delegation. Furthermore they admitted that they would be prepared to serve in a Lloyd George administration instead. They urged him to do the same.

Asquith was cornered. He had no alternative but to resign, after eight years and 241 days in office. From Sunday 3 December 1916, assured in Downing Street, by Tuesday 5 December he was out. He went back to see the King at Buckingham Palace ('It is a great blow to me & will I fear buck up the Germans,' George V wrote in his diary).

For a day there was uncertainty as to who would succeed him. There was a conference of party leaders at Buckingham

> **King George V** (1865–1936). The younger son of Edward VII and Queen Alexandra, he became Prince of Wales on the death of his brother Prince Albert Victor, giving up a promising naval career. He was an exemplary monarch during the First World War, becoming a symbol of national unity and determination and taking a personal interest in the Army and its commanders. The 'King's Pledge', his example of abstention from alcohol for the duration, was certainly not taken by Asquith! He was the only European monarch who came out of the First World War with his throne strengthened.

Palace. At one stage Bonar Law indicated his willingness to form a government if Asquith would serve in a subordinate position within it, a suggestion that understandably did not meet with his approval. Asquith, whose manner was said to resemble a schoolboy 'who has got an unexpected half-holiday', is said to have retorted: *What is the proposal? That I who have held first place for eight years should be asked to take a secondary position?*

And then the mantle passed to Lloyd George, who was able to form a new coalition, though without any other Liberal members of the old Cabinet. As Churchill wrote many years later: 'The vehement, contriving, resourceful, nimble-leaping Lloyd George seemed to offer a brighter hope, or at any rate, a more passionate effort.'[34] The economist J M Keynes dined with the Asquiths two nights later and told Virginia Woolf that 'though Asquith himself was quite unmoved, Margot started crying into the soup.'

On the night of his resignation Asquith sat down in Downing Street to write a letter. This time it was to Sylvia Henley, Venetia's older sister, who was now in receipt of his confidences: *You see, I am using up my stock of official paper ... I have been through a hell of a time for the best part of a month and almost for the first time I begin to feel older. In the end there was nothing else to be done, though it is hateful to give even the semblance of a score to our blackguardly Press ... So we are all likely to be out in the cold next week.*[35]

> 'Though Asquith himself was quite unmoved, Margot started crying into the soup.'
>
> JOHN MAYNARD KEYNES

He was right: the Asquiths could not even move back into their old home in Cavendish Square as it was let out and badly in need of renovation.

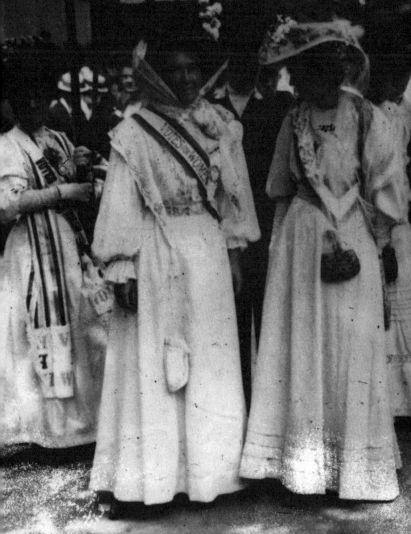

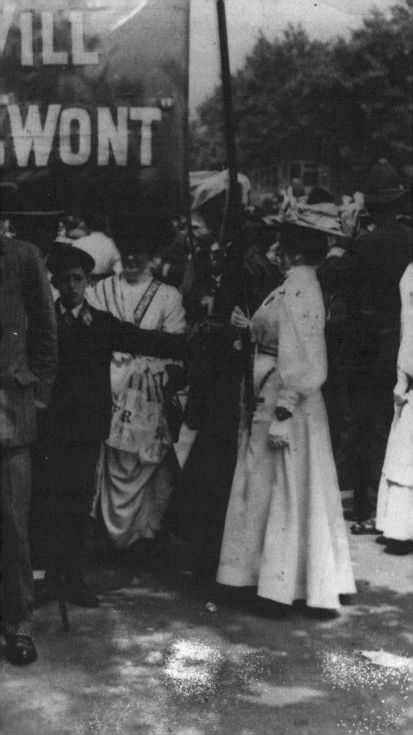

Part Three

THE LEGACY

Chapter 7: Decline

Asquith's leadership of the Liberal Party was confirmed three days after he left office. He declined a peerage (and the Order of the Garter) and now found himself, after nearly 11 years continuously on the government front bench, effectively leader of the opposition to Lloyd George's new government. It was an anomalous position, not only because he and the Prime Minister were in the same party, but because until only a few days before, he had been the leader of the government and the war effort and privy to all its secrets: in Matthew's words in the *DNB*: 'he knew too much and could say almost nothing'. Anything he did say was likely to be misinterpreted as sour grapes. From being indispensible, he was suddenly unwanted.

As instinctively a ministerial man, he could not bring himself to wage the sort of captious or unscrupulous opposition that the Conservatives had had no hesitation in adopting and indeed for all Lloyd George's bluster about conducting the war differently, there was little change in either the military strategy or in the direction of the war effort at home: 1917 would bring Passchendaele, a battle quite as horrific and protracted as the Somme.

Asquith found himself very much out of things. If he was hamstrung in criticising the war, so were his Liberal colleagues on the benches around him. There were periodic half-

hearted approaches for Asquith to join the government but he responded bleakly after one such: under *no conditions wd I serve in a Govt. of wh. Ll.G. was the head. I had learned by long and close association to mistrust him profoundly ... In my judgement he had incurable defects, both of intellect and character wh. totally unfitted him to be at the head.*[1] He declined the offer of the Lord Chancellorship in 1917 and subsequently found himself sidelined, devoting his attention to giving the Romanes Lecture at Oxford in 1918 and chairing a royal commission into the future of Oxford and Cambridge. The one job he would have liked, being part of the British delegation at the Versailles peace conference, was denied him.

In Parliament in the last year of the war he did lead calls for a select committee of inquiry into whether Lloyd George had misled Parliament about the number of troops available for deployment in the battle of Passchendaele, such as he had conceded for the Dardanelles and Mesopotamia campaigns earlier in the war. The proposal outraged Lloyd George who used the Commons vote (Asquith's motion was defeated by 108 votes to 295) as a litmus test of loyalty to his leadership – a 'coupon', Asquith called it – when it came to endorsing sitting candidates in the 'khaki' general election in November 1918.

The Liberal Party machine had atrophied during the war but there was never any likelihood of Lloyd George's coalition being unseated. Asquith was given a tough ride in East Fife, a constituency he had rather taken for granted for many years, scarcely visiting it during the war, but he does not seem to have contemplated the possibility of actually being defeated. Churchill, campaigning in Dundee, wrote to his wife that Asquith was having a very rough time 'subjected to abominable baiting by a gang of discharged soldiers'. Placards in the constituency claimed; 'Asquith nearly lost you the war.

Are you going to let him spoil the peace?' Nevertheless the former Prime Minister himself claimed he had never known such enthusiastic and crowded gatherings during the two days he troubled to spend in the constituency: *The heckling was for the most part of the feeblest and most contemptible kind*. Defeat by 2,000 votes after 32 years as an MP, therefore came as a shock. Only 29 non-couponed Liberals survived the landslide.

Still Asquith clung on to the party leadership. By now the Liberals were not only divided but also outflanked, by the Labour Party. In February 1920 he was prevailed upon to stand in a byelection for the Scottish seat of Paisley (shades here of his biographer Roy Jenkins who came back to British politics as leader of the SDP 60 years later in a by-election at Glasgow Hillhead) which he won, despite confiding privately: *I am not very fond of going back to Scotland.*

On the register were 15,000 women voters who, bearing in mind his opposition to giving them the vote a decade before, were *a dim, impenetrable, for the most part ungettable element – of whom all that one knows is that they are for the most part hopelessly ignorant of politics, credulous to the last degree and flickering with gusts of sentiment like a candle in the wind*.[2] Nevertheless, with the fervent help of his daughter Violet, he won with a majority of nearly 3,000 votes.

Asquith held on to the seat through two general elections, in 1922 and 1923, but with increasing difficulty. In the former campaign there were effectively two Liberal parties with similar policies, one led by Lloyd George and the other by himself and although the following year they managed to agree a common programme, by that time the party had been supplanted by Labour. It was indeed Asquith's last decisive act in his political career to persuade the Liberal parliamentary party to stand aside after the second election and allow a Labour administration to take power as a minority

government, discounting, it was said, the threat of Socialist guillotines in Trafalgar Square. Asquith was not being entirely disinterested: he told Edmund Gosse that he would not rob Ramsay MacDonald, the Labour leader, 'poor man, of an hour of his brief rule; let him enjoy it while he may, for once out and he will never be heard of again'. Liberal votes sustained Labour in office for nine months but, when in the autumn of 1924 a new general election was called, the timing could not have been worse for the Liberals. Short of money, the party was also distracted by one last wrangle between Asquith and Lloyd George over how to spend what resources there were.

What is that melancholy dirge they are crooning now?

H H ASQUITH

Asquith fought the campaign in Paisley at the age of 72 'languid to the point of indifference'. *What is that melancholy dirge they are crooning now?* he asked Violet as his words were drowned out at a public meeting by hecklers singing the Red Flag. Thereupon, she wrote in her diary, 'he would evince mild interest ... lean back in his chair again with a sniff and a shrug and resume his own train of thought'. He was defeated by 2,000 votes by the Labour candidate, a former Liberal named Rosslyn Mitchell, who came up to him at the count awkwardly apologising: 'I am so sorry, so terribly sorry this has happened.' Loyal local Liberals sang: 'Will ye no'come back again?' but they and he knew his Parliamentary career was over.[3]

In compensation, the King now offered, and Asquith finally accepted, an earldom and the Garter. Even this however was not without controversy. Asquith chose the defunct title of Earl of Oxford ('like a suburban villa calling itself Versailles', sniffed the future Lady Salisbury) but the Tory descendants of Robert Harley, the minister who had held the title in the

reign of Queen Anne 200 years before objected – 'perhaps you consider old traditions and sentiments to be of no account in these days', wrote one insultingly – and he was required to become Earl of Oxford and Asquith as a means of differentiation instead.[4]

And there was one further humiliation. In 1925 the Chancellorship of Oxford University fell vacant (another position that Jenkins would subsequently hold) and Asquith was invited to stand for election by the MAs of his old university. He was, in the words of Lord Birkenhead – formerly his old enemy F E Smith – 'the most distinguished living Oxonian'. But it did him no good. Conservatives put up Lord Cave, the then Lord Chancellor ('the least distinguished occupant of the Woolsack of the first 30 years of the century', in Jenkins's magisterial estimation[5]) and the Tory Masters of Arts turned out in force to reject the old Prime Minister, vindictively, narrow-mindedly and discreditably. It was his last electoral defeat. Partisanship has never been a handicap in even the most ceremonial of Oxford elections, as Margaret Thatcher discovered 60 years later when the dons voted her down for an honorary degree.

One reason why Asquith clung on in politics for so long was that he was by no means rich and had no other career left open to him. He had not benefitted financially from office and it was a time before the sinecure of well-paid directorships was available to former Prime Ministers. He really did not have enough money to sustain the earldom, or indeed maintain the old, long-accustomed way of life that he and Margot had enjoyed. Their home at Cavendish Square was sold in 1919 and they moved to the somewhat less affluent area of Bedford Square, Bloomsbury instead. Both wrote for money: Margot brought out two candid and outspoken volumes of autobiography between 1920 and 1922 and, in due course, Asquith

published his war memoirs: four volumes in all, though none as boastful or sensational as those of Churchill and Lloyd George. They bore titles such as *The Genesis of the War*, *Fifty Years of Parliament* and *Memories and Reflections* instead.

The Asquiths still moved in the artistic and youthful circles in which their children were involved. His son Herbert (Beb) was a novelist and poet (as was Beb's wife Cynthia, who was J M Barrie's secretary). Anthony – Puffin, Asquith's youngest son – became a film director, Elizabeth, his second daughter, married a Romanian count, befriended Proust, wrote poems and novels and eventually took to drink. Margot would write a novel too and sustain herself financially until her death in 1945 by occasional articles and handouts from old friends such as Lord Beaverbrook. His older daughter Violet, who married his former private secretary Maurice 'Bougie' Bonham Carter, was a doughty Liberal and defender of her father's reputation until her death in 1969. Helena Bonham Carter, the actress, is the latest artistic member of the family.

> The films of Anthony Asquith (1902–68) include *Brown on Resolution* (1935) with John Mills, *Pygmalion* (1938) with Leslie Howard, *French Without Tears* (1939), *Channel Incident* (1940), *We Dive at Dawn* (1943) with John Mills, *Fanny by Gaslight* (1944) with James Mason and Phyllis Calvert, *The Way to the Stars* (1945), *The Winslow Boy* (1948), *The Browning Version* (1951) with Michael Redgrave, *The Importance of Being Earnest* (1952), *The Young Lovers* (1954), *Carrington VC* (1954) with David Niven, *Libel* (1959) with Dirk Bogarde, *The Millionairess* (1960) with Sophia Loren and Peter Sellers, *The VIPS* (1963), and *The Yellow Rolls Royce* (1964).

There is a memoir by the famous beauty, Lady Diana Cooper, of joining the party to celebrate Asquith's 67th birthday in Venice in 1919: 'we dressed him up as a Doge and hung the sala with Mantegna

swags of fruit and green leaves and loaded him with presents, tenderness and admiration. I think he was ecstatically happy that day.' Of another occasion when he was still in Downing Street, she added: 'I really loved Mr Asquith. He delighted in the young and the young's conversation and would talk of poetry and people and weddings and jokes and he wanted to hold one's hand and feel equal and comforted.'[6]

The last 18 months of Asquith's life were painful ones. He had a stroke in June 1926 and finally that autumn, reluctantly, gave up the leadership of the Liberal Party – 'he had stayed too long in an impossible situation,' says Jenkins. In 1927, he was still visiting shows (he enjoyed Puffin's films) and playing occasional golf, but one of his legs began to fail and he was confined to a wheelchair. He went into slow decline: there was a visit to York to receive the freedom of the city, a final call on Venetia Montagu, now living in Norfolk and then, as his ill-health increased, a retreat to the Wharf. Over the winter as his arteries hardened his mind became confused.

During a visit by Vivian Phillipps, his former private secretary, in January 1928, he grasped his hand and said: '"You will come and see me again – right to the end," and then quickly – as if he had said more than he meant to – "I mean right to the end of this Parliament".'[7]

H H Asquith died a month later, on 15 February 1928. He is buried in the village churchyard at Sutton Courtenay, near his home. In his will he left £9,345.9s.2d.

Chapter 8: Summary

Nearly 90 years after his ejection from office and 80 years since his death, Herbert Henry Asquith is an almost forgotten figure among 20th-century Prime Ministers, even though his administration was one of the most important and far-reaching of the entire period. His domestic achievements are dim memories now while his role in the early years of the First World War is scarcely mentioned in the plethora of books on the military aspects of the conflict. Yet it is entirely arguable that no prime minister of the 20th century had a more lasting impact on the lives of British citizens.

Many of the issues with which he wrestled, more imaginitively and less frenziedly than most of his successors, remain potent nearly a century onwards – Ireland, Constitutional Reform, Welfare – but that they do so is scarcely his fault. At a time when media scrutiny and the pressure of multiple news outlets drives ministers and prime ministers to act ever more frenetically, his measured and magisterial response to critical events seems benign indeed.

Domestically, the first Asquith administration's greatest achievement was the introduction of the old age pension, implemented with determination despite prolonged Conservative opposition. This was a social reform which did more than any other before the introduction of the National Health Service nearly 40 years later to improve the condition

of the country's neediest and most vulnerable citizens and to ameliorate the end of their lives, alleviating the fear of ending in the workhouse that clouded so many's thoughts. It was all of a part with the government's cautious intervention in other areas of national life and attempts to improve and regulate working conditions, not least its preparedness to become involved to try to bring an end to industrial disputes. Although Lloyd George is usually credited with the People's Budget of 1909 which inaugurated the pension plan, Asquith had actually first introduced the measure in his last budget the previous year and, as Prime Minister, he gave it sturdy support into implementation, without trumpeting it as his own initiative. Many of the Liberal government's other domestic reforms – its education legislation, licensing reform, Welsh disestablishment, Irish Home Rule – were either defeated or emasculated by a protracted and ruthless campaign of parliamentary opposition by the Conservative Party using their inbuilt majority in the House of Lords to wreck the programme of a democratically-elected government. Even a century on the recklessness, even obtuseness, of the tactics still have the ability to take the breath away.

The Lords was a weapon the Conservatives had deployed in opposition for many years and, if popular suffrage meant anything, it was a tactic that had to be faced down. That the Liberal government was able eventually to do so and that it achieved its goal moderately and largely without direct confrontation – or, ultimately, having to create a majority of Liberal peers – was largely due to Asquith's leadership. He received little thanks for it, of course – and it was no thanks at all to the Tories – but the Parliament Act helped to safeguard British democracy during the challenges of the 20th century.

The Liberal government was ultimately not successful in

its search for a constitutional solution to the Irish problem, which had bedevilled British politics for several generations, but it is at least possible to argue that, despite the confrontations of 1912 to 1914, by the time of the outbreak of the war, Asquith's government had reached a compromise – indeed one which has essentially been in place ever since – splitting off Ulster from the rest of the island in allowing Home Rule to the South. While it is perfectly possible to argue that Asquith and his ministers underestimated and misinterpreted the passions that Home Rule induced, their behaviour was at least well-meaning and sincere.

Home Rule would have been implemented had there been no war – and had the Easter Rising not precipitated a wholly new stage in the old conflict. It is at least evident that Home Rule could probably have been achieved without the bloodshed that occurred, or the mutual bitterness and recrimination and that today Ireland would be an independent state, just as it is now but without the legacy of violence that has taken 80 years to overcome. Events which were certainly not of Asquith's making conspired to destroy that possibility.

Even in the case of the First World War, it is now possible for historians to look beyond the contemporary attacks on Asquith's government and the subsequent revisionist phase of regarding the conflict as entirely incompetent and unnecessarily brutal – the 'lions led by donkeys' tradition – to see that the Prime Minister played a significant part in developing the strategy and organisation that ultimately led to an Allied victory. The proof of that rests in the fact that Lloyd George's government did not substantially alter policy or personnel in the last two years of the war and faced similar problems in a similar way. Where Asquith is much more culpable is in not initially grasping the scale of the conflict or adopting a more interventionist approach to leading the nation's war effort.

Shortcomings in the government's decision-making processes gave scope for rivalries to develop and for the Prime Minister's own position to be undermined.

Sir Maurice Hankey, the secretary of the war committee, who worked with Asquith as closely as anyone, wrote that the causes of the coalition government's failure lay more 'in an inherent political weakness than in the leadership'. Asquith, he said, 'never wavered in his unswerving determination to see it through to final victory' and built up 'a military machine ... on which his successor in office was able to build so successfully as to achieve final victory within less than two years of Asquith's fall ... His powerful and sonorous eloquence enabled him to exercise a leadership which was at the time unsurpassed in any of the nations at war.'[1]

Of course Asquith had his faults and failures. Perhaps his greatest blind spot was in not extending the vote to women before the war – an action which would have cost little and saved much aggravation, besides cementing his reputation as a major social reformer and visionary. That he did not do so, as we have seen, was precisely because he never courted easy popularity or bowed to what he saw as unreasonable pressure and, once he had made up his mind intellectually (in this case that women's position would not be improved by having the vote) he was obstinately hard to shift.

He was certainly a man of his time in that, as he was in his casual but not vicious anti-semitism towards, for instance, Edwin Montagu (though that did not stop him appointing him private secretary and later bringing him into the Cabinet). There were strands of intellectual arrogance and complacency too, which did not help him, certainly either as a man-manager or as a wartime leader. His other personal character traits: his drinking and his correspondence with attractive younger women, do not seem to have undermined

his work, while his more public characteristics: his intelligence and fluency, his probity, loyalty and resolution, certainly enhanced it. He clearly played a role in the decline of the Liberal Party – party organisation was never much interest to him – but it may well have been beyond saving in the light of the rise of Labour.

What Asquith certainly lacked – and perhaps did not need to cultivate in the days before television appearances and the soundbite culture – was a common touch or a desire to appear dynamic or relentlessly active. This did not stop him being an extremely able and efficient administrator and manager, but it did not stand him in good stead once Britain went to war and public leadership was required. His colleagues and successors, Lloyd George and Winston Churchill, both very different characters, certainly learned from that when they came to lead the country in war.

There is no doubt that Asquith was traduced, both during the war and afterwards, by the press and by certain of his colleagues and opponents. That has helped to overshadow his reputation, as indeed has the great divide of the First World War itself, but it was unfair then and it remains unfair today.

He held power during some of the most daunting years of the 20th century and, for almost all the eight years of his administration, was regarded as both a dominant leader and an indispensible one. He thought so himself but he was under no illusions as to the durability of his reputation. In January 1915 as he was being driven down to Walmer Castle in Kent for the weekend, his car avoided what he described to Venetia Stanley as *two or three very narrow shaves of collision & disaster. And after each, I said to myself – suppose it had gone wrong and I had (as Browning says) 'ended my cares', what would have been the consequence? Lots of stuff in the press – a nine days' wonder*

in the country: violent speculation as to who was to succeed me …
many obituary notices and, after a week or 10 days (at the outside)
the world going on as tho' nothing had happened … a few ripples,
even, if you like, a bit of a splash in the pool – but little or nothing
more.[2]

In that, at least, he was mistaken.

NOTES

Introduction: The Noblest Roman

1. British Library sound archive, *Voices of History* tape, 2005.
2. Kenneth Rose, *King George V* (Macmillan Papermac edition, London: 1983) p 71.
3. Colin Clifford, *The Asquiths* (John Murray, London: 2003) p 32, hereafter Clifford.

Chapter 1: The Means of Ascent

1. Clifford, p 3.
2. Speech by H H Asquith at Balliol dinner to celebrate premiership, 1908.
3. Roy Jenkins, *Asquith* (Collins, London: 1964) p 23.
4. Stephen Koss, *Asquith* (Columbia University Press: 1976) p 8, hereafter Koss.
5. Jenkins, *Asquith*, p 25, quoting H H Asquith, *Memories and Reflections* (Mackintosh, London: 1928) p 25, hereafter Asquith, *Memories*.
6. Clifford, p 9, quoting letter written to Frances Horner, 17 October 1892.
7. Jenkins, *Asquith*, p 34.
8. Clifford, p 5.
9. Clifford, p 6.
10. H A Asquith, *Moments of Memory* (Scribners, London: 1938) p 22.
11. Koss, p 12.

Chapter 2: The Coming Man

1. Jenkins, *Asquith*, p 43.
2. Jenkins, *Asquith*, p 44.
3. H H Asquith, *Studies and Sketches* (Mackintosh, London: 1924) p 206, hereafter Asquith, *Studies*.
4. Jenkins, *Asquith*, p 45.
5. Koss, p 28.
6. Asquith, *Memories*, pp 79–80.
7. Clifford, p 35.
8. Jenkins, *Asquith*, p 75.
9. Clifford, p 37.
10. Clifford, p 51.
11. Jenkins, *Asquith*, p 60.
12. Koss, p 32.
13. Jenkins, *Asquith*, p 61
14. *Dictionary of National Biography*, hereafter *DNB*.
15. Jenkins, *Asquith*, p 69.
16. Koss, p 38.
17. Jenkins, *Asquith*, p 83.
18. Jenkins, *Asquith*, p 89.
19. Koss, p 52.
20. Koss, pp 54–5.
21. Koss, p 59.
22. Shaw, *Letters to Isabel*, quoted in Paul Johnson (ed), *The Oxford Book of Political Anecdotes* (OUP, Oxford: 1986).
23. Koss, p 71.
24. Jenkins, *Asquith*, p 155.

Chapter 3: Into Office

1. Koss, p 74.
2. *DNB*.
3. John Wilson, *CB: A Life of Sir Henry Campbell-Bannerman* (PBS edition, London: 1973) p 608.

4. Jenkins, *Asquith*, p 198.
5. Koss, p 86.
6. Jenkins, *Asquith*, p 180.

Chapter 4: Prime Minister
1. Koss, p 90.
2. Koss, p 88.
3. Koss, p 139.
4. Koss, p 112, and Roy Jenkins, *Mr Balfour's Poodle* (Collins, London: 1968 edition) pp 76–7, hereafter Jenkins, *Poodle*.
5. John Campbell, *F.E. Smith* (Pimlico edition, London: 1991) p 201.
6. Jenkins, *Poodle*, p 89 and Clifford, p 150.
7. John Grigg, *Lloyd George, The People's Champion, 1902–1911* (Penguin edition, London: 1997) p 208.
8. Koss, p 117.
9. Jenkins, *Asquith*, p 207.
10. Jenkins, *Asquith*, p 210.
11. Jenkins, *Asquith*, p 212.
12. Koss, p 125.
13. Clifford, p 184.
14. Campbell, *F.E. Smith*, p 243.

Chapter 5: Local Difficulties
1. Koss, p 138.
2. Clifford, p 186.
3. Clifford, p 194.
4. Michael and Eleanor Brock, *H.H. Asquith, Letters to Venetia Stanley* (OUP, Oxford: 1982) pp 184–5, hereafter Brock, *Letters*.
5. Clifford, p 207.
6. Jenkins, *Asquith*, p 234.

7. Koss, p 130.
8. Koss, p 133.
9. Fulford, *Votes for Women*, p 184, quoted Jenkins, *Asquith*, p 247.
10. Jenkins, *Asquith*, pp 249–50.
11. Campbell, *F.E. Smith*, p 322
12. Campbell, *F.E. Smith*, p 222
13. Koss, p 134.
14. Jenkins, *Asquith*, p 278.
15. Koss, p 138.

Chapter 6: Wartime
1. Koss, p 143.
2. Robert K Massie, *Dreadnought: Britain, Germany and the Coming of the Great War* (Random House, London: 1991), Ch 26.
3. Koss, p 146.
4. Koss, p 149.
5. Hew Strachan, *The First World War* (Simon and Schuster, London: 2003) p 16.
6. Jenkins, *Asquith*, p 324.
7. BBC Tape: *Eyewitness 1910–19*, Harold Nicolson.
8. Brock, *Letters*, p 151.
9. *DNB*.
10. Jenkins, *Asquith*, p 329.
11. Jenkins, *Asquith*, p 343.
12. Koss, p 171.
13. Robert Rhodes James, *The British Revolution, British Politics 1880–1939* (Methuen, London: 1978) pp 299–300.
14. Clifford, p 230.
15. Koss, p 168.
16. Koss, p 186.

17. Jenkins, *Asquith*, p 355.
18. Jenkins, *Asquith*, p 352.
19. Jenkins, *Asquith*, p 363.
20. Jenkins, *Asquith*, p 362.
21. Jenkins, *Asquith*, p 360.
22. Koss, p 186.
23. Sheffield, Gary, and John Bourne (eds), *Douglas Haig, War Diaries and Letters* (BCA edition, London: 2005) p 228.
24. Jenkins, *Asquith*, p 379.
25. Koss, p 188.
26. Koss, p 205.
27. Koss, p 207.
28. Clifford, p 369.
29. *DNB*.
30. Jenkins, *Asquith*, p 416.
31. Jenkins, *Asquith*, p 430.
32. Koss, p 219.
33. Jenkins, *Asquith*, pp 447–8.
34. Clifford, p 386.
35. Jenkins, *Asquith*, p 460.

Chapter 7: Decline
1. Koss, p 234.
2. Koss, p 246.
3. Koss, p 268.
4. Jenkins, *Asquith*, p 508.
5. Jenkins, *Asquith*, p 511.
6. Koss, p 141.
7. Jenkins, *Asquith*, p 519.

Chapter 8: Summary
1. *DNB*, quoting Hankey papers.
2. Koss, p 176.

CHRONOLOGY

Year	Premiership
1908	6 April: Herbert Henry Asquith, aged 55, is summoned by the King to his holiday home at Biarritz to 'kiss hands'. He returns the next day with his list of Cabinet ministers already approved.
1909	Lloyd George proposes his People's Budget, to raise money for defence and social expenditure. After six months of debate it goes to the House of Lords and is rejected.
1910	King Edward VII dies, and is succeeded by George V. House of Commons resolves that the House of Lords should have no power to veto money bills. Liberals win General Election.

History	Culture
King Carlos I of Portugal and the Crown Prince assassinated. Manuel II becomes King.	Colette, *La Retraite Sentimentale*.
	E M Forster, *A Room with a View*.
Edward VII and Tsar Nicholas II meet at Reval.	Kenneth Grahame, *The Wind in the Willows*.
Ferdinand I declares Bulgaria's independence and assumes the title of Tsar.	Anatole France, *Penguin Island*.
	Marc Chagall, *Nu Rouge*.
	Maurice de Vlaminck, *The Red Trees*.
Union of South Africa is established.	Bela Bartok, *String Quartet No.1*.
The Daily Telegraph publishes remarks about German hostility towards England made by Kaiser Wilhelm II.	Elgar, *Symphony No. 1 in A-Flat*.
William Howard Taft elected US President.	
Kiamil Pasha, grand vizier of Turkey, forced to resign by Turkish nationalists.	Marinetti publishes *First Futurist Manifesto*.
State visits of Edward VII to Berlin and Rome.	Strauss, *Elektra*.
	Delius, *A Mass of Life*.
Anglo-German discussions on the control of Baghdad railway.	Bellows, *Both Members of this Club*.
	Matisse, *The Dance*.
Plastic (Bakelite) is invented	Vasily Kandinsky paints first abstract paintings.
	H G Wells, *Tono-Bungay*.
	Maeterlink, *L'Oiseau Bleu*.
	Thomas Mann, *Königliche Hoheit*
	Frank Lloyd Wright builds Robie House, Chicago.
Egyptian Premier Butros Ghali assassinated.	E M Forster, *Howard's End*.
	H G Wells, *The History of Mr. Polly*.
South Africa becomes a dominion within the British Empire with Botha as Premier.	Karl May, *Winnetou*.
	Fernand Leger, *Nues dans le foret*.
King Manuel II flees Portugal to England. Portugal is proclaimed a republic.	Modigliani, *The Cellist*.
	Elgar, *Concerto for Violin in B Minor, Op. 61*.
Marie Curie publishes *Treatise on Radiography*.	Puccini, *La Fanciulla del West*.
	R Vaughan Williams, *Sea Symphony*.

Year	Premiership
1911	Lloyd George introduces National Health Insurance Bill in Parliament. Coronation of King George V. Winston Churchill appointed First Lord of the Admiralty. A J Balfour resigns leadership of Conservative Party. Ramsey MacDonald elected chairman of the Labour Party.
1912	Ulster Unionists resolve to repudiate the authority of any Irish parliament set up under Home Rule Bill. House of Commons rejects women's franchise bill.
1913	House of Commons rejects a women's franchise bill.

History	Culture
US-Japanese and Anglo-Japanese commercial treaties signed.	Cubism becomes public phenomenon in Paris.
Arrival of German gunboat *Panther* in Agadir triggers international crisis.	Max Beerbohm, *Zuleika Dobson*.
	D H Lawrence, *The White Peacock*.
Peter Stolypyn, Russian Premier, assassinated.	Saki, *The Chronicles of Clovis*.
	Renoir, *Gabrielle with a Rose*.
Italy declares war on Turkey.	George Bracque, *Man with a Guitar*.
	Strauss, *Der Rosenkavalier*.
	Stravinsky, *Petrushka*.
The liner *Titanic* sinks; 1,513 die.	Alfred Adler, *The Nervous Character*.
Montenegro declares war on Turkey.	
Turkey declares war on Bulgaria and Serbia.	C G Jung, *The Theory of Psychoanalysis*.
Turkey asks Great Powers to intervene to end Balkan War.	Marc Chagall, *The Cattle Dealer*.
	Franz Marc, *Tower of Blue Horses*.
Woodrow Wilson is elected US President.	Marcel Duchamp, *Nude descending a staircase II*.
Armistice between Turkey, Bulgaria, Serbia and Montenegro.	Schoenberg, *Pierrot Lunaire*.
Lenin establishes connection with Stalin and takes over editorship of *Pravda*.	E M Dell, *The Way of an Eagle*.
	Gerhart Hauptmann, *Atlantis*.
	Arthur Schnitzler, *Professor Bernhardi*.
	Ravel, *Daphnis and Chloe*.
Bulgarians renew Turkish War.	D H Lawrence, *Sons and Lovers*.
King George I of Greece assassinated and succeeded by Constantine I.	Thomas Mann, *Death in Venice*.
	Marcel Proust, *Du côté de chez Swann*.
Second Balkan war opens.	
US Federal Reserve System is established.	Igor Stravinsky, *Le Sacre du Printemps*.
Mahatma Gandhi, leader of the Indian Passive Resistance Movement, is arrested.	'Armory Show' introduces cubism and post-impressionism to New York.
	Grand Central Station in New York is completed.

Year	Premiership
1914	Liberal Unionists unite with Conservatives. 4 August: Britain declares war on Germany and later on Austria and Turkey. Battle of Mons.
1915	Western Front: Battles of Neuve Chappelle and Loos. The 'Shells Scandal'. Asquith forms a coalition government with A J Balfour and Reginald McKenna. Winston Churchill leaves the Admiralty for the Chancellorship of the Duchy of Lancaster; a new Ministry of Munitions is created with Lloyd George as minister. Gallipoli Campaign.
1916	The Battle of Jutland. The Battle of the Somme. 5 December: Asquith leaves office, having served 8 years and 244 days as premier.

Asquith has received remarkably little attention from biographers in recent years. Despite all the interest in the First World War and in personalities such as Winston Churchill, the major biography of Asquith remains that by Roy Jenkins – a politician who rather self-consciously resembled him – and that dates back to 1964. It had to pull some punches over, for instance, Asquith's relationship with Venetia Stanley (because Violet Bonham Carter was still alive. but it is a magisterial, judicious and sympathetic study.

Stephen Koss' much shorter biography was published in 1976 and was revisionist and much more critical, even acerbic, in its judgements, but does not substantially change the picture of events.

Much more recently Colin Clifford's *The Asquiths* (2002. is more gossipy and very readable but it concentrates much more on Margot and the careers of the children than it does on the politics of the day.

What really changed Asquith's repuation in the last 40 years was the publication in 1982 of his letters to Venetia Stanley. Although Jenkins had seen them too, and quoted discreetly from them, it was their unveiling in the raw, so to speak, which revealed a new picture of the old boy: no longer stiff, formal and rather cold as many of his contemporaries thought, but passionate, romantic and frustrated. They opened an astonishing new window into the man's soul and into his decision-making process during the critical three-year period between 1912 and 1915.

Books Consulted

Asquith, Herbert A, *Moments of Memory* (Scribners, London: 1938).

Asquith, H H, *Studies and Sketches* (Mackintosh, London: 1924).

—, *Memories and Reflections* (Mackintosh, London: 1928).

Barton, Brian, *From Behind a Closed Door, Secret Court Martial Records of the Easter Rising* (Blackstaff Press, London: 2002).

Blake, Robert, *The Conservative Party from Peel to Churchill* (Fontana edition, London: 1972).

Brock, Michael and Eleanor, *H.H. Asquith, Letters to Venetia Stanley* (OUP, Oxford: 1982).

Campbell, John, *F.E.Smith* (Pimlico edition, London: 1991).

Caulfield, Max, *The Easter Rebellion* (Gill and Macmillan edition, London: 1995).

Chambers Biographical Dictionary (1993 edition).

Clifford, Colin, *The Asquiths* (John Murray, London: 2003).

Dangerfield, George, *The Strange Death of Liberal England* (Paladin edition, London: 1972).

Dictionary of National Biography (Oxford University Press, Oxford: www.oxforddnb.com, 2005).

Gilbert, Martin, *First World War* (Harper Collins paperback edition, London: 1995).

Grigg, John, *Lloyd George, The People's Champion, 1902–11* (Penguin edition, London: 1997).

—, *Lloyd George, From Peace to War 1912–16* (Penguin edition, London: 1997).

Jenkins, Roy, *Asquith* (Chilmark Press, London: 1964).

—, *Mr Balfour's Poodle* (Collins, London: 1968 edition).

—, *Gladstone* (Macmillan, London: 1995).

—, *Churchill* (Macmillan, London: 2001).

Johnson, Paul, *The Oxford Book of Political Anecdotes* (Oxford University Press, Oxford: 1986).

Keegan, John, *The First World War* (Hutchinson, London: 1998).

Koss, Stephen, *Asquith* (Columbia University Press: 1976).

Massie, Robert K, *Dreadnought. Britain, Germany and the Coming of the Great War* (Random House, London: 1991).

Rhodes James, Robert, *The British Revolution, British Politics 1880–1939* (Methuen, London: 1978).

Rogers, Colin, *The Battle of Stepney* (Robert Hale, London: 1981).

Rose, Kenneth, *King George V* (Macmillan Papermac edition, London: 1983).

Sheffield, Gary, and John Bourne, *Douglas Haig, War Diaries and Letters* (BCA edition, London: 2005).

Strachan, Hew, *The First World War* (Simon and Schuster, London: 2003).

Townshend, Charles, *Easter 1916* (Allen Lane, London: 2005).

Wilson, John, *CB: A Life of Sir Henry Campbell-Bannerman* (PBS edition, London: 1973).

Wilson, Trevor, *The Downfall of the Liberal Party 1914–35* (Collins Fontana edition, London: 1968).

Audio Sources

BBC, *Eyewitness, 1910–1919*, Audio Books Radio Collection (2004).

British Library, *Voices of History*, recordings from the sound archive (2005).

PICTURE SOURCES

Page 6
A policeman salutes as Asquith leaves the War Office in London, 1 October 1915.
(Courtesy Getty Images)

Pages 50–1
Herbert Asquith pays his taxi fare at the roadside, circa 1915.
(Courtesy Getty Images)

Pages 130–1
One of the seven processions on their way to Hyde Park on 2 June 1908 for the suffragettes' 'Monster meeting'. The banner refers to Asquith's reluctance to meet their demands.
(Courtesy Getty Images)

INDEX

Balfour

E H H GREEN

HAUS PUBLISHING • LONDON

First published in Great Britain in 2006 by
Haus Publishing Limited
26 Cadogan Court
Draycott Avenue
London SW3 3BX

www.hauspublishing.co.uk

Copyright © E H H Green, 2006

The moral right of the author has been asserted

A CIP catalogue record for this book is available from the British Library

ISBN 1-904950-55-8

Designed by BrillDesign
Typeset in Garamond 3 by MacGuru Ltd
info@macguru.org.uk

Printed and bound by Graphicom, Vicenza

Front cover: John Holder